Beyond Loving

Beyond Loving

Intimate Racework in Lesbian, Gay, and Straight Interracial Relationships

AMY C. STEINBUGLER

OXFORD
UNIVERSITY PRESS

OXFORD
UNIVERSITY PRESS

Oxford University Press is a department of the University of Oxford.
It furthers the University's objective of excellence in research, scholarship,
and education by publishing worldwide.

Oxford   New York
Auckland   Cape Town   Dar es Salaam   Hong Kong   Karachi
Kuala Lumpur   Madrid   Melbourne   Mexico City   Nairobi
New Delhi   Shanghai   Taipei   Toronto

With offices in
Argentina   Austria   Brazil   Chile   Czech Republic   France   Greece
Guatemala   Hungary   Italy   Japan   Poland   Portugal   Singapore
South Korea   Switzerland   Thailand   Turkey   Ukraine   Vietnam

Oxford is a registered trademark of Oxford University Press
in the UK and certain other countries.

Published in the United States of America by
Oxford University Press
198 Madison Avenue, New York, NY 10016

Library of Congress Cataloging-in-Publication Data
Steinbugler, Amy C.
   Beyond loving : intimate racework in lesbian, gay, and
straight interracial relationships / Amy C. Steinbugler.
      p. cm.
ISBN 978–0–19–974356–8 (pbk. : alk. paper) —
ISBN 978–0–19–974355–1 (hardcover : alk. paper)
1. Gay couples.   2. Lesbian couples.   3. Heterosexuals.   4. Interracial marriage.
5. Race relations.   6. Race awareness.   I. Title.
HQ76.34.S74 2012
306.76′6—dc23   2011050183

ISBN 978–0–19–974356–8
ISBN 978–0–19–974355–1

9 8 7 6 5 4 3 2 1
Printed in the United States of America
on acid-free paper

CONTENTS

ACKNOWLEDGMENTS

This book would not exist without the eighty-two people who agreed to sit with me and share the details of their lives and intimate relationships. They invited me into their homes, introduced me to their families, and talked to me about their lives. Occasionally they even fed me dinner. Their generosity and candor move me still. I especially owe profound thanks to the four couples who allowed me to "sit in" on their lives for five weeks. They showed unfailing patience and trust in me that there was something sociological about all of this. I am sincerely grateful.

This project began as a dissertation at Temple University. In the beginning stages of that process I was fortunate to be mentored by Julia Ericksen, who pushed me to develop my own focus and interests and ask the questions that I wanted to ask. Her intellectual guidance and friendship have been invaluable; her confidence and generosity mean more to me than she could know. At a critical stage in the development of this project, France Winddance Twine provided crucial support. She challenged me to take my own ideas seriously; this was a tremendous gift. I was sometimes guided and propelled forward by an outstanding committee, including Julia Ericksen, Michelle Byng, Kim Goyette, Sonja Peterson-Lewis, and France Winddance Twine. My graduate school peers helped me finish with my sanity intact. I am indebted to Janice Johnson Dias, Wendy Sedlak, Vincent Louis, Nicole Gossett-Cousin, Danielle Farrie, Frances Barlas, Tami Nopper, Maggie Ussery, and Mary Stricker. I also want to thank Allie Armstrong, Jessica Savage, and Rasheeda Phillips for their excellent transcriptions and Damien Frierson for assisting me with some of the early interviews.

For the past several years, I have had the pleasure of working with wonderful colleagues at Dickinson College. Thank you to Dan Schubert, Susan

Rose, Helene Lee, Erik Love, Stephanie Gilmore, Megan Yost, and Vickie Kuhn. I also had the extreme good fortune to work with Maggie O'Brien, whose detective skills, persistence, and quick wit made her an invaluable research assistant. Helene Lee, Erik Love, Susannah Bartlow, Greg Howard, Maggie O'Brien, Stephanie Gilmore, Suman Ambwani, and Jennifer Froelich-Schaefer made Carlisle, Pennsylvania, feel more like home.

As I reimagined my dissertation as a book, I was inspired by three qualitative studies that I believe exemplify the power of nesting everyday lives in a social-structural context. For countless months, I carried copies of Annette Lareau's *Unequal Childhoods*, Prudence Carter's *Keepin' it Real*, and Karyn Lacy's *Blue-Chip Black* back and forth from Philadelphia to Carlisle. I thank these women for their thoughtful and critical analyses. In revising the manuscript, I was aided immeasurably by colleagues who read individual chapters, often more than once, and offered their feedback. Thank you to Heather Dalmage, Stephanie Gilmore, Mary Hickert Herring, Rosanna Hertz, Janice Johnson Dias, Karyn Lacy, Helene Lee, Robin Leidner, Erik Love, Heather Love, Mignon Moore, Kevin Mumford, Anna Muraco, Eileen O'Brien, Salvador Vidal Ortiz, Mara Steinbugler Pohl, Kerry Ann Rockquemore, Renee Romano, Leila Rupp, R. Tyson Smith, and Maggie Ussery. I also benefited from the extraordinary editorial eye of Katherine Mooney. Her meticulous attention to both the finer points and the bigger picture made my writing clearer. James Cook at Oxford University Press was a strong ally throughout the process. As the project came together, Julia Ericksen, Annette Lareau, Antonia Randolph, and Dan Schubert read the entire manuscript and offered incisive, detailed comments. I am incredibly grateful to them for their time and careful attention. I extend heartfelt thanks especially to Annette Lareau, who swooped in at crucial points and unfailingly stood right by me when I needed her support most.

During the final months of writing, the line between extreme focus and extreme isolation was very fine and hard to see. Without the patience, generosity, and love of a small group of people, I might have been forever stuck on the wrong side of that line. Thank you to Erica Lee, Mara Steinbugler Pohl, Rebekah Kilzer, Christie Whisman, Etta Pearl Kilzer-Whisman, Helene Lee, and Erik Love. You made all the difference.

And finally, I am indescribably indebted to my family who have loved, forgiven, and supported me, and offered patience that I have not always deserved. My sincere love goes to Eileen Altieri, Richard Steinbugler, Mary Steinbugler, Mara Steinbugler Pohl, David Pohl, Willem Pohl, Donnamarie Cooper, McKenna Cooper, Jamison Cooper, Lee Connolly, Helen

Altieri, Richard Polo, Jimmy Altieri, Jocelyn Altieri, Jim Altieri, Eleanor Antonucci, Mary Altieri, and Carolyn Altieri. Erica Lee has generously made room in our lives for this work. Her warmth and humor inspire me every day.

To Mom, Dad, Mary, Mari, and Erica, who have believed in me from the beginning, I cannot thank you enough. This book is for you.

INTRODUCTION

Our upbringings [were] so different. [Kirk] was raised in a family,
there was six of them and there was one of me.... There is something
about his energy in that upbringing. He tends to be more generous.
I tend to be more selfish, in my own perception. He's always thinking
about other people's birthdays and anniversaries, and I can barely
figure what I'm going to have for dinner the next night.... At times,
I'm more superficial and he's less superficial; that's an oppositeness
that we have. Although it's funny because I have taken on some of his
qualities and he has taken on some of mine.... I like the difference.

WHEN WALTER BELTON-DAVIS DESCRIBES his relationship with his partner,
Kirk Belton-Davis, he is thoughtful about their differences.[1] They have
different temperaments, ways of expressing themselves, and perceptions
of what counts as tidy. Though he is Black and Kirk is White, in the epi-
graph above, Walter does not describe the racial difference between them
as significant. Their racial difference is meaningful to each of them, but
they think of it more as an aesthetic variation than a source of conflict.
They enjoy being interracial; it brings them pleasure. Sometimes, Kirk,
who is forty-four, and Walter, who is forty-six, function like an old married
couple. By most counts, they are. They have been together for twenty-four
years and are officially registered as domestic partners in the state of New
Jersey. Spending time with them reveals their settled intimacy—when they
talk together, they play off each other's memories, frequently interrupting
with corrections, and anticipating stories' endings.

Race is a part of their relationship, but it is not the only part. They are animal lovers, gardeners, film buffs, and travelers. They squabble about money and whose turn it is to do the laundry. Yet their racial difference has unavoidable consequences. Racial segregation characterizes many of the social spaces they frequent, including some in Philadelphia, which is just fifteen minutes from their suburban New Jersey townhouse. They do not talk about their racial difference in terms of social power, but these two men are unequally positioned in a social context that privileges Whiteness and marginalizes Blackness within other categories, such as gender, sexuality, and social class. As the interracial narratives in this book demonstrate, such differences in power arise in the most ordinary moments of everyday life. Racial difference is also meaningful to this couple and other couples like them because interracial intimacy itself is stigmatized.

Walter and Kirk, like the other partners whose experiences this book explores, are part of a growing trend. The percentage of U.S. couples who are interracial has risen markedly over the last several decades, although such unions are still rare in absolute terms. According to the 2010 U.S. Census, 6.9 percent of heterosexual married couples are interracial.[2] A much smaller percentage of all heterosexual married couples (less than 1 percent) are Black/White.[3] Cohabitants are more likely to be interracial—among all heterosexual unmarried-partner households, 14.2 percent are interracial.[4] The percentage of interracial gay and lesbian unmarried-partner households is 14.1 percent and 11.4 percent, respectively.[5] Yet, as with heterosexual couples, the percentage of lesbian and gay couples who are Black/White is much smaller. Two percent of interracial gay couples and 1.7 percent of lesbian couples are Black/White pairs.[6] But interracial couples—especially heterosexual ones—hold symbolic value greatly disproportionate to their numbers. The increasing frequency of interracial partnerships and the "mixed" children that come from these unions are interpreted by some as proof of a profound shift in U.S. race relations.

Some commentators characterize the first decades of the twenty-first century as the dawn of a "postracial" era in which racial differences will become less and less important until, eventually, Americans will have moved beyond race completely. Those who make this claim marshal evidence from a wide swath of social life, including the tremendous achievements of the civil rights movement, the demise of de jure discrimination, and survey research showing a decline in racial hostility among White Americans, especially in younger generations. These analysts find the increasing numbers of interracial families and multiracial people especially relevant, for they seem to promise to change the face of America itself.[7] Critics, however, argue that a postracial world is a fantasy—a future that we are never likely to encounter. These voices remind us of the enormous gulfs that still separate racial groups in the United States. Structural inequalities in education, employment, health care, housing, and rates of incarceration persist. Critics also point to the vastly different cultural meanings that groups attach to patterns of racial inequality.[8] From this standpoint, interracial unions and multiracial children are no panacea for enduring problems of stratification.

Debates about the possibility of a postracial society threaten to devolve into a standoff between those who focus on decades of racial progress and those who stress the persistence of inequality. This polarized discussion obscures a more complex reality. Racial dynamics in the United States have shifted in complicated ways, leaving vestiges of old racial systems within contemporary racial formations. Our racial present is a mix of enduring inequalities and new cultural messages. To understand this contemporary reality, we must set aside the simplistic notion of a postracial society and move on to more sophisticated questions: In the first decades of the twenty-first century, how do people experience race in their everyday lives? How do individuals engage one another across racial lines? Can intimate relationships bridge racial boundaries, or do they inevitably reproduce the tensions that characterize broader racial hierarchies?

Beyond Loving addresses these fundamental questions about the contemporary significance of race in the United States by examining the everyday lives of same-sex and heterosexual Black/White interracial couples. It extends the work of researchers who for decades have looked to micro-level interactions for clues about macro-level race relations. Various forms of interracial relationships, such as Asian American/White, Native American/Black, Native American/White, have existed throughout history. Intimacy between Blacks and Whites, however, is a crucial point of inquiry, because this color line has historically been the most rigorously surveilled and restricted.[9] Indeed, it is precisely because of this history of fierce contestation that the rising number of these unions generates both hope and skepticism.

My analysis focuses on what I call "racework": the routine actions and strategies through which individuals maintain close relationships across lines of racial stratification.[10] Interracial partners are not the only people who do racework—interracial friendships and parent-child relationships are also close relationships in which people negotiate racial differences. Yet intimate romantic relationships are a crucial site at which to explore this practice, because these are often the most central and deeply rooted bonds that people form in their lifetimes. This book explores the practice of racework within public spaces, intimate interactions, and identities. I examine the following four types of racework: navigating racial homogeneity, visibility management, emotional labor, and boundary work. Conceptualizing these social practices as "work" makes interracial intimacy visible as an ongoing process, rather than as a singular accomplishment. This analytic shift also reveals how race "works" in intimate spheres and draws attention to the complexity of interracial interactions in other areas of social life, including schools, neighborhoods, and workplaces.

This book also charts new territory by bringing gay and lesbian interraciality into focus. Whereas research on interracial couples in the United States has traditionally looked almost exclusively at heterosexual couples, I analyze how everyday racial practices are shaped by sexuality and gender. I examine how being lesbian, gay, or heterosexual influences the ways in which partners attach meanings to being an interracial couple, experience racial difference, and engage in racework. This allows me to foreground the experiences of same-sex Black/White partners, a type of interracial relationship that has been almost completely neglected in sociological studies of interracial intimacy.[11]

Highlighting lesbian and gay interracial experiences also creates an opportunity to consider the significance of racial difference outside and apart from the influence of stigmas associated with heterosexual interraciality. Because qualitative scholars of interracial intimacy in the United States have focused almost exclusively on heterosexual couples, their observations typically center on how partners respond to cultural anxieties attached to heterosexual Black/White intimacy.[12] Observing these cultural anxieties has too often kept researchers' gaze trained on social prejudice. Privileging the problem of prejudice obscures other important ways in which racial difference shapes personal relationships. For instance, when two people establish intimate relationships across racial lines, they must negotiate each other's differential access to status and power. Interracial relationships are not miniature models of racial hierarchy in which the person of color is subordinate to the White partner, and yet neither are these relationships raceless spheres in a racialized world. Interracial partners also must navigate racially divided social environments to find spaces where both are comfortable. Researchers who have focused primarily on longstanding prejudice against heterosexual Black/White couples have failed to explore these other formidable challenges. Critically examining the experiences of lesbian and gay partners therefore opens up at least two new vantage points in the study of interracial intimacy. Expanding our view to include lesbians and gays pushes us to acknowledge other daily challenges to interracial lives in addition to the problems of prejudice. That is, it forces us not only to look at more kinds of interracial partners, but also to look at them differently. Further, by attending to crucial issues of sexuality and gender, we see how race intersects with other dimensions of inequality, including heterosexism and sexism. This broader lens reveals the true complexities of interracial unions.

Love Myths, Assimilation, and the Importance of Seeing Race as Structure

The day-to-day lives of interracial couples involve a myriad of issues besides race. The women and men in this study contended with challenges large and small: adjusting to a new job, managing a long commute, helping a son with grade-school math, planning a wedding, feeding dinner to a two-year-old, trying to get pregnant, finding standing room on the subway, and creating time to be together. So I was not surprised when some interracial partners told me that the racial difference between them was not a major concern.

Yet, as a researcher, I also recognize that our contemporary ideologies about race and romance de-emphasize the significance of race and racism. The practice of avoiding discussions about race or diminishing its importance by insisting that "we are all just people" who share an equal and common humanity reflects what Eduardo Bonilla-Silva calls "abstract liberalism," a key component of colorblind racism.[13] Abstract liberalism enables individuals to de-emphasize their membership in racial groups whose members share a common social location or material interests, and instead to see interracial intimacy as a coincidence of skin color, a partnership between two people who "happen to be" of different races. The popular notion that love and romance exist in an emotional space beyond the realm of rational cognition typically affirms the serendipity of romantic love. In recent decades, sociologists have identified cultural and gendered patterns in how Americans think about romantic love and intimacy.[14] Popular "love myths" characterize love and desire as at once "natural and supernatural," situated within "the mysterious realm of romance, where all that occurs is deemed to stand apart from and often to be arrayed against social convention."[15] Rachel Moran conceptualizes this perspective as one of "romantic individualism," a vantage point from which love can be not only blind, but colorblind as well.[16] This framework emphasizes that categories like race, ethnicity, class, and religion cannot tell us either how or whom to love.[17] In the popular imagination, love has the potential for bringing about radical social transformation, because it is believed to supersede group differences and render them trivial. These two discourses—abstract liberalism and romantic individualism—share a common thread. From both perspectives, romantic love is a great equalizer that rises above the supposed banalities of color and class.

Some of these popular ideas about love mesh easily with assimilation theory. Classical assimilation theorists considered interracial intimacy a measure of the social distance between racial groups and an important site of structural and cultural assimilation. They expected that only through such cross-cutting unions could individuals from ethnic groups become sufficiently enmeshed in White American communities that they would lose all traces of what made them distinctive.[18] Intermarriage with Whites was interpreted as a clear signal that minority group members had adopted the language and customs of the dominant White population and had been economically and politically absorbed into mainstream society.[19] This theory was modeled on the experiences of European immigrants from countries such as Germany, Ireland, and Italy. It never adequately captured the racialized realities of African Americans, or of Chinese, Japanese, or Filipino immigrants. A trajectory of gradual absorption was not a viable option for groups who were visually coded as indelibly different and inferior.[20] The benign absorption of racial minorities is untenable in the presence of the kind of intensive, systemic racism that exists in the United States.

Despite the discrediting of classical assimilation theories, the idea that the "mixing" of Blacks and Whites will bring the two groups closer together and dissolve racial differences continues to hold great symbolic power. This is true even though the one-drop rule (the racial classification system in which a person with *any* African ancestry is considered "Black") has never blurred, let alone broken, the color line. It has simply positioned children of Black and White parents as Black. Only now, when multiracialism and hybridity have come to be seen as potentially transformative, are Black/White couples cast as part of an intimate "vanguard" who "work on narrowing the divisions between groups in America, one couple at a time."[21] From this perspective, the differences that separate social groups geographically, politically, and culturally are expected to erode and eventually disappear in the context of long-term, stable, romantic relationships.

It is a curious idea that in a world where racial conflicts are widespread, romantic love can be assumed to create an intimate sphere in which racial differences do not matter. Social scientists have long demonstrated that equal status is not a prerequisite for marriage, nor does marriage itself have an equalizing function.[22] For example, we know that heterosexual marriage does not neutralize status differences between women and men. Some of the same assumptions that have traditionally segregated men and women in particular labor markets also organize the division of housework inside the home.[23] Within most heterosexual marriages, women still perform more housework and have primary responsibility for childcare, whether or not they also hold a full-time job.[24] These and similar findings suggest that social inequalities that exist in our broader society also shape intimate relationships.

My perspective on race is markedly different from popular imaginings of love and romance and from the predictions of classic assimilation models. White supremacy in the United States is not primarily a set of malicious attitudes or misunderstandings. It is a social system. For centuries, Whites have structured social institutions—education, law, housing, criminal justice, employment—to benefit Whites. Racism is therefore not primarily a problem of prejudice, although this may be what is easiest to see. As a system, it involves both institutional inequalities and patterns of ideas—or ideologies—that justify or naturalize these inequalities. Making this distinction is important because how we define racism shapes how we think about interracial intimacy. When social scientists (and others) understand racism entirely as racial *prejudice*, as a collection of resilient, negative generalizations, then intimacy seems to promise a way to neutralize racial differences. Contact theory is based on this very premise: It proposes that anti-Black racism has its basis in ignorant, faulty generalizations and that social intimacy corrects erroneous stereotypes, conferring acceptance and equality.[25] But if we recognize racism as a *social system*, one that shapes not only individual attitudes and perceptions but also how people are materially rewarded or disadvantaged within social institutions, we are left with many more difficult questions. How do White and Black partners maintain intimate relationships when they do not share equal levels of racial power and privilege? Can familiarity, empathy, and intimacy erode racial differences within interracial couples? Do interracial relationships have the potential to change broader dynamics between Whites and Blacks? This study explores these questions by asking *how* people establish and maintain bonds of trust, love, and communication across systems of stratification.

Conceptualizing Racework

The approach I take in this book differs from other research on interracial intimacy. In analyzing interracial narratives, I have tried to understand not only the social context in which lesbian, gay, and heterosexual interracial partners live their lives, but also how these partners go about sustaining intimacy across systems of stratification (White supremacy, sexism, and heterosexism). The concept of racework, described earlier, helps bring into sharp relief the commonplace practices through which interracial partners deal with being racially different in a society where African Americans and Whites are spatially segregated and persistently unequal. Racework also draws attention to the dynamic nature of intimate relationships and helps us understand the countless ways in which race shapes social interactions. I am particularly concerned with four types of racework that people use to maintain close relationships across racial lines. I categorize these as boundary work, visibility management, emotional labor, and navigating racial homogeneity.

For many partners, the existence of longstanding interracial stigmas makes particular forms of racework necessary. Despite sometimes being heralded as symbols of a more progressive racial future, in everyday life—at work, on city sidewalks, at the mall—interracial partners often face a different perception. Their relationships are viewed as ill-fated, based purely on sexual attraction, or simply immoral. In response, Black and White partners take steps to assert a counter identity for their relationship, one that distances them from these stereotypes. This process of drawing boundaries between themselves and others—to assert who they are and who they are *not*—is a form of work. I identify these social practices as *boundary work*.

The same negative stereotypes that partners actively challenge as they talk about themselves and their relationship also shape their behavior in public spaces. In order to move safely through the streets, neighborhoods, and social spaces in which they live, some interracial partners, especially lesbian and gay partners, take one of two approaches. Some assume a defensive posture, modifying their actions in order to mask their intimacy. Others, conversely, take proactive measures to make their intimacy more visible. Although these may seem to be opposite strategies, both are means of obtaining some control over situations in which being recognized brings potential vulnerability. This form of racework is best characterized as *visibility management*. We can think of visibility management as partners' public strategy for dealing with some of the same prejudices evaded at the level of their identity as a couple through boundary work. Conceptually separating boundary work from visibility management clarifies the extent to which the problems of racism necessitate modification of both identities and public behaviors.

Stigma is not the only manner in which racial difference manifests for interracial couples. Stigmas and stereotypes come from the outside—from strangers, coworkers, neighbors, members of church congregations, family members, and so on. Racial differences are also a reality *inside* the relationship itself. In the United States, along with social class, gender, and sexuality, "membership" in a racial group shapes people's life chances, as well as the vantage point from which they view racial inequality. In the context of an intimate relationship, interracial partners must negotiate their different racial—and sometimes gender—statuses, as well as the particular orientations that arise from these statuses. I identify this form of racework as *emotional labor.*

The final form of racework is *navigating racial homogeneity.* More than two-thirds of the interracial partners in this study live in racially segregated neighborhoods (specifically, in neighborhoods that are at least 70 percent White or 70 percent Black). Living in a place where one's racial group is in the minority did not bother every partner. For many, though, this experience engendered race fatigue—the stress that results from always feeling conspicuous and repeatedly having to consider the racial undercurrents in ordinary social interactions. I call the work of managing this fatigue and feeling of relative isolation *navigating racial homogeneity.*

Lesbians, Gays, and the Experience of Racial Difference within a Heterosexist Social World

Qualitative studies have provided rich details about the contours of everyday interracial life.[26] By privileging the narratives of interracial partners, they illuminate the challenges of establishing relationships and families across racial boundaries. But the vast majority of these studies have taken heterosexual interracial couples as their only subjects.[27] The near-exclusive focus on heterosexual interraciality limits these studies' analytic power in two main ways. First, researchers who fail to examine how heterosexuality itself shapes the experiences of the straight Black/White couples they study overlook the fact that interracial partners have a sexual status, as well as a racial one. This is a significant oversight, given that U.S. society is heteronormative. When heterosexuality is assumed to be the "normal" mode of sexual and social relations, heterosexual persons, relationships, and families are privileged as healthy, legitimate, and natural, whereas those with same-sex desires are often marginalized as deviant, unnatural, or criminal.[28] Historically, heterosexuals have had—and continue to have—innumerable customary privileges that are amplified or diminished by their race, gender, and social class. Examples of these privileges include having one's sexuality affirmed in most religious traditions, enjoying legal recognition of one's marriage throughout the United States and the world, and knowing that employment benefits (e.g., health and life insurance) will cover one's spouse.[29] Researchers' failure to explore how heterosexuality itself shapes interracial life is akin to studying the history of White labor unions without considering their Whiteness, or analyzing all-male sports teams without examining the production of masculinity. In this way, heterosexuality is further normalized, and these couples—though they have been historically stereotyped as sexual deviants—are not seen as possessing a notable sexual identity, just as Whites are often not seen as possessing a particular racial identity and men are not seen as possessing a particular gender identity.

Studying only straight interracial couples, and not examining how their lives are shaped by their "straightness," has led researchers to misinterpret the experiences of straight couples as representative of all interracial couples, including lesbian and gay ones. Specifically, because it is often true of heterosexual couples, these researchers erroneously assume that racial difference is the "master status" for all interracial partners and that racial difference between intimate Black/White partners is almost always highly visible.

The second main limitation of qualitative research on interracial couples that focuses exclusively on heterosexuals is that it has shaped interraciality into an area of intellectual inquiry where heterosexual assumptions go virtually unchallenged. I include gay and lesbian couples in my study to explore how racial difference is experienced in the context of entrenched and widespread marginalization of lesbian and gay relationships. As I noted above in my discussion of racial stratification, how we conceptualize this marginalization shapes our understanding of gay and lesbian interracial lives. When people assumed to be lesbian or gay are openly harassed—for example, by strangers yelling hurtful words from car windows—or are ostracized by family members who believe their relationships to be immoral or unnatural, we call these actions and attitudes homophobic. Homophobia is defined as an extreme and irrational aversion to homosexuality. Commonly used, the term refers to emotional, angry, or fearful reactions to lesbians and gays, as well as to bisexual and transgendered persons. But if we focus on homophobia as a set of stubborn, negative associations held by certain individuals, we miss the systemic nature of gay and lesbian subjugation and underestimate the scope of the problem. Homophobic acts are not isolated aberrations from an otherwise egalitarian sexual system. Sexual stratification *is* the system, and its norms are embedded in the structures of our culture and laws. In other words, the lesbian and gay partners in this study are marginalized not only by strangers' overt hostility or family members' hurtful comments, but also by state laws that forbid them to marry or by employment policies that prevent them from sharing health insurance benefits. In this book, I refer to the systemic subjection of lesbian and gays as *heterosexism*, which has been defined as "the pervasive cultural presumption and prescription of heterosexual relationships—and the corresponding silencing and condemnation of homosexual erotic, familial, and communitarian relations."[30] Making clear the extent to which heterosexist assumptions are embedded within social institutions is an important, ongoing project that will enable researchers to see connections between discrimination in marriage and adoption laws, immigration laws, housing and employment policies, and welfare policies.[31]

The Study

At its core, this study is about how people maintain relationships across lines of stratification and how they establish intimacy in the context of inequality. To explore these topics, I used a qualitative approach—one that would allow me to understand how interracial partners interact with their social worlds and how they interact with each other. I wanted to understand how people interpreted the racial difference between themselves and their partner. What does it mean? Under what circumstances does it become important? When is it *not* important? How do sexuality and gender shape these experiences? To investigate these and related questions, I conducted interviews and gathered accounts of what it means to be interracial in everyday life.

This book is based on the narratives of eighty-two interracial partners, as well as ethnographic observations conducted among a smaller subset of this group. (Methodological details are provided in appendix A, and key characteristics of the sample are provided in appendix B.) Because it was important to talk with the members of each couple separately, the eighty-two interviews represent both partners of forty couples, plus two additional interviews with Black women whose White husbands were unavailable. Of the forty couples, ten are lesbian, ten are gay, ten are heterosexual couples in which the woman is Black and the man is White, and ten are heterosexual couples in which the woman is White and the man is Black. I chose to compose the sample this way so that I could compare nearly equal numbers of Black partners with White partners, same-sex partners with heterosexual partners, and women with men. The composition of the sample also represents an effort to prevent the experiences of Black men with White women from becoming representative of every other type of relationship, as has happened in numerous qualitative studies of interracial intimacy.[32]

The interracial partners in this study share several important characteristics. The sample is almost exclusively urban and suburban. Over half the couples live in the Philadelphia metropolitan area, about one-third live in the New York metropolitan area, and the rest live in Washington, D.C. The sample is also distinctly middle class. This was intentional. I designed the study to not introduce too many competing factors into a project aimed at analyzing intersections of race, sexuality, and gender. What do I mean by middle class? Sociologists often look to income and education as important reflections of a person's class status. Over 90 percent of these partners attended college and 70 percent of the respondents have college degrees.[33] The typical couple in my sample, as measured by the median, jointly earned between $60,000 and $75,000 (in 2004–2005). Occupational prestige is also important. Middle-class people like those in this study tend to have occupations with relative autonomy and are often responsible for supervising others in their workplaces. Constructing a sample in which respondents have similar class positions does not, however, lessen the influence of social class on the narratives as a whole. Economic resources provide these couples with numerous choices in deciding where to live and whether to send their children to public or private schools. Partners who have attended college and received their degrees have likely been instilled with the dominant colorblind discourse that pervades higher education. In these and other ways that I highlight throughout the book, the "middle classness" of the participants' interracial stories is plainly apparent.

The scope of this book is inevitably limited, in that all the interracial couples I interviewed involved one African American and one White partner, to the exclusion of other forms of interraciality, such as Black/Asian, White/Native American, Asian/White, and so on. As I noted earlier, there are good reasons for focusing on Black/White couples—theirs are the relationships that have been most forcefully prohibited. And yet in placing these two groups at the center of my analysis, I contribute to a longstanding pattern of framing racial politics in the United States as a matter of Black and White. Unavoidably, I join other researchers in reproducing a binary notion of race and excluding the experiences of non-Black communities of color. Numerous scholars have insisted upon the need to push beyond the Black/White paradigm and incorporate other groups—especially Asians and Latinos—into models of race and racism.[34] Some of my findings may contribute to that effort. The practice of racework has much to offer those interested in other types of relationships in which partners routinely negotiate intimacy across racial lines of power and privilege. For example, as with African Americans and Whites, intermarriage between Asian Americans and Whites has historically been prohibited. Partners in these couples therefore may also engage in boundary work to disassociate themselves from pejorative stereotypes about their relationships or from stigmas attached to gay and lesbian Asian/White pairs.[35] Similarly, conceptualizing the emotional labor through which partners negotiate racial difference may be useful for these other relationships as well.

One other brief comment on scope is necessary. Some readers may expect that a book about interracial intimacy will focus extensively on family—on the issues that interracial partners experience with their own children or with their families of origin, who may or may not be accepting of their relationship. These are crucial issues, and I do address them. My analysis, however, is limited to the ways in which interracial partners employ racework to deal with these interactions. I do not focus on the reactions or acceptance of families of origin except to examine how this shapes the relationship between interracial partners. Similarly, I investigated the racial identity of couples' children only to the extent that it was a subject of discussion or contestation between parents.[36]

A Note on Language

In social science research, "Black" is commonly capitalized because it refers not merely to skin pigmentation but also to a cultural heritage and identity that is often as meaningful as the ethnic identities that are conventionally capitalized. But "White" is also a social category that has engendered strong ethno-racial identification, and not simply a physical description. In this book, I capitalize both White and Black. In describing individuals of African descent, I alternate between "African American" and "Black" because these are the words my respondents used to describe themselves. The two terms, however, are not synonymous. African American is a term that describes persons whose African ancestors came, forcibly or not, to the United States. "Black" is a broader term, including not only African Americans but also those of Afro-Caribbean descent and African immigrants. I also use the words "gay," "lesbian," and "queer" because these are the terms used by my respondents, though they too mean different things. "Lesbian" and "gay" both connote same-sex attraction. "Queer" is a more expansive term that suggests the fluidity of both sexual orientation and gender identity as well as the instability of binary categories. Finally, in this book I use the term "White supremacy" to describe persistent racial stratification in the United States. By White supremacy, I mean the social system that oppresses and exploits people of color for the purpose of maintaining White wealth, power, and privilege. Some readers may be surprised by my use of this term or may infer that I am describing the kind of racial order advocated by extremists like the Ku Klux Klan, but this is not the case. We do not live in the Jim Crow era. I use this term because it draws our attention to the fact that dramatic racial inequalities still define our daily lives. As a researcher who studies race and ethnicity, I am convinced that the magnitude of evidence merits the use of this particular, weighty language.

Organization of this Book

Qualitative studies of social life bear the challenge of analyzing the nuances of individual stories while nesting them within the structural context that gives them meaning. Chapter 1 provides a historical framework for the narratives in this book by examining the variable position of heterosexual and same-sex interracial intimacy in a racial system characterized by segregation and stratification. Moving into the next chapters, I consider how interracial partners use racework in crucial social spheres—in public spaces, inside their relationships, and at the level of identities.

Chapter 2 explores how interracial partners live their everyday lives in neighborhoods and social spaces that are often racially segregated. In this environment, racework takes the form of navigating racial homogeneity. I identify and assess the work that partners do in seeking out racially diverse neighborhoods and the race fatigue that can develop when partners live in racially segregated neighborhoods. I argue that middle-class African Americans are much more familiar with this sort of fatigue, and that middle-class Whites' frustration with this sensation is an element of White racial privilege. In this chapter, I also discuss how couples navigate racially separate social spaces and explain why this can take an emotional toll, especially on Black partners.

Chapter 3 considers how interracial partners deal with racial prejudice and homophobia in public places. Here, the racework that partners do centers on visibility management. Although heterosexual couples in this study were aware of others' negative judgments, they rarely acted to manage their visibility in public spaces. Lesbian and gay partners, on the other hand, were more likely to feel a pronounced invisibility in social spaces. These couples' intimacy breaks with normative conventions in two ways—it is not heterosexual and it is not monoracial. They managed potential conflict by monitoring how openly they displayed their relationship. Sometimes this involved assuming a defensive posture; they modified behaviors in order to keep their intimacy unseen. Other times they overtly asserted their relationship through public displays of affection or even dressing alike.

In chapter 4, I shift the analysis from public spaces to the social interactions within the relationship itself. This shift reveals a third type of racework: the emotional labor through which interracial partners negotiate race in their relationship. I examine the extent to which interracial intimacy resolves racial differences between partners. I position this examination within Pierre Bourdieu's framework of habitus (and Eduardo Bonilla-Silva's extension of that term), for it is through racial habitus that race becomes a meaningful element of everyday interraciality. Within intimate interactions, lesbian/gay and heterosexual partners engage in very similar forms of emotional labor. So, in this chapter, I emphasize the importance of racework to individual partners across sexual identities. I also discuss the minority of interracial partners who do not engage in these practices. Although racial difference does not beleaguer all interracial couples or manifest uniformly in all relationships, my analysis clearly demonstrates that imbalances in power and privilege emerge in the most ordinary circumstances. Intimacy does not erode differences in racial status.

Chapter 5 explores the fourth and final type of racework: the boundary work through which partners construct an identity for their relationship and for themselves that is outside and in opposition to negative stereotypes about interracial intimacy. These include negative images that rely on sexualized gender and racial stereotypes that have been historically associated with both coercive and consensual interracial sexuality, as well as stereotypes about the cultural politics of interracial partners that position them as less "authentic" racial subjects. I investigate how partners in my study use symbolic boundaries both to distance themselves and their relationships from interracial stereotypes and to blur distinctions between themselves and same-race couples. The chapter's final section considers how sexuality influences the ways in which interracial partners think about the racial difference in their relationship.

Chapter 6 steps away briefly from the analysis of racework to consider whether intimacy shapes the ways in which individual partners view their own racial identity. Because Black racial identities were far less affected by interracial intimacy, in this chapter, I focus on White partners and situate them along a continuum of racial awareness. Using a social-psychological perspective, I show that although interracial intimacy has little effect on the racial subjectivities of some partners, for others it acts as a catalyst that begins to move Whites toward a more critical awareness of race. For a third group, this shift is profound. Examining how these intimate relationships shape perceptions of Whiteness allows us to consider the extent to which interracial contact actually shapes racial orientations.

In the conclusion, I revisit my central question about the capacity of interracial intimacy to dissolve racial differences between partners or racial groups more broadly. I point to the trust and compassion I witnessed between partners and the ways in which partners build lasting intimacy across lines of inequality. Overall, however, I identify the significance of the social practices through which interracial partners negotiate racial differences. I believe that we should be careful not to interpret increasing numbers of interracial unions as unambiguous proof of racial progress. Instead, we might re-examine our investment in interracial intimacy as a symbol of racial transcendence by looking more carefully at what happens *inside* these relationships. Interracial intimacy has much to show us about how race functions in the contemporary United States, but not because of the simple fact of its existence. Establishing an interracial partnership is only the beginning. What happens after that is far more significant and much more complex.

CHAPTER 1 | The Historical Roots of Lesbian, Gay, and Heterosexual Black/White Intimacy

THE NOTION THAT INTERRACIAL couples are a symbol of racial progress is part of an ideological shift that occurred in the United States in the middle of the twentieth century. Older representations of interracial sexuality dating back to the eighteenth and nineteenth centuries are strikingly different. In these other imaginings, sex and marriage between White and Black persons were characterized as dangerous, deviant, and—until 1967—criminal.[1] Interracial sex between Black women and White men was almost always a form of sexual violence, more accurately described as "rape," not "intimacy."[2] Even sexual encounters that were not violent took place within a context in which White men had power and authority and Black women did not. These old forms of racial thinking did not abruptly end as new racial logics took hold. Instead, shifts in racial ideologies have involved an overlap between old and new—or what Patricia Hill Collins has called "past-in-present racial formations."[3] Thus, any attempt to understand contemporary interracial experiences must take a longer, wider look back into U.S. history. Historical accounts of sexual relations between Blacks and Whites provide a structural and cultural context in which to understand the power differences that have long existed between interracial partners, as well as the interracial stigmas that linger even at the beginning of the twenty-first century.

Exploring the history of gay and lesbian interraciality alongside heterosexual interraciality reveals a vastly uneven record. Heterosexual interracial sexuality has been the subject of political and legal discourse since the first laws against interracial sex, then more likely to be called "fornication," were enacted in Virginia and Maryland in the 1660s. Gay and lesbian interracial sexuality, on the other hand, is barely perceptible within historical records before the end of the nineteenth century. As I explain below, the notion of sexual identities as such—apart from sexual desire and sexual behavior—did not emerge in the United States until the 1880s. Because same-sex sexuality was highly marginalized, some of the earliest evidence of lesbian or gay interraciality emerges in psychological reports from penal institutions and in official accounts from vice squad investigations in cities such as New York and Chicago.

My goal in this chapter is not to provide a systematic history of either heterosexual or same-sex interracial intimacy, for such an undertaking is beyond the scope of this book. Instead, my intent is to reveal enough about the events, laws, and struggles over the meaning of Black/White intimacy to contextualize the relationships of interracial partners who were born in the middle of the twentieth century and after. I begin with a brief consideration of interracial sex and marriage in the United States before the Civil War.

Power, Property, and Privilege: Heterosexual Interracial Sex before the Civil War

In Southern states during the seventeenth and eighteenth centuries and most of the nineteenth century, the differences in status between White Americans and people of African descent were stark.[4] The line between Whiteness and Blackness was the boundary between freedom and enslavement, between owning property and being considered property. In the late seventeenth century, these status differences were mapped onto differences in skin color and physical characteristics such as facial features, hair, and physique. Thus, sharply defined differences in social status became embodied as racial differences.[5] In most areas within the Northern states, racial differences did not reflect the contrast between freedom and enslavement, but the alleged superiority of Whiteness over Blackness was unequivocal. Importantly, power differences between Blacks and Whites have always been shaped by social class. In both slave-holding and non-slave-holding states, many White men and women did not belong to the land-owning class and were marginalized as yeoman farmers or sharecroppers. Yet even poor Whites enjoyed a "psychological wage" as members of the dominant racial group.[6]

In addition to being deeply influenced by class, the social inequalities embodied by racial differences were intrinsically gendered. Sexual relations between White women and Black men occurred within a distinctly different social-political context than sexual relations between White men and Black women. From the beginnings of chattel slavery until the mid-1800s, Black women enslaved by White families experienced an institutionalized form of sexual violence. Although both Black men and women performed strenuous physical field labor, Black women's bodies were further exploited by sexual coercion and rape.[7] When Black women gave birth to children sired by slave masters, White men benefited economically from the reproduction of their enslaved labor force. In this way, White men owned Black women's sexuality and fertility as property.[8] The end of formal slavery in 1865 emancipated Black women from the sexual violence of their White owners, but this "liberation" left them open to a wider range of sexual predators. Instead of being dominated by one man to the exclusion of others, Black women were now owned by none and vulnerable to many.[9]

The pervasive reality of institutionalized rape was undeniable in Black communities. It was embedded in the suffering of generations of Black women, and it was visible on the faces of thousands of light-skinned children born in the South. In White communities, however, this violence was treated as a private indiscretion on the part of propertied White men. Although these coercive sexual relationships often did not go unnoticed by the assailants' spouses, neither the sexual acts nor the children that resulted from them evoked punitive action from local officials or from other elite Whites.[10] The official response was silence. To justify and rationalize the violent treatment of Black women, they were castigated as loose, hypersexual, and animalistic. The power and privilege of propertied White men and the secrecy and silence surrounding their actions ensured that no similarly negative cultural stereotypes were created to demean *them*. Instead, the collusion of White communities protected constructions of White masculinity as strong, honorable, and restrained.

Sexual relations between White women and Black men, on the other hand, were much more infrequent and had a markedly different character. During the era of slavery, children inherited the status—enslaved or free—of their mother.[11] Thus, sexual relations between White women and Black men threatened to blur the lines of race and status in a way that the institutionalized rape of Black women by White men did not. As mothers, White women were held responsible for maintaining White racial purity and a family structure that kept wealth and property within White families. In the centuries before the Civil War, the formal system of slavery was largely sufficient to discourage sexual relationships between Black men and White women, though such relationships did sometimes take place.[12] After emancipation, Whites erected legal and ideological structures to maintain this color line. In the crucial 1883 case of *Pace v. Alabama*, the Supreme Court upheld the states' right to regulate interracial relationships, or "miscegenation."[13] In addition, Whites cultivated the myth of the Black male rapist—a frenzied narrative framing Black men as violent, hyper-sexual aggressors who would defile the innocence of White women (who were, of course, portrayed as fragile, virtuous, and pure). This myth fueled a new system of social control over Black male bodies enacted through lynching and castration.[14]

Examining interracial sexual relations in this time period reveals power differentials at their most severe. Most of these sexual encounters were sexual assaults in which the most privileged members of society—White men of the land-owning class—exploited those with virtually no social power—enslaved African and African American women. The status difference between Black men and White women was only slightly less acute. Although entrenched racism continued to pervade social life in the United States beyond the Civil War and Reconstruction, interracial intimacy at the turn of the twentieth century and beyond took place in a more complicated racial environment.

Heterosexual Interracial Sexuality and Marriage from the 1880s to World War II

The overt nature of Jim Crow racism that characterized the late-nineteenth-and-early-twentieth-century United States made it difficult for individuals to establish intimate relationships across racial lines. Until the 1950s and 1960s, formal segregation characterized public places such as restaurants, buses, hotels, schools, bars, and performance halls in many towns and cities.[15] Marriage itself was often a segregated institution.[16] In towns such as Anna, Illinois, and Appleton, Wisconsin, African Americans were threatened with violence if found within town limits after dark. Blacks and Whites would be unlikely to pass one another on the streets of "sundown towns" like these, let alone develop a close connection.[17] In the first decades of the twentieth century, especially in the South, the Ku Klux Klan used racial terror to dissuade Black men and White women from engaging in sexual relationships. Extralegal vigilante groups lynched thousands of Black men, ostensibly for having raped or had sex with White women.[18]

In cities in the North and Midwest, however, interracial contact was more frequent and less often marked by overt violence. The Harlem Renaissance that flourished in New York City between 1920 and 1935 provides insight into the racialized sexual dynamics of urban centers during this period. Harlem's distinction as a cultural mecca was in many ways unique, but the demographic shifts that made it a hub for interracial contact shaped other

U.S. cities as well. At the turn of the twentieth century, thousands of African Americans fled to Northern states, pushed by the brutality of the Jim Crow South and pulled by the burgeoning opportunities for industrial jobs that resulted from American participation in World War I. This demographic shift, called the "Great Migration," created sizable Black communities in Chicago, Detroit, and Buffalo, but the largest and most spectacular settlement was in Harlem. Harlem was a "city within a city, populated entirely by Blacks."[19] This was the era of "New Negroes." Blacks manifested a new militancy and pride, derived in part from the experiences of Black servicemen who had been treated with respect and near-equality while serving in Europe during the war. The Renaissance that African American women and men created involved jazz musicians, artists, writers, and entertainers. These demographic and cultural transformations coincided with the enforcement of Prohibition, beginning in 1920.[20] This legislation forbid the production and sale of alcohol, and ultimately resulted in the development of an underground economy in Harlem and other urban areas, where speakeasies became popular sites for drinking and socializing.

This vibrant urban center attracted the attention of Whites. Among rich and middle-class Whites, "slumming" in Harlem came into vogue.[21] The influx of White urbanites into Black neighborhoods for leisure and sexual amusement in the late 1920s was precipitated in part by the 1926 publication of *Nigger Heaven* by White author Carl Van Vechten. This widely popular narrative about slumming eroticized Harlem and its residents as at once forbidden and lurid.[22] Ironically, when visiting Harlem, many Whites felt most comfortable witnessing "authentic" Black culture in White-owned clubs, where Black women and men performed but were not permitted to enter as patrons. In these clubs, Whites enjoyed highly contrived versions of Black culture and watched elaborate floor shows. A New York City guidebook from 1925 entices visitors with this description: "One of the New York evening pastimes is to observe the antics of members of its enormous [N]egro population, many of whom show great ability in song, dance, and comedy performance.... Their unfailing sense of rhythm, their vocal quality, something primitive, animal-like, and graceful in their movements, combine to make their performances interesting to all who can put racial prejudice out of their minds."[23] In these settings, club owners played on White visitors' desire to feel as if they were transgressing racial boundaries, even as they resolutely confirmed them.[24] Accounts of White slumming suggest a desire to consume racial difference in a neatly commodified form. The same belief in racial difference that undergirded the separation of places where Blacks and Whites ate, slept, prayed, shopped, and learned was fashioned in Harlem night clubs as exotic and seductive.

Some White visitors strayed from White-owned clubs to visit "Black and Tans," saloons that catered primarily to Black men and White women, or to buy sex from Black prostitutes.[25] Interracial sexual encounters, both commercial and social, heightened the allure of slumming for many White visitors. Yet beyond actual intimate acts, this eroticization of racial difference—for Whites and for some Blacks as well—demonstrates how racial power and subordination became sexualized in the context of racial stratification. Crossing racial boundaries from White into Black communities signified, in slumming narratives such as *Nigger Heaven* and in the regular lives of White men and women, a sexual transgression.

During this time, some Blacks and Whites did create lasting relationships and, in states that permitted it, married. These relationships were somewhat tolerated because they occurred infrequently. As isolated examples of intermarriage, they did not threaten the general pattern of segregation.[26] But interracial couples faced various social sanctions. It was often necessary to conceal such relationships from White employers. Moreover, unless the Black partner was light-skinned enough to pass for White, these couples usually lived in (traditionally more accepting) Black neighborhoods. Securing a place to live could be difficult for those who were not legally married, however. Such couples often found it hard to convince their Black neighbors that they were "respectable."[27]

The regional differences in interracial relations during this period may seem striking. In some Southern or rural areas, the Ku Klux Klan massacred Black men and created a public spectacle out of the ritual, while in New York City, Blacks and Whites might sit at adjoining tables at a Black-owned Harlem speakeasy. Indeed, across rural areas, towns, and cities, the segregation and acts of racial violence that characterized this era were uneven in their scope and intensity. Yet it is important to recognize that the fear and aggression that fueled racial terror and the erotic fascination that propelled White visitors toward Harlem were part of the same racist impulse: Eroticization is the flip side of loathing.[28] Desire and fear both stemmed from the same deeply rooted belief that Blacks were intrinsically different from Whites.

Same-Sex Interraciality from the 1880s to World War II

To consider the events of this same time period with a focus on lesbian and gay Black/White couples necessitates a careful examination of scattered pieces of historical evidence. Further, because our contemporary categories of "lesbian" and "gay" are relatively recent inventions, examining the history of same-sex interraciality in the United States requires familiarizing ourselves with alternate models for understanding sexuality. While sexual acts between men and between women have a long history, they did not cohere around a specific identity until the late 1800s. Before then, these behaviors were only that—practices or activities in which some people and not others took part. Falling in love or engaging in a same-sex sexual act did not necessitate a specific label or make one a special kind of person. Identity categories like "homosexual" and "heterosexual" did not emerge until the 1880s, as the expanding field of medical science began edging into the domain of the sexual. This new discipline was termed sexology.[29]

Early sexologists understood same-sex desire through the lens of what we now recognize as gender. For these scientists, what impelled men to want other men and women to want other women was a gender dysfunction. Within the strict logic of heterosexuality, any person with sexual attraction toward women must have essential male tendencies and any person with sexual attraction toward men must have essential female tendencies. This phenomenon was termed "sexual inversion," a complete gender identity of which erotic behavior was one small part.[30] Prominent sexologist Havelock Ellis argued that the tendency toward same-sex desire was more than a passing inclination. It was congenital—inverts were born that way.[31] By the 1920s, the dominant model for understanding sexuality had shifted to our current framework that emphasizes the sex of the person toward whom sexual desire is directed.[32]

Early evidence of gay/lesbian interraciality comes from social reformers who were particularly appalled at the interracial relations they found among inverts. At the turn of the twentieth century, officials charged with eradicating illegal alcohol production and sale, prostitution, and other forms of vice from city neighborhoods found same-sex interracial socializing and carousing morally abhorrent. In 1893, a prominent doctor referred to "drag dances" attended by both Black and White male inverts as "an orgy of lascivious debauchery."[33] One expert on sexual disorders called these men "homosexual complexion perverts," arguing that they suffered from a kind of "social reverse complexion" syndrome in which color or racial difference substituted for the gender difference found in heterosexual relationships.[34] Twenty years later, another medical expert identified a similar pattern among women. In 1913, a medical journal published an article by psychologist Margaret Otis that focused on "the love-making between white and colored girls" within an institution for "delinquent" young women.[35] While others had observed the "ordinary form [of homosexual relation] ... found among girls even in high-class boarding schools," Otis proposed a different interpretation. She asserted that the racial difference between young women was a reflection of "a perversion not commonly noted."[36] Like the medical expert who observed drag dances, she too believed that within these interracial romances, "the difference in color ... takes the place of difference in sex, and ardent love affairs arise between white and colored girls in schools where both races are housed together."[37] For social reformers just before and just after the turn of the century, the compulsion toward a heterosexual logic was so strong that if gender difference in intimate relationships could not be achieved physically, it must be approximated symbolically. From this perspective, a simple analogy between race and gender sufficed to restore symbolic order: Black was to White as masculine was to feminine.[38]

Did Black/White intimacy between men or between women trouble social reformers because it was homosexual or because it was interracial? The two factors—homosexuality and racial difference—may well have worked together to position these sexual relations as especially deviant in the eyes of both reformers and police. For vice squad investigators, all Black/White intermixing was immoral, but these observers seemed especially disturbed by same-sex interraciality, which they documented in their reports as "the worst."[39] A careful analysis of Otis's article suggests that it was indeed the racial difference between these young, institutionalized women that lent special significance to her report. At the turn of the twentieth century, in an American society where Jim Crow racism structured taboos against any public (nonwork-related) interracial relationship, schoolgirls who were visibly from different racial backgrounds and yet publically intimate became marked as scientific oddities needing further study.[40] In a cultural context in which social intimacy between women was common, racial difference evolved into an overt marker of sexual intimacy. Given the existing backdrop of racial segregation and stratification, these interracial romances between young women became legible as "perverse."[41]

By the 1920s, evidence of same-sex interraciality appears in several gay and lesbian histories, and the Harlem Renaissance is an especially rich context for these sources.[42] Harlem was home to a thriving homosexual community. Black gay men and women built an extensive homosexual world within their own neighborhoods. Notably, their commitment to local establishments was made necessary by their exclusion from most of the restaurants and speakeasies that White gays frequented. Ironically, racial segregation created a homosexual culture that, in its scope, visibility, and boldness, surpassed that of largely White gay communities like Greenwich Village.[43] As a dynamic center for same-sex sociability and sexuality, Harlem became a favorite destination of White gays and lesbians as well. Some White visitors frequented Black/White homosexual clubs that, according to a vice squad report from 1927, catered to "specialized types of degeneracy and perversion."[44] These "dives" might contain one room designated for the purchase and consumption of alcohol, with a few other rooms in the back where people engaged in sexual activities, sometimes with prostitutes.[45]

Racial crossings brought significant tensions. The White gay men and women who visited these neighborhoods left behind the families and communities that normally might have constrained their behaviors. This provided White patrons a form of privacy—even in the overtly public space of jazz clubs and drag balls—that Black gays and lesbians, who frequented Harlem's shops and churches as well as its nightclubs, could not enjoy. In this way, White gays and lesbians shared some of the same racial and class privileges as White heterosexuals who had become fascinated with African American culture and sexuality.

Heterosexual Interracial Intimacy after World War II

After World War II, heterosexual interracial intimacy continued to be rare, but relationships developed within a racial landscape substantially changed by the war. Some changes resulted from demographic shifts. The war fueled industrial growth and created a demand for new workers. Over five hundred thousand Blacks left the South between 1942 and 1945, joining thousands of Whites who moved from rural hometowns to cities in the North and the West.[46] In these areas, Blacks and Whites who had never before had any interracial social contact might work next to each other in factories or, in some cases, live in the same city neighborhoods. Other changes in the racial landscape were of a more intellectual or ideological nature. The United States' participation in World War II highlighted important ideological inconsistencies in its racial policies. As America fought Adolf Hitler and his ideas about a "master race" abroad, at home Black troops and civilians were denied service in restaurants. These contradictions highlighted America's entrenched racism, making it visible to a worldwide audience. Similarly, as details of the horrific genocide of European Jews at the hands of Germans became fully known, fury at these events further discredited the biological notions of racial superiority that had once been championed by American eugenicists and social scientists.[47]

In combination, the postwar demographic and ideological shifts changed the social environment for interracial partnerships in subsequent decades.

Yet interracial intimacy continued to produce anxiety among many Whites. Especially in the South, the fear of interracial sexuality and marriage was a fear of social equality, a fear of being forced to interact with African Americans as equals not only in the public sphere but also in the more intimate sphere of social and family life.[48] When sociologist Gunnar Myrdal surveyed Americans and asked them to rank the forms of discrimination that Blacks experienced *in order of importance*, White Southerners placed restrictions against intermarriage and sex with White women at the top of the list.[49] By the mid-twentieth century, White anxieties about miscegenation were heightened by the prospect of integrated schools and public spaces.[50] Indeed, it is notable that marriage was the last social institution to be desegregated—the Supreme Court's ruling in *Loving v. Virginia* came more than a decade after *Brown v. Board of Education* and several years after the passage of the Civil Rights Act. At every step, opposition to integration was linked to opposition toward interraciality. As a 1954 article in one Southern newspaper phrased it, "Mixed schools lead to mixed sex."[51] The image that triggered White animus was, of course, not the image of a White man in a relationship with a Black woman, but that of a Black man involved with a White woman. "Would you want your daughter to marry one?" was the question that haunted White families, invoking deep-seated racist fears about Blackness and Black masculinity.[52]

Compared to Whites, African Americans have been more ambivalent about interracial intimacy. Twentieth-century attitudes toward these relationships have ranged from acceptance to tolerance to disdain. In the 1940s and 1950s, Blacks struggled against de jure segregation. As Black activists pushed for equal access to public spaces such as buses, trains, lunchrooms, and schools, it was difficult to argue that intimate relationships should remain segregated, though some Blacks did maintain this stance.[53] But whether Blacks lobbied for the *right* to intermarry or not, there was no special interest in intimate intermingling with Whites. For many middle-class Blacks, relationships between Blacks and Whites were unseemly and carried no special social currency.[54] In some circles, deep distrust and skepticism toward Whites who established relationships with African Americans were mixed with revulsion. Nonetheless, during this period, as in others, Blacks' "grudging acquiescence" to interraciality stood in marked contrast to the "near-hysterical disapproval" of Whites.[55]

The 1967 *Loving v. Virginia* decision represented a beginning of sorts. The Supreme Court's ruling insisted that interracial marriage be considered a fundamental personal right, and it made clear that heterosexual inter-racial couples deserved the same privacy and state protection given to heterosexual same-race couples. Yet *Loving* was also the culmination of changes that had been brewing in the United States in response to the social activism of the civil rights movement. Although organizations like the Student Nonviolent Coordinating Committee (SNCC) and Congress on Racial Equality (CORE) did not directly encourage interracial rela-tionships, they advocated a transformation in social relationships between Blacks and Whites, as demonstrated by SNCC's slogan "Black and White together."[56] The Supreme Court's decision influenced White opposition in important ways. In 1965, 72 percent of Southern Whites and 42 percent of non-Southern Whites told Gallup pollsters that they agreed with laws for-bidding intermarriage. By 1970, only 56 percent of Southern Whites and 30 percent of non-Southern Whites agreed with these laws.[57]

In addition to the changes wrought by *Loving*, the emergence of Black nationalism in the 1960s and 1970s led Blacks to a new way of thinking about interracial sex and marriage. Black nationalists fed up with the slow pace of social change and wary of White allies in the fight for racial justice promoted a separatist agenda. African Americans "wanted to know the time and place of their own triumph over both institutional racism and the burden of everyday insults."[58] Black people, nationalists argued, should jettison efforts to integrate racist White organizations and instead form their own social institutions. According to some leaders, integration simply reinforced the notion of White superiority by assuming that Blacks should change themselves to better fit into White institutions.[59] Honoring Black beauty and African traditions was integral to this nationalist perspective. Interracial relationships were seen as a threat to pride and cohesion within Black communities; they represented the worst form of integration. For some, interracial intimacy amounted to an attempt to reject Black culture and assimilate into Whiteness.[60]

Gay and Lesbian Interracial Intimacy after World War II

Some of the same broad shifts that increased interracial contact between Blacks and Whites in the period immediately following World War II also facilitated the expansion of gay and lesbian communities, especially in cities such as New York, Washington, D.C., Detroit, and Buffalo.[61] The deployment of U.S. troops overseas and the growth of war industries cre-ated sex-segregated work environments that heightened the chance that men and women with unexpressed or unacknowledged same-sex desires would make contact with others who shared those feelings.[62] The growth of gay and lesbian bars and the continued popularity of house parties and drag balls in the 1940s and 1950s gave people with same-sex desires additional opportunities to find each other and socialize publicly. The war had special consequences for lesbians because, with the loosening of social conventions for *all* women, the behavior of lesbians did not stand out as vividly.[63] Heterosexual women working in cities began to do things that "respectable" women had not previously done, like going to bars without male escorts and wearing pants on the street. This normalized some aspects of lesbian behavior.

Yet those who frequented lesbian and gay bars made themselves vulnerable to police raids, street harassment, and public exposure. This was especially true for African Americans, who were already the target of police harassment in many urban areas. In the 1950s and 1960s, police raided lesbian bars and arrested women who were not wearing at least three pieces of women's clothing. They were charged with impersonating men.[64] Similarly, laws against "sexual misconduct" or "lewd and lascivious acts" were used to arrest women who were dancing together or holding hands.[65] Women arrested in bars sometimes had their names published and their employers notified of their transgressions.[66] The police were not the only threat, however. Women had to be careful when entering and leaving lesbian bars, because public displays of affection in parking lots or on city sidewalks could provoke homophobic violence.[67] Socializing in public was a risky pursuit.

Beyond increasing the risk of harassment, the rise in the number of bars with a White lesbian, gay, or bisexual clientele resulted in the entrenchment of racial segregation.[68] Blacks were not served in downtown Washington, D.C., restaurants until a 1953 Supreme Court ruling barred this kind of discrimination. In the absence of formal exclusion, informal exclusionary practices often arose. For example, White owners had a strategy of leaving "Reserved" signs on every table in their establishments so that Black patrons could be told there was no available seating.[69] The persistence of White racism and a strong collective sense of Black racial identity steered Black gays and lesbians toward the few Black gay bars that existed, but it also created alternative social opportunities.[70] For those who were not comfortable in bars or could not afford to frequent them, Black gays and lesbians in urban areas held "rent parties."[71] At these gatherings, held in private homes or apartments, the host might charge a few dollars' admission for dancing, jazz, and the opportunity to buy bootleg liquor. By the end of the night, the host might have accumulated enough money to pay the next month's rent.[72] Sometimes these parties were just for gays and lesbians, but frequently they included a mix of African American hetero-sexuals, lesbians, and gays. This underscores the fact that many Black gays and lesbians did not frequent bars with primarily gay clientele or social-ize exclusively with other gays. Their strong sense of unity and belonging within Black communities allowed them to establish vibrant gay commu-nities inside Black neighborhoods, while keeping their sexuality separate from other facets of Black social life.[73]

Some historical evidence suggests that Black and White lesbians did socialize with each other in lesbian bars or at house parties. In Buffalo, New York, in the 1950s, Black lesbians purposefully desegregated what had formerly been White lesbian bars.[74] Whereas individual Blacks and Native Americans had visited these bars in the 1940s, by entering these bars in large groups, African Americans forced White patrons to notice and accept their presence. These actions made Black lesbians vulnerable, as racial prejudice continued to exist in Buffalo bars, just like it did in New York, Detroit, and Washington, D.C. Among these working-class "tough bar lesbians," Black and White women interacted frequently, both at the bars and in the house parties in Black neighborhoods that began when the bars shut down. Interracial couples became "quite common" in this crowd.[75] Though fighting and violence were common in tough bar culture, there was a marked lack of overt racial conflict in mixed spaces. Yet we should be cautious about interpreting this limited interracial contact—both social and sexual—as evidence that a common sexual marginaliza-tion diminished the significance of racial divisions. Among some Buffalo working-class lesbians, a conscious lesbian solidarity was strong enough to override racial tensions, but this accomplishment was limited. Even though some bars were desegregated, there is no evidence that they ever truly belonged to *both* White and Black lesbians.

In some cases, those who crossed the boundaries of racial communi-ties were specifically looking for interracial sex or romance. In Washing-ton, D.C., in the 1940s and 1950s, for instance, Blacks and Whites rarely occupied the same social spaces for any reasons other than interracial sex.[76] Similarly, White lesbians in Detroit rarely entered Black lesbian bars unless they were looking for sexual or romantic relationships with Black women. Indeed, interracial sexual desire has had an overt place in same-sex communities, though more so for gay men than for lesbians.[77] In a racially stratified society in which Whiteness has been valued over Black-ness, Black men's desire for White men has caused conflicts about racial authenticity and pride in Black gay communities.[78] While White men who exclusively sought out relationships with Black men may have been regarded with envy, curiosity, or disgust by other Whites, interracial desire did not create the same tensions within White gay communities.

A Historical Framework for Contemporary Interracial Lives

Examining the history of Black/White sexuality and marriage provides a valuable context in which to understand contemporary interracial narratives. It also gives rise to multiple questions. The violence associated with heterosexual interracial sex in previous centuries—both the institutionalized rape of Black women and the lynching of thousands of African American men justified in the name of protecting White women—demonstrates that sexual relations across the color line may be deeply symbolic for Blacks, as well as for Whites. How meaningful is this violent history for Black/White heterosexual couples in the twenty-first century? Have these events been relegated to a far-distant past, or do they hold social currency in the present day? Making sense of present-day heterosexual interracial intimacy requires that we take into account its relationship to a vicious past.

So then, what of gay and lesbian interracial intimacy? In important ways, it has a history in the shadows, away from mainstream racial politics and legal prohibitions against miscegenation. Indeed, lesbian and gay "race-mixing" has been a practice that is difficult to see, even for historians of interracial intimacy. It is notable, I believe, that same-sex interracial intimacy is virtually absent from the historical literature on interraciality.[79] Those scholars who have looked into the past in search of evidence of intimate encounters across the color line have tended to find only information about heterosexual relationships.[80] In contrast, historians with intellectual lenses primed to recognize same-sex sexuality have been able to document lesbian and gay interracial intimacy. This is the case even though historians of sexuality have been rightly critiqued for their tendency to focus on White lesbian and gay subjects to the exclusion of lesbians and gays of color.[81] I draw attention to this pattern not only to address the heterosexual bias within scholarship on interracial intimacy, but also because it speaks to a broader pattern that emerges within these histories, namely that gay and lesbian interracial partners were most visible to other gays and lesbians. Tensions arising from racial difference became visible in same-sex communities in which a couple's intimacy was already legible.

Finally, although we observe substantial divergences when we position these histories side by side, there are significant commonalities as well.

During the Harlem Renaissance, for example, the desires of White gay men may have been considered deviant in relation to the desires of White heterosexual men, but both groups enjoyed racial and class privileges when they visited Harlem for sexual amusement. Both enjoyed the spatial mobility accordant with their social standing, and both could indulge their fantasies and then return home to a separate community where their sexual encounters would not be known. Further, by eroticizing Harlem as exotic and Black men as hypersexual, White straight and gay men simultaneously invoked and perpetuated racist myths about Blackness. Similarly, though lesbian bars were considered marginal or immoral sites during the 1950s, the racial exclusion practiced in White lesbian bars during this time granted White lesbians a form of racial power that heterosexual Whites enjoyed when they prohibited Blacks from entering their lunch counters, movie theaters, or swimming pools. In these contexts, both White gays and White lesbians approached interracial intimacy from a position of privilege. For the most part, race-based power differences between Whites and Blacks endured across gay, lesbian, and heterosexual relationships.

The social and cultural history of interracial intimacy I have examined in this chapter brings us to the brink of contemporary interracial life. We cannot accurately interpret the present without a clear recollection of what has come before. With this history as a foundation, the stage is set for an analysis of how racial difference affects contemporary lesbian, gay, and heterosexual Black/White relationships. Moving from the outside in, this book explores the shape and texture of everyday interracial life. I begin by investigating how interracial partners negotiate racial divisions within their social environments.

CHAPTER 2 | Public Interraciality: Navigating
Racially Homogeneous Social Spaces

Like going to church, I didn't realize it, um, before I knew Neil,
that it was such an issue, that there was such, that church was so
segregated, it really is.... There's no—you can't find a setting that
you feel comfortable in, that it's a nice mix, a balance, racial balance.
It's either all Black or all White. You know or all, you know, whatever
the race is. I mean we're dealing with Black and White basically, you
know, um, you can very easily find a church that's predominantly
Jamaican. You're happy and comfortable in there, but I know that
Neil's not, wouldn't be comfortable.... Right now we're not really
um, we don't really go to church on a regular basis.... I would be
more comfortable going to church if, as a family, if we were able to
find a more diverse church.

IN THIS QUOTATION, Mary Chambers laments the scarcity of racially
integrated churches that she can attend with her White husband, Neil
Chambers, and their three children. She draws our attention to a form
of social organization that troubles many interracial couples: the spatial
separation of White and Black social environments. Though these racial
divisions characterize everyday life for most Americans, not just Black/
White couples, interracial couples often have a particular investment in
racially mixed spaces, because generally in such spaces neither partner
feels conspicuous and both can be comfortable. But mixed environments
are hard to find, as Mary's observation about places of worship indicates.
Couples in my study navigated racially homogeneous barber shops, restaurants, subway cars, convenience stores, dance classes, theaters, activist
group meetings, post offices, Little League practices, video stores, block

meetings, and so on. In many instances, if one partner is uncomfortable in a racially separate space, the couple is able to find a mutually accept-able alternative. But these situations become trickier when couples cannot avoid certain settings, as when children's activities require their presence, or when one partner's connection to a setting is very important, or, as in Mary's case, there is no available alternative. Monoracial spaces can be stressful for one or both partners. In this chapter, I explore how interracial partners address the daily challenges of being interracial in racially homo-geneous environments.

Racial Residential Segregation and Neighborhood Preferences

Social scientists study the racial segregation of neighborhoods, towns, and cities because where we live and with whom we live have tremendous sig-nificance for our life chances. Neighborhoods are not only a reflection of the economic standing of their residents; they also shape residents' eco-nomic opportunities. The quality of local schools is dependent on the tax base of the surrounding community. Neighborhoods also provide social networks through which individuals may exchange information, oppor-tunities, and resources. In other words, because our homes exist within a physical and social network in which resources are unevenly distributed, where we live both reflects and shapes our place within this hierarchy.

Research shows that American neighborhoods are persistently segre-gated, with Black communities remaining the most isolated from other racial groups.[1] This pattern has a long history. In the 1920s and 1930s, residential segregation was enforced by discrimination in both housing and lending policies. "Neighborhood improvement associations" main-tained racial divisions in residential areas through restrictive housing cov-enants and restrictions on sales to interracial partners.[2] By 1940, urban neighborhoods in the largest metropolitan areas in the North were sub-stantially segregated. In the two decades that followed, the Federal Hous-ing Administration (FHA) and the Veterans Administration (VA) spurred suburban development by insuring loans and easing the process of buying a home—for Whites.[3] Even after these formal avenues of discrimination were closed, informal discriminatory practices, such as real estate agents' efforts to steer Black buyers away from White neighborhoods or their use of "blockbusting" strategies, have maintained racial segregation.[4]

The material consequences of these residential patterns are quite seri-ous—historically unequal access to home ownership has contributed to the tremendous gap in wealth that exists between White and Black Americans.[5] This segregation also has indirect social consequences—when neighborhoods are segregated, so too are the commercial, religious, civic, and recreational spaces used by people in those neighborhoods. Even at the beginning of the twenty-first century, it remains fairly unusual to see White and Black people interacting together socially, whether they are friends, lovers, partners, or family members.[6]

Institutional forces have excluded Blacks from majority-White neighborhoods, but research on racialized neighborhood preferences suggests that other factors play a role as well. African Americans and Whites have competing conceptions of what "mixed" is and different tolerances for what kind of racial balance is ideal. Whites prefer to live in predominantly White neighborhoods, although they are willing to live with a small number of Blacks, Asians, or Latinos. In contrast, Blacks are willing to live in neighborhoods where they are the minority. Studies suggest that Whites are willing to live with Blacks up to a threshold of 80 percent White and 20 percent Black.[7] Although social class divisions overlay racial divisions in the separations of neighborhoods, Whites appear to be much more averse to living with Blacks than with Asians and Hispanics. Sociologist Camille Zubrinsky Charles argues that communities with relatively high concentrations of African Americans are viewed as undesirable to Whites, even when those communities are relatively affluent.[8] In contrast, African Americans are willing to live with higher percentages of other racial groups, including Whites, especially if they perceive the area to have a comfortable and safe racial climate. Earlier studies suggest that a 50 percent Black/50 percent White split is tolerable for most Blacks.[9] These marked differences in what constitutes a desirable neighborhood help account for why interracial partners must expend effort to find a place that is comfortable for them both.

Racework in Public: Navigating Racially Homogeneous Social Spaces

The interracial partners in my study live in or in close proximity to large metropolitan areas—New York, Philadelphia, and Washington, D.C. Because these are racially and ethnically diverse areas, they contain numerous racial communities. There are not only White and African American enclaves, but also African, Latino, Eastern European, Asian, Asian American, and others. Racial segregation continues to ensure that such groups inhabit racially distinct neighborhoods and spaces within these cities and their surrounding suburbs. This increases the likelihood that neighborhoods, schools, churches, grocery stores, and playgrounds will be Black *or* White, not Black *and* White. Racial segregation also forces interracial partners to navigate neighborhoods and social spaces that are racially divided, and to make decisions about how to live their lives within these spaces.

The segregated nature of neighborhoods and the racial separation within other regular public spaces brings into play a particular form of racework—*navigating racial homogeneity*. This involves the energies that interracial couples expend deciding what types of environments, from neighborhoods to churches, restaurants, holiday parties, etc., are comfortable for each partner. Those who desire racially mixed spaces must first agree on what kind of racial mixture counts as "diverse," "mixed," or "integrated." These negotiations, which often involve two distinct perspectives, are a form of racework that interracial partners jointly undertake when they decide where to live. Most partners in my sample, however, live in racially segregated neighborhoods. This means that one partner is unmarked (as part of the racial majority) and the other partner is much more conspicuous (as part of the racial minority). In these instances, the partner in the racial minority engages in the work of navigating racially homogeneous spaces alone. Black partners in majority-White spaces and White partners in majority-Black spaces both experience race fatigue. They contend with the stress of always feeling conspicuous and of having to attend to the presence of racial undercurrents in everyday social interactions. The race fatigue that Black and White partners endure, however, is not equivalent. In the context of White supremacy, Whiteness still yields privilege, even in a non-White context, and Blackness may be most consequential in an all-White context.

Like other forms of racework, navigating racial homogeneity enables interracial partners to deal with some of the social costs connected to the racial difference in their relationship. But unlike the boundary work that partners use to create interracial identities apart from longstanding stigmas, and in contrast to the emotional labor by which partners negotiate differences in racial habitus, navigating racial homogeneity is a form of racework that is a direct response to the racial divisions that characterize public spaces. As I explain later in the chapter, at times these responses resemble other forms of racework, but they are unique in that they are strategies that shape how interracial partners negotiate their social landscapes.

I begin the analysis by describing the experiences of interracial couples who seek out mixed neighborhoods in which to live. I then discuss the realities of partners who are the racial minority in their segregated neighborhoods. Stories of both racially mixed and homogeneous neighborhoods provide examples of the kinds of actions and efforts that make navigating segregated space a form of racework. I also consider the experiences of interracial partners in other racially divided social settings, particularly queer establishments. For Black lesbians in my sample, the importance of these spaces created potential tension within their relationships.

In analyzing the narratives in this chapter, I follow sociologist Heather Dalmage's important distinction between racial *segregation* and racial *separation*.[10] Dalmage uses the term "segregation" to describe the effects of almost a century of discriminatory housing and lending practices imposed by White-controlled institutions. When discussing some Blacks' preference for all-Black spaces as a response to this exclusion and as settings where people can find safety and community, she uses the term "separation." I make the same distinction in this chapter.

Seeking Mixed Neighborhoods

In my conversations with interracial partners, I often heard people espouse the virtues of "mixed" neighborhoods. Many asserted that a neighborhood with both African Americans and White residents is where they would feel most comfortable and welcome and that, by contrast, they felt "conspicuous" being racially different from the community in which they were living. As Julianna Tyson, a White heterosexual woman in her mid-thirties explains, "We always try to live in an environment where it's more of a mix. I mean, I don't think I would like to move into an all-Black neighborhood or I would like to move into an all-White neighborhood." Julianna states her racial preference in a manner that resonates with many other couples in my sample—racial heterogeneity is more desirable than racial homogeneity, whether it be all-White or all-Black.

Wanda Maxwell is a thirty-year-old Black woman who lives with her White husband, Ethan Smolen, in an area of Philadelphia with a reputation for being historically racially integrated. They bought their house shortly after they got married, six years ago. Wanda is tall, wears stylish eyeglasses, and has dreadlocks. She describes herself as "determined, stubborn, and driven." When I ask her why she chose a racially mixed neighborhood, she explains, "I think people who are willing to live in a mixed neighborhood are a little more comfortable with people different than them. It doesn't mean they are 100 percent comfortable, but I feel in daily interactions that you're going to get stared at less, whether it's me or Ethan." Ethan is a twenty-nine-year-old White middle-school science teacher. He has short brown hair, blue eyes, and wire-rim glasses with round lenses. Although he describes himself as "goofy," as we talk, I sense a calm confidence beneath his self-deprecating humor. Ethan's feelings about the neighborhood are similar to Wanda's. He says that in a racially mixed neighborhood, "You get all that richness; you get all that diversity. And then when you live in a neighborhood that's predominately one way or the other way, you lose some of the interest of everything. Like, for example, living in an all-Black neighborhood, Wanda is really perceived as the lady with the White husband; in an all-White neighborhood, I'm the guy with the Black wife. You know you don't have as much of that here."

On the whole, Wanda and Ethan are very pleased with where they live. In addition to a number of aesthetic priorities—they were looking for a neighborhood with a lot of trees and a house that was "architecturally beautiful"—they had a specific set of racial criteria. They wanted a racially mixed neighborhood where they would both be comfortable; finding such a neighborhood required concerted effort. Wanda tells me, "We did a lot of research before we bought our house, in terms of neighborhoods, a lot." They compared the racial composition of several neighborhoods, using census tract data they found on the Internet. They drove around prospective neighborhoods in both the daytime and nighttime. They even went to a local Irish pub—a social space they deemed potentially problematic—"on purpose, to see how it would feel."

The work in which Wanda and Ethan engaged primarily centered on researching and identifying racially mixed neighborhoods, and they are both satisfied that they found one. Their conception of "mixed" does not necessarily mean equal numbers of Blacks and Whites. According to the U.S. Census Bureau, Ethan and Wanda's mixed neighborhood is 25 percent White and 68 percent Black.[11] Defining "mixed" can be challenging. Researchers who study integration disagree about what constitutes a mixed neighborhood. Some believe that for an area to be truly mixed, it should have equal representation from each group. That means that in a neighborhood comprised mainly of African Americans and Whites, true integration would involve 50 percent Whites and 50 percent African Americans.[12] Others use different guidelines.[13]

Some interracial partners made deliberate efforts to find a diverse neighborhood but ended up in a racially homogeneous environment anyway. Kristie Kelley is a forty-six-year-old African American woman who lives with her forty-nine-year-old White husband, Burton Connell, and their teenage daughter, Ivy, in Woodsdale, an affluent community less than thirty miles north of New York City.[14] Kristie is an attorney and Burton, who has a Ph.D. in biology, works in a research laboratory. When the couple was searching for a house, they were looking for a neighborhood that, as Burton explains, was "racially diverse and somewhat economically diverse." Like Wanda and Ethan, they had researched the racial composition of potentially attractive neighborhoods. They also took time to make careful observations. Kristie describes this process:

> That was Burton's job. ... The different communities we were thinking of living in, he went to the schools, he did the tours. He sat out[side] and watched the playgrounds, [to] see who was there, what was the racial mix, 'cause you can't really get that from the guided tour. So he did all of that.

For Kristie and Burton, as for other couples in the study, racial diversity was one priority among a number of desirable characteristics. As Kristie explains, "We had a list of these are all of the things we want, these are the things that we have to have, and these are the things we could do without." Kristie works in Manhattan and commutes by train, so she was looking for a town not too far from the city and a neighborhood in close proximity to a train station. She and Burton were also very concerned about the school district that Ivy would attend, because moving to this northern suburb would mean sending their daughter to a public school instead of the private school she had attended when they lived in Harlem.

In the midst of these competing pressures, racial diversity lost out. Burton tells me that when they moved into their neighborhood nearly ten years ago, it was about 5 percent Black. Now it is a little less than that. He and Kristie are most concerned with the racial homogeneity of their neighborhood as it relates to Ivy's school. The private school Ivy used to attend was much more diverse. According to Kristie, that was inevitable. "Private schools get to pick, so you can create your diversity. [In] public schools, diversity comes from your housing stock." Kristie would prefer a more racially mixed school, but she believes that, at least, her neighbors are "all keen on diversity." Burton expressed a similar point about the "liberal, open-minded" people in their neighborhood, when he told me that there is "not that much diversity, but [there are] people who like the *idea* of diversity."[15]

For couples who prioritize mixed neighborhoods, part of the work of navigating racially homogeneous social spaces is to try to avoid them. This is why they focus their energies on seeking out diversity. This kind of racework is more about the process than the result. Wanda and Ethan were able to find a neighborhood that fit their ideals, whereas Kristie and Burton were less successful. Yet both couples engaged in a similar process of conducting research, driving around, making observations, discussing pros and cons, and so on. Interracial partners are not alone in valuing diverse environments, or in commodifying diversity. But as Black and White couples, many do have a special interest in finding neighborhoods where each will feel comfortable.[16]

Segregated Neighborhoods and Separated Social Spaces

Although many interracial partners invoked this ideal of a "mixed" neighborhood, most of the couples in my sample lived in neighborhoods that were fairly homogeneous. More than two-thirds lived in neighborhoods that were at least 70 percent White or 70 percent Black.[17] Some lived in extremely homogeneous environments. Just over a quarter of the respondents lived in neighborhoods that were at least 90 percent White or 90 percent Black. Interracial partners had varied experiences within these racially homogeneous neighborhoods, depending not only on their race, but also on their social class and sexuality.

White neighborhoods in my study were also, on average, wealthier than the predominantly Black neighborhoods in which other interracial partners lived. The middle-class interracial partners who lived in neighborhoods where at least 70 percent of residents were Black resided in areas where the average median household income was only $29,700, compared with an average median household income of $70,100 in neighborhoods where over 70 percent of the residents were White. In other words, in this study, social class differences in neighborhoods map onto racial differences in neighborhoods. Research suggests that this residential pattern is firmly rooted in a history of segregation, in which White Americans have preserved exclusive access to neighborhoods with valuable homes and high-quality public services. When Black Americans were formally excluded from purchasing homes in the burgeoning suburbs during the 1940s and 1950s, they were denied an opportunity to make the kind of investment that would secure a middle-class status.[18]

Managing Race Fatigue: White Partners

White partners who live in majority-Black neighborhoods experience a pronounced sense of race fatigue prompted by feeling racially conspicuous in the social spaces surrounding their homes. Feeling racially marked is something to which most White Americans are not accustomed. Helen Rutkowski, for example, is a fifty-year-old White woman with brown eyes and straight, sandy-blond hair that just reaches her shoulders. She is employed as the fiscal director for a community health organization. Her partner, Benjamin Walters, is a tall, fifty-seven-year-old Black man with closely cropped hair. Ben works as a community advocate for homeless people. The couple lives in a Philadelphia neighborhood that according to census data is 76 percent Black, 12 percent White, and 9 percent Asian. The streets in this neighborhood are lined with row houses, a popular style in Philadelphia, in which each dwelling shares a barrier wall with the home on either side, leaving no open space between any two dwellings. Helen and Ben's block, which is almost entirely residential, has some vacant storefronts at the corner. Although there are very few trees in the neighborhood and none on their block, down the street from Helen and Ben, several residents have placed potted flowers along the sides of their concrete steps.

Helen notices the racial homogeneity of the surrounding city blocks. She comments, "Sometimes when I'm moving around my neighborhood, I'm very aware that I'm the only White person." She tells me about a conversation she often has with herself when she gets on the bus to go to work in the morning. "I sometimes think that [people think,] 'She's going to sit next to the other White person on the bus.' But I really try to figure who is the less fat, so I have a seat or whatever. That's my criteria for the bus. It's all about that, it's not about the White person or the Black person. Sometimes I think the Black people are looking at me for that. Like, 'Where is she going to sit?' Because it's predominately Black ... there are very few Caucasians.... It's weird that I think that they're thinking that." The racial difference between Helen and her neighbors is something that she notices and assumes they notice. She is conscious of it in casual conversation with people on her block and when she gets on a crowded bus. She reports that she is not distressed by these experiences, but being in the localized minority makes her acutely conscious of her Whiteness.

Neil Chambers shares some of Helen's experiences, even though the middle-class Black neighborhood where he, Mary, and their children live seems worlds away. The Chambers house sits back on a giant, grassy lot on a tree-lined street in Oakton, a small city less than thirty miles north of Manhattan.[19] Although their two-story colonial is sizable, the adjacent sprawling, three-story Tudor houses with landscaped hedges and bird baths make their home look modest. With over 70 percent African American residents, its racial composition is one of the only things that might differentiate the Chambers's neighborhood from many other older suburban neighborhoods in Westchester County. Another notable difference is that it is in close proximity to neighborhoods with working-class and poor residents.[20]

When I speak with Mary on the screened-in porch the day before Easter, she explains that she grew up in this house, which she and Neil bought from her parents. Neil had earlier confided that they would never have been able to afford the house with their own income. Referring to Neil, Mary tells me, "I think that he would prefer to live in a community where he's more comfortable with the people, in a community where he can look around and see his own race. ... With more White people, absolutely, he'd be more comfortable."

When I ask Neil about the neighborhood, he tells me it is impossible for him not to think about race in everyday social interactions. It is entirely usual, he says, for him to go into the grocery store or the post office and be "the only White guy there." He continues:

> It's hard for me to kind of put it into words. Where it's not a bad thing, you know, it's not like I feel like I'm going to get mugged or um, I'm going to get hurt. But you have to understand, it's kind of like when you deal with White people, they have their prejudice, they have their—they have what they're used to. And then when you deal with Black people, it's really the same thing, you know? ... And you don't always have an awkward exchange—as a matter of fact it's more often than not it's not, it's not an awkward exchange, but there are times where maybe you get a little vibe that's negative. It's not like a big deal, but you know, that is something, that, it's part of the equation.

For Neil, it is difficult to separate the numerous interracial exchanges he has at the gas station, post office, shopping center, Little League field, etc., from the "larger context ... of race relations within the United States." He adds: "I'd be lying to you if I said, 'Oh, I don't see any difference, it doesn't matter, it's all the same.' That's bullshit, excuse my language."

In addition to feeling tension in his everyday interactions, Neil also laments the poor quality of the schools in his area and connects this more generally to the economic condition of the neighborhood. "The high school is a disaster. You know, it has a metal detector—it's a bad high school. This whole school system is bad, so that the property value really suffers. Well, let's say our house is, which I know this'll sound nuts, but it's like $500,000, if that was three miles away, four miles away, you're looking at $750,000 [or] $800,000." Like his African American neighbors, Neil loses out economically because of a housing market that devalues homes located in predominantly Black neighborhoods.[21]

When White partners discuss their discomfort with living in poor or working-class Black neighborhoods, their class prejudices sometimes magnify their perceptions of racial difference. For example, Marie Thomas is a thirty-two-year-old White heterosexual woman who lives with her twenty-nine-year-old Black husband, Frank Thomas, about ten blocks from Helen and Ben. She and Frank have been together for two years; they moved into this neighborhood just over a year ago. The landlord is a friend of Frank's mother. Marie explains that if it were not for this personal connection, they probably would have cancelled the appointment to see the apartment as soon as they saw the rundown state of the neighborhood. They showed up at six o'clock on a Sunday night in March to walk through the place. The inside of the apartment had been beautifully remodeled, with granite countertops and stainless-steel appliances. More importantly, the rent was well within their means. At the time, Marie and Frank were engaged and were saving money for their upcoming wedding. Renting this apartment allowed them to put aside a few hundred dollars per month.

Marie, like Helen and Neil, experiences race fatigue. As a White person who has always lived in White neighborhoods, feeling racially conspicuous is not something with which she had much experience before moving to this apartment. This racial difference makes her feel like an outsider. "I'm always the only White person getting off or on [at] the bus stop, pretty much in a five block radius. ... I get some looks when I get off the bus. To me it's the same looks [I get] at work when I say that I don't have a car. Like, 'What?' It's not so much anger. It's like, 'What are you doing here?'" As she continues, she tells me that there are some "older ladies that are very cordial" and that the crossing guards have begun to warm up to her. But like Neil, she assumes that Black people hold prejudice toward White people, just as White people hold prejudice toward Black people. "All these years Black people have had to suffer total injustice and the nightmarish treatment, I guess they are saying that, 'We didn't deserve that,' and [now] treat White people the same way."

Marie's experience of being racially isolated, much like Neil's, is shaped by the class differences she perceives between herself and her working-class and poor Black neighbors. The litter and vandalism she observes in the blocks that surround her apartment are not things she experienced when she and Frank were living in other, more upscale areas. Perhaps because she and her partner have the financial means to live elsewhere but have chosen to live in this setting temporarily, the problematic aspects of the neighborhood make Marie's time here seem to her like an unwarranted sacrifice. She says,

> I said something really mean the other day, but we walked out when the [car] windows were broken out, [and] I was so frustrated. We have mice now that we can't get rid of because of this vacant house next to us, and I'm like, "[I have] done my year in the Peace Corps. I'm tired of this. Get me out of here." [Frank] said, "That is the worst thing you ever said." But sometimes it feels like that. Like it's pretty hostile around here.

By comparing her Philadelphia neighborhood to a Peace Corps region, Marie positions the social class difference between her (and Frank) and their neighbors as immense—as different as a first-world nation is from a third-world nation.

As we continue talking, she makes the link between her neighbors' economic struggles and their Blackness more explicit. In recounting a conversation she had with her mother when she and Frank first moved in, she remembers saying,

> "Living here is making me racist." I'm fighting it with everything that I have. I'm obviously not racist. It's a hard thing to be the outsider here. ... I could probably say the same thing about the White version, or we could live in a rural area of Appalachia. To see the lack of male role models, the lack of family. ... Lately it has been bothering me more because I really don't like getting on the bus. I like to—my walk from work has been my time to unwind and relax—and if I have to get on the bus and hear people yelling, and swearing, and everything else, when I'm trying to do my unwind, or I have to put my [headphones] on, it's a horrible experience.

Although she acknowledges that White people live in areas with similarly acute levels of poverty and hardship, Marie associates behaviors that make her uncomfortable with Blackness. In this case, she is unable to see how material constraints shape social behavior. She does not see her own neighbors as fellow commuters traveling to and from work while managing the additional strain of negotiating public transportation with children in tow. Instead, she observes a "lack of family," a "lack of role models," and then makes generalizations about the health and character of entire communities from a small set of observations within one, hectic public space.

Like the majority of Whites in the United States who are accustomed to being part of the dominant racial group, the White partners I have described in this section are used to thinking of their Whiteness as invisible or race-neutral, if they think about it at all.[22] But unlike the majority of White Americans, these White partners live in majority-Black neighborhoods. Although it is impossible to know for sure where these White partners would be living if their significant others were not Black, research suggests that they would be likely to live somewhere surrounded by other White people.[23] Being in racial environments in which their Whiteness marks them as overtly visible is a new and uncomfortable experience. Managing the fatigue that comes from constantly wondering about the racial subtext of every social interaction is a form of work. It involves a set of emotional practices—assessing social interactions, analyzing their racial dynamics, and deciding upon the proper outward response—that are largely unnecessary for Whites who live in majority-White neighborhoods. I consider these emotional practices a form of the racework of navigating racial homogeneity, because these White partners would be less likely to live in Black racial environments if they were not in interracial relationships.

Managing Race Fatigue: Black Partners

Racist slights and assumptions are pandemic in our society, and they are certainly common in racially diverse locales. Yet Black partners may feel especially vulnerable to everyday racism when they are one of only a few African Americans in their neighborhood. Scholar Philomena Essed defines everyday racism as practices that are familiar, recurrent, and systematic. Everyday racism includes "injustices recurring so often that they are almost taken for granted, nagging, annoying, debilitating, seemingly small injustices one comes to expect."[24] These practices are generally not extreme, but their mundane nature does not mean that they are not harmful. Research shows that the psychological distress caused by experiencing racism on a day-to-day basis can adversely affect mental and physical health.[25] Kalvin Oster, a thirty-year-old Black financial analyst whose wife is White, attests that even for "a person who has been shown racism all their life … it's still alarming when you feel it. It still has that same response … that same gut-wrenching feeling when it happens. You want to act out or just vent until it's gone."

Black partners in my study recount subtle incidents that highlight the racial difference between themselves and their neighbors. These events provide insights that are useful for understanding the experience of being a person of color with a White partner in a predominantly White neighborhood. The narratives reveal the energy that Black partners routinely expend in order to protect themselves and manage the stresses of racism.

We can clearly conceptualize these survival strategies as a form of work—they involve anticipating racist incidents, interpreting events that could be of a racial nature, evaluating possible reactions, suppressing sometimes intense emotions of anger or fear, and deciding on the best response. But, in many instances, these strategies are *not* forms of racework because they are actions in which African Americans engage independent of whether they are in an interracial or a same-race relationship. They are behaviors that are not necessarily part of maintaining a close relationship with their White partner. Kristie Kelley's experiences in her Woodsdale neighborhood are illustrative. For the most part, Kristie feels comfortable in her neighborhood. She acknowledges that she may have felt "more comfortable" in their old neighborhood on 125th street in East Harlem but she says, "There haven't been any particular experiences" in Woodsdale that make her dislike the neighborhood. Like some of the Black middle-class suburban residents in sociologist Karyn Lacy's ethnographic study, Kristie blurs the lines between herself and her White neighbors by emphasizing her social class status and staking a legitimate claim to her White upper-middle-class suburban neighborhood.[26] She says, "I felt like, 'Hey, I bought a house. It's my neighborhood. So what are you going to say? You can't say anything really.' I mean [they] could, but it's very 'liberal' for lack of a better word, and people aren't going to say anything. They're not."

Yet even in the absence of overt racial conflict, racialized assumptions and comments arise in daily life that make Kristie aware that she is one of very few people of color who live in this quiet neighborhood. At a birthday party at a house down the street, while having a casual exchange with a neighbor's White father, the racial dynamics of the conversation became evident. She explains:

> He says, looking to me, [that] he plays the piano and he asked me about some old Negro spiritual. Now I don't think if I wasn't Black he would have asked me that question. And no, I didn't know the song he was talking about but I'm convinced he would not have asked me that if I was not Black ... and I was the only Black person in the room at the time. ... And I'm sure he was just making conversation, you know it wasn't a derogatory thing, but there was nothing about our conversation that would lead us to that discussion. ... Only because you see a Black person you're going to ask me this stupid, what felt like a stupid question at the time, given there was not context for it.

These moments are ubiquitous for middle-class African Americans in daily life. Economic resources and the ability to access previously racially exclusive locales do not protect members of the Black middle class from everyday racism.[27] Kristie acknowledges the surface ambiguity of this exchange by explaining that this elderly man was not trying to be "derogatory." She prefaces this story by telling me, "It could be my paranoia, but. ..." Yet she is confident that the White man assumed that her brown skin conferred upon her expertise about all things African American.[28]

Other African Americans in predominantly White middle-class neighborhoods had similar experiences. When Kalvin Oster recounts to me a racist joke that his White neighbor told him, he seems not to have been intimidated by the experience, but he clearly found it bewildering. On occasions when Whites "get up close" to Mabel Renault to see her dreadlocks during the summer months that she, her White husband, Hank, and their three children spend in New Hampshire, she is vexed. When a White stranger asks Nadine Allen, who is a Black lesbian, which tenant she works for as she is riding the elevator up to her new apartment in a high-rise building in Washington, D.C., she summons a practiced patience and tells him she works at a local private high school. Then she asks him whom *he* works for.[29] On these occasions, like so many others in which middle-class Blacks encounter racist slights in the familiar spaces of their own neighborhoods, these partners consciously worked to not become upset, and they moved on.

Most of the predominantly White neighborhoods in my study are middle class or upper-middle class. Some of the everyday racism that Black partners experience, however, comes from working-class White neighbors. When Leonard Umbers, a Black gay man, talks about the White men who live next door to him and his White partner, Victor Renford, in an area about fifty miles north of New York City, he expresses an uneasy caution. "There's diversity within economic level, I'll put it that way. Um, you have a lot of probably people like us—you know, people that make good money moved up here, have, you know, resources. ... But then you equally have, um, people that don't have money.... There's an element of I don't know what the word is—'redneck' or what[ever], but there is that element, too." By using the disparaging term "redneck," Leonard suggests that lower socioeconomic status is coupled with less tolerance and a greater likelihood of racist and homophobic antagonism. He recounts a story that he believes justifies these assumptions: "One night we were out in the garden in the front there, and somebody was yelling at somebody, and it was like, "Blah, blah, blah and blah, blah, and I don't care if that nigger blah, blah, blah." We're like [mimes shock] so like [our] radar went up.... I mean nobody seems to have come rushing over here to burn a cross, so we ... just sort of put it on the back burner." Like Marie and Neil,

Leonard laments his proximity to working-class people. He describes the neighbor's house as "really ramshackle. ... It's like eight cars in the road, broken refrigerators. ... There's a difference in terms of economics."

The experiences with everyday racism that I have recounted so far—between Black partners like Kristie, Kalvin, Mabel, and Nadine, and their White neighbors—require work. These experiences demand deliberation, introspection, and examination, all of which take time and emotional and psychological energy. Yet they do not fit within my definition of racework, because the racial tensions these partners are dealing with arise from everyday racism and are not part of maintaining their interracial relationship in a racially stratified society. African Americans who live in White neighborhoods with their African American partners are likely to have similar experiences. It may be that the feeling of being racially conspicuous or isolated is more acute when one has a White partner, but my respondents did not say or even imply that in our conversations. Further, it is possible that the middle-class Black partners in my study would still live in these mostly White neighborhoods even if their partner was Black. Pushing against decades of formal and informal discriminatory practices, some middle-class Black couples move into White suburban neighborhoods. As I noted at the beginning of the chapter, research shows that African Americans have more flexible neighborhood preferences than do Whites. Although the most desirable neighborhoods may be those that are both middle class and have more than a handful of Black residents, Black Americans also rate neighborhoods with high median housing values as desirable, even if very few Blacks reside there.[30] In other words, the experience of managing everyday racism in White neighborhoods is certainly a form of work, but it is not necessarily a form of racework.

When *do* Black partners undertake racework in White settings? These practices are much easier to discern in the context of social spaces like parties, meetings, and churches. In the excerpt that opens this chapter, Mary Chambers expresses her frustration with the difficulty of finding a church that she and her husband Neil would both feel comfortable attending. This challenge demonstrates why social spaces necessitate racework for so many interracial partners—racially mixed environments are often difficult to find and, in the absence of such places, one partner must manage the burden of being in the numerical minority in that place, whether that burden involves curious looks or overtly racist actions.

Partners in my study reported places of worship (churches, temples, synagogues, and Quaker meetings) as commonly racially segregated spaces. This mirrors a much broader trend within the United States.[31] Indeed, Martin Luther King Jr. famously observed that the most segregated hour in America is eleven o'clock Sunday morning.[32] Segregation of this kind creates difficulty for some interracial couples that same-race couples do not face. How can Black/White couples find places to worship where each partner is comfortable and neither feels conspicuous? Mabel Renault faces precisely this challenge. She and Hank, her White husband, attend Quaker meetings each Sunday, often with their children in tow. The meeting hall is close enough that they walk from their house, yet once they pass through the hall's large, open wooden door, the racial diversity that characterizes their Philadelphia neighborhood all but disappears. Mabel grew up in a predominantly Black neighborhood and attended Catholic school from elementary through high school. Although she laments the "Catholic guilt" her education instilled in her, she misses some things about Catholic services. Music is one; at Quaker meetings, there is none. She tells me that she is thinking about more regularly attending an African American Catholic church a few miles away that "has music. I like the music." Mabel shares her misgivings about the Quaker meetings with Hank's mother. Both were raised Catholic but attend Quaker meetings with their husbands. "His mother and I talk about race and a lot of different things. In the Quaker—I don't totally feel comfortable in the White Quaker situations." Mabel mentions that she and Hank "pray differently. He's a Quaker, so you pray silently. My family doesn't do that. … I'm not a Quaker." Sometimes she gets up early and goes to the nine o'clock mass at the African American Catholic church, but most Sundays she attends the Quaker meetings with Hank and their kids. Mabel's participation in the religious life of the Quaker community, even though she does not identify as a Quaker, is a form of racework because it involves a deliberate engagement with a White racial space that she would not be in if her partner were not White.

Although Mabel does not report experiencing any overt hostility at the Quaker meetings, the environment is not comfortable for her. Being the only person of color in a space can be taxing, even in the absence of noticeable negativity. Whether or not Black partners actually encounter racist comments, questions, or assumptions, remaining alert to the possibility of racism or even just feeling racially conspicuous involves expending significant energy. Velena Julien, who is Black, sometimes has to remind her White husband, Brent Isley, that it is tiring to be the only person of color in otherwise White places, such as holiday parties. As Velena explains, the emotional effort involved in navigating racially homogeneous places can be frustratingly hard to convey to a partner:

> I was telling him [that] it gets really difficult being the only Black person in the room. And not because anyone is being unpleasant or not because …

it's just tiring for some reason. But then he was saying, "Everyone is being really pleasant and everyone likes you and everyone is friendly, so why is this a big deal?" "It's not a big deal, but it's just a feeling. It's exhausting, I'm self-conscious. ... I can't explain it to you. It's just an emotional reaction and you're not accepting what I'm saying." And then have us both be frustrated and just to have to not deal with it for a while.

For Velena, like other Black partners in my study, an all-White environment may feel uncomfortable whether or not anyone present intends that. In spaces like these, the race fatigue that Black partners experience is a result of their interracial relationship.

It is important to recognize that, like the fatigue that White partners develop, the persistent weariness that Black partners feel is very much rooted in their structural location. Experiencing Whiteness as conspicuousness tires middle-class Whites whose privilege has enabled them to rarely feel racialized or racially marked. Race tires African American partners for the opposite reason—because anticipating, managing, and responding to racism is so much a part of everyday life. The continual expenditure of energy on race is exhausting. The consequences of feeling racially conspicuous are a different and additional burden. For Whites like Neil, Helen, and Marie, always feeling their Whiteness weighs on them, but it does not exact a material or physical cost. In contrast, being the only Black person in sight has historically left Blacks vulnerable to verbal or physical abuse. Although these sorts of overt racial hostility are less common in our era of colorblind racism, persistent prejudice ensures that being in the numerical minority is not an equivalent experience for Whites and Blacks.

Implicit in my analysis of Kristie's, Mabel's, and Velena's narratives is the assumption that African American partners are most comfortable in the presence of other African Americans. Although this is true for many of the partners in my sample, I spoke with some Black partners who were equally or more comfortable in White racial spaces. For them, a White racial space *is* their comfort zone. These Black partners have White friendship networks; frequent largely White restaurants, bars, and clubs; and spend almost all of their time in White social settings. They do not experience White racial spaces as particularly trying. Blackness is not the most salient feature of their identities, and they establish strong social bonds with non-Blacks. Tara Hilliard, for example, has always felt ambivalent about Black social spaces. A twenty-seven-year-old Black lesbian, Tara tells me that it was not her sexuality that made her think other African Americans considered her "that weird Black girl." It was the cultural differences—her

White friends, the heavy metal music she listened to, the way she danced, the fact that she cursed. Now, spending time in majority-White spaces is not unusual for her. She explains, "[When] I'm the only Black person, it's like I'm kinda used to it. ... Most of my friends were [White] mostly 'cause I just surround myself with people who I have the most in common with, and like, I don't care what they look like. So it's like a lot of times I find myself like being the only Black person. And I'm kinda used to it."

Other African American partners who frequent White social spaces began with pronounced caution but eventually developed a strong sense of belonging. Lionel Ivers, a thirty-five-year-old heterosexual Black man, has been practicing Judaism with his White wife, Meryl Agassi Ivers, for five years. Lionel did not grow up in a Jewish family, but in the years since he converted, Judaism has become an important focus of the Ivers's relationship. Lionel recalls his initial fears about joining the synagogue he and his wife attend, which he describes as "an older congregation ... born in the early 1900s." He says, "These people never had Black people in their homes besides butlers and servants. ... Before you converted you'd go in [the synagogue] and see everyone is White. And I'm like, why did I think about doing it?" But the interactions he has had with members of the community have eased his concerns. "I did have these fears. I thought I would get some resistance somewhere. I just was sure it was going to come but didn't know from who and when. I kind of waited and waited and it never came." By the time I meet him and Meryl, Lionel is completely at ease. "They're like my family. I walk into synagogue, I feel like it's home. It feels that warm when I walk in there. After the service is over, people look for me. Even when I'm not there, they ask Meryl, 'Where's Lionel?' ... I don't know if they feel so amazed there's a young Black male who converted who's in this all-White synagogue. These people are so open that I wish there were more Black dudes out there that would come to this synagogue. Because you could feel at home here."

Negotiating Racial Separation and In-group Unity

The long history of anti-Black exclusion in White communities has necessitated the creation of all-Black social spaces. This is true in a literal sense—African Americans developed separate restaurants, churches, social clubs, dance halls, voluntary associations, hotels, doctors' offices, and clothing stores as a response to being physically denied entrance to White establishments.[33] It is also true that the dangers and pressures of

White supremacy have created the need for symbolic zones of safety, unity, and refuge. But these spaces offer more than just safety—they are places where diverse African American cultures thrive and people simply enjoy being with other Black people. This is what Dalmage captures when she uses the term racial "separation."[34] Although White exclusion is one impetus for in-group solidarity among Blacks, it is not the only force. Blacks who choose to establish and maintain all-Black social spaces are not engaged in "segregation" as it has been practiced by White institutions, but rather in a form of "separation" that marginalized groups have long created as a source of strength and pride.

For some of the African Americans in my study, having a White partner sometimes conflicts with their desire to be in all-Black settings. Deciding whether to visit these spaces, whether to bring along their White partner, and how to negotiate these tensions involves racework. For instance, Sylvia Chabot, a Black lesbian in her late twenties, has always loved to dance. For the past several years, she has taken classes in traditional African dance. Depending on the history and politics of individual dance communities, these spaces are more or less racially homogeneous. Even though her White partner, Leslie Cobbs, rarely attends these classes, the racial dynamics of these spaces matter to Sylvia when she looks into the future. She tries to picture how she, Leslie, and the child they are expecting will fit into these dance communities. She reflects:

> [Would it be] so wrong for [the] baby to just come dance with me every now and then? [Leslie's] like, "Maybe I'll start dancing," but that's not an automatic thing. I mean, I guess it depends too on who are the dancers that we kind of align ourselves with. ... There's a lot of drama in African American dance communities that are, not *separatist*, but in my experience, if I'm dancing with African Nationals, they're a lot more open to people of European and Asian descent dancing with them, versus dancing with African Americans who are like, "No, we have to preserve this culture for ourselves," and are a lot more closed to other folks dancing with them. We're trying to find the right balance of dance community, and finding the right dance community [that] could be like, you know, our family.

The politics that Sylvia refers to are complex. Traditional cultural practices like African dance and drumming are sites of debate about issues of access, authenticity, and appropriation. The debates are more than philosophical; they have concrete, practical significance to those who practice and perform these traditional arts. For Sylvia, tensions, both among people of African descent and between those of African descent and those of European and Asian descent, make it difficult to figure out where she and her family fit in. She wants to include Leslie, but she is also sensitive to the cultural dynamics at play. Sylvia does not articulate her desire to be in all-Black dance spaces as directly related to their racial homogeneity, but part of her appreciation for this dance form is the connection she feels to it as a "Black lesbian of African descent."

Leslie supports Sylvia's desire to be a part of these African dance communities. She occasionally accompanies her to the dance studio, which is located a few blocks from their Brooklyn neighborhood. She tells me, "It's been interesting to get to see these dance communities in each of the places that Sylvia and I have lived together—Kansas City, Los Angeles, Stamford, and here. Wherever we have lived, Sylvia has sought out other dancers. And each community has been different. It's been interesting to see how inclusive different communities are and what their racial politics have been. Like this [studio in Brooklyn] is probably the most inclusive place that Sylvia has ever done African dance." Because Leslie knows how important dance is to Sylvia, she is willing to engage in the racework it takes to figure out her own role. Together they consider how the family they are building will fit into these spaces and what kind of involvement would make each of them comfortable. Though the dance communities in which Sylvia has been involved are not exclusively lesbian, in my sample, Black lesbians showed the strongest investment in racially separated Black social spaces. As the next section shows, negotiating the racial divisions within queer spaces requires significant emotional energy.

Negotiating Racial Separation in Lesbian and Gay Social Spaces

As I explore in the next chapter, same-sex partners seek out lesbian and gay spaces as a sort of refuge, a place where they feel recognized and where they can be open in their affections. But in Philadelphia, Washington, D.C., and New York City, as in towns and cities across the United States, lesbian and gay spaces have historically been racially divided. The same exclusionary racist practices that kept African Americans out of White schools, luncheonettes, and restrooms also barred them from the small number of bars and restaurants that catered to lesbians and gays. Racial separation in queer spaces continues today.

Sociologist Mignon Moore argues that younger generations of Black lesbians and gays are faced with new opportunities and challenges. Those who grew up in the 1960s or early 1970s came of age amid public representations of gays and lesbians in film and television and dramatic increases in women and men choosing to live openly gay lives.[35] These younger Black gays and lesbians, including many of the partners in my study, do not face the violent or overt racial exclusionary practices that characterized the experiences of older generations. Instead, they must navigate more subtle forms of White racial exclusion within mainstream gay and lesbian communities. At the same time, those who are embedded within Black communities and social networks must figure out for themselves how to "enact a modern gay identity" within a particular cultural context.[36] They must determine how to situate themselves between gay and lesbian communities whose needs are driven by Whites, and Black racial communities whose needs are driven by heterosexuals.

The contemporary prevalence of racial separation between Black and White gay and lesbian communities makes it unlikely that one queer establishment will be a refuge for both interracial partners. For some partners in my study, informally segregated queer spaces are particularly difficult to negotiate because there is so much at stake. Heterosexual partners generally do not need to seek out special locations where they can feel comfortable expressing affection, or expect their relationship to be recognized and respected, or attempt to establish new romantic relationships. For some gays and lesbians, by contrast, queer spaces are a precious commodity, and the racial homogeneity of these spaces makes it difficult to find contexts in which both partners feel comfortable.

Monique Gilliam tells me that if New York City, where she has lived nearly all her adult life, were less segregated, she probably would think less often about being interracial. Monique is a Black lesbian in her mid-thirties who lives in a middle-class Black neighborhood in Brooklyn. Her partner of two years, Barbara DiBacco, an Italian-born White woman in her early forties, lives in Queens. Monique sees significant racial divisions within queer spaces:

> If Black people and White people were much more social or interactive on a much more social level—Black heterosexual, Black lesbian, Black gay, Black bi[sexual], Black trans[gender], Black queer, and Whites—[if] all these groups interacted on a much more social level, maybe I wouldn't think about it so much. But as diverse as the city is, to me still it's pretty segregated. . . . And when I go to lesbian spaces or lesbian clubs it still feels so segregated. . . . This past summer, there were two really, really, really big lesbian pride parties and I looked at the ad and I said [to Barbara], "Baby,

you know who's going to go to this one and you know who's going to go to that one, right?" She looked at me [and] said, "What do you mean?" I said the Black women and the Latino women are gonna go to that one. And the White women are gonna go to that one. You just need to look at the ads, look at who's in the ads. So I think about it in social settings. ... It enters my consciousness much more in social settings.

Monique and Barbara sometimes attend Black and Latina social events, but they also frequent White gay and lesbian spaces. In fact, Monique tells me that the only time they are in predominantly White spaces is when they are at gay and lesbian events. For Monique, there is a tension between wanting to be at Black and Latina parties with Barbara and not wanting to violate the intraracial sanctity of those spaces. She explains, "To me there's something very beautiful about having a Black pride, you know, what is it like to be in this place that's mostly Black people dancing and doing their thing and, you know, I mean, I love that. I miss that. And so I would love to share that with her." But Monique also feels a strong reluctance to bring Barbara into these spaces and did not do so during either of the Black pride festivals that took place during the two summers the women have been together. "I remember what it's like being in Black space or Black queer space and how I felt when people who were not Black came into the space. And I know how important that space is." Monique recognizes the importance of a place where African American lesbians and gays can be together in a community apart from the immediate stresses of homophobia and racism. She also knows that other Black lesbians may engage in "border patrolling" to enforce the safety and privacy of these spaces.[37] The opinions of others in these communities are meaningful to her, and to be criticized in these environments would hurt. "I have thinner skin than [Barbara] does," Monique tells me. "So I'm more sensitive to what people say." Sensitivity to this anticipated disapproval has led to her decision not to attend these celebrations at all. "I may say okay, well, you know I'm not going to go to that event and it's not even a conversation. ... I might just not go at all. Because I feel weird saying, 'Okay, baby, I'm going to go, I'll see you later.' So I'd rather just not go." That she chooses not to discuss this with Barbara means that Monique must do this racework alone. Though on any given night, they decide as a couple what social events to attend or to avoid, the emotional toll of the racial tensions in queer spaces is something that only Monique experiences.

Onika Marsh is a twenty-six-year-old Black lesbian who is quite aware of the racial dynamics of social spaces. When we meet, she is living in

Philadelphia a few blocks from her White partner, Margaret Otterlei, and pursuing a master's degree in fine arts at a nearby art school. Her experiences growing up in Rhode Island and attending a majority-White boarding school in Vermont have given Onika many opportunities to consider how race shapes her interactions. Negotiating racial dynamics with Margaret can be difficult. "Sometimes it's really, really hard. Really hard." For Onika, this plays out in both informal social settings—friendship networks and parties—and queer establishments like bars or clubs. "In our daily lives, when we're interacting, like one of the places that it comes up has to do with friends and like comfort level of friends." She has "a relatively small group of friends," who are "not all people of color—but [who] definitely have a very intense dynamic about how they articulate and understand race." When Onika's friends and Margaret are together, the atmosphere is strained. Onika attributes part of this tension to the fact that Margaret is "very awkward socially." Margaret has had close friendships with African Americans, but in Philadelphia, her social circle is predominantly White. Onika recounts to me how she explained to Margaret the tension she feels interacting with Margaret's group of friends:

> I don't want you to feel like you have to go out and get, you know, get a bunch of Black friends. ... It's more like I feel uncomfortable as like the only Black person in the room. And I don't really know them and that kind of makes me uncomfortable. So you go and have your friends; that's fine. I'm not saying there's something wrong with them. And when you want to have a big party that you really want me at, then I'll be there.

Being interracial with racially different friendship networks makes it difficult to decide where and with whom to socialize. When Onika considers the broader social landscape of queer bars and clubs in Philadelphia, this tension is further heightened. She is adamant that she would be too uncomfortable to even consider bringing Margaret into a Black queer space:

> I feel like in terms of queer spaces, there's queer spaces that tend to be largely White and there's some that are more mixed, and we're in those two sorts of spaces. And then there are spaces that are queer that are largely people of color, and we're never there together. And we sort of talk about this like a little bit. Like there's this Black dyke bar in [a Black neighborhood in Philadelphia] and I'm like, "I'm not going to be the girl who brings her White girlfriend into that bar. I'm sorry. It's not gonna happen."

Onika perceives gradations of racial homogeneity within queer spaces, and she has considered what types of racial discomfort she will tolerate and what types she will not. Though she is not at ease in predominantly White gay and lesbian spaces, like other Black partners I spoke with, Onika nevertheless visits these spaces and sometimes enjoys herself. The type of discomfort that she anticipates feeling if she brings her partner into predominantly Black spaces, however, is one that she is unwilling to endure. She would prefer to deal with the problematic racial politics of White queer spaces than to bring Margaret into Black queer spaces and experience alienating or disapproving looks from people in that community. Making this decision involves racework for both partners.

The racework in which Onika engages with Margaret is a process of demarcating which queer spaces they will enter together and which ones she will go to alone. Margaret, Onika says, understands her concerns:

> And I think, she's perfectly fine with that, you know. ... And she respects that. That that's something I need and want and take seriously. And I don't think—you know, I've asked her, and I don't think it makes her feel like I'm going out of my way to like exclude her. ... I think she recognizes and appreciates the importance of those things and is fine with it, and wants to be friends with my friends and all that, but like, kind of is like, "That's fine."

Together they have agreed that Margaret will not go with Onika to Black queer spaces. They were able to come to this decision in part because Margaret understands that those spaces give Onika a validation she needs and does not get elsewhere. Onika acknowledges that this decision would create more problems if she chose to be in these spaces all the time, or if there were not other spaces where they could interact socially with common friends. But she also admits that managing these issues about race, friendships, and social settings requires a lot of work: "I think we just generally have a hard time maybe figuring out how to interact as a couple in the world, like in social situations. I think there are a lot of factors too, and race is one of them."

Nadine Allen, who was introduced earlier in this chapter, lives with her White partner, Nancy Taylor, in Washington, D.C. Nadine has a different perspective than Monique or Onika on racial separation within queer communities. She and Nancy go to events in both White and Black social settings. Nadine believes that the gay community in Washington is racially segregated "for the most part." She explains, "Frequently I will go [to gay] places where I'm the only Black person," but she would rather go to some dances that are predominantly Black because she prefers the music at those events. "Although I don't usually go to some all-Black events but ... I like the music better. When I go dancing, I like the music. But you know, in places like that I do sometimes get that negative energy because I'm with a White woman. But I'm usually partying and dancing so I don't focus on that too much."

Nadine professes a clear preference for integration over separation, both on a practical and ideological level:

> I don't join a group that's all Black, that specifically says this [is a] Black women's group. I don't join it. As a matter of fact, my sister, my youngest sister, has joined this investment group and it's Black women. ... And although this is information that I need and I want, I don't want to join something that's all Black or all anything because I believe integration is important. That while people need spaces to deal with whatever they need to deal with, I just can't be a part of that, it's against my core. And so that's how I just don't join those groups any more. ... But it took me awhile to come to that because I [kept] getting into those situations, like I would join a writing group. ... I couldn't deal with people referring to [White] people as "them" and I knew who the "them" they were referring to, who they were. And I know that's my partner. There's a kind of a conflict, it creates a conflict to be in an environment like that and then go home.

Nadine's struggle with racially segregated spaces differs from that of the other Black lesbians I have discussed. Her concern is not whether to bring her White partner into these spaces but whether Nadine herself belongs in them. Her investment in integration is both political and personal. A group specifically framed around Black womanhood—even if it is queer-friendly and designed as a safe place where Black women can be at ease—makes her feel conflicted.

It is striking that the most passionate concerns about separated social settings come from Black lesbians. None of the Black gay men in my study articulate similar concerns. This may be because the two groups are in different structural positions. Compared to the Black lesbians, the Black gay men in my study are older, have a higher median family income, and are in relationships that began earlier. These factors may make them less invested in Black queer spaces.[38] There are social patterns that support this explanation. Most of the Black gay men in my sample live in predominantly White areas and have almost exclusively White social circles. These men appear to feel less intensely connected to Black social spaces and communities.

If these structured patterns influence Black queer partners' investment in Black queer spaces, then what looks like a gendered pattern may really be an extension of social class and the racial character of social networks. In this case, we might assume that on the whole, Black lesbians and gay men have similar ties to Black queer spaces and that my sample only picked up on part of this pattern.[39]

Another explanation is that the gendered pattern in my sample is part of a broader difference in how Black lesbians and gay men relate to Black lesbian and gay spaces. Black feminists have argued that intersecting vectors of oppression create a position of triple jeopardy for Black lesbians— they are at once marginalized by their race, gender, and sexuality.[40] For this reason, Black lesbians may feel a special investment in Black queer spaces as refuges where they can connect with other Black queer *women*. Black women's invisibility relative to White women in many White lesbian spaces and Black women's relative invisibility to Black gay men in Black gay spaces may make these connections especially important and these sites especially valuable.

Other research on interracial intimacy identifies a similar gender pattern between heterosexual Black women and men. Dalmage, for instance, writes that some of the heterosexual Black women in her study felt conflicted about whether to bring their White husbands to Black-centered events.[41] Like Monique and Onika, they wanted to participate in Black cultural spaces and were sensitive to the ways in which White partners might disrupt the shared investment in all-Black environments. Dalmage does not report any of the Black men in her sample mentioning similar concerns and interprets this pattern as distinctly gendered. As Black women, these partners may take on a more intensive role in building connections within and between Black families and Black communities.

It is also notable that White lesbians and gays generally did not mention experiencing tensions about whether their Black partners would be welcome or feel comfortable in White queer spaces. There are many possible reasons for this. First, many White lesbians and gay men do not see White social spaces as having a racial character. Brett Beemyn has argued that White gay communities are typically defined by same-sex sexual attraction and are rarely examined through a racial lens. This makes it difficult to see that the communities created by White gays and lesbians are also structured by race, as a result of both racial exclusion and White racial privilege.[42] Further, if White gays and lesbians do perceive a particular space as being overtly discriminatory, they can choose to visit another establishment. This is especially true for White gay men, who are most visibly represented in gay and lesbian public spaces. The number of Black gay and lesbian bars and clubs is much smaller, making each one more valuable.

In an important way, these stories about racial divisions within gay and lesbian spaces reveal alternate narratives about racial separation and belonging. Nadine laments the lack of more diverse queer environments. But for Onika and Monique, racially separate social spaces can be positive. Each of these women articulates the potential tension this separation creates within their relationship, but they each see all-Black queer spaces as important, valuable, or "beautiful." There is pleasure and security in these communities where the realities of homophobia and racism are temporarily kept at bay.[43] And though they evaluate the benefits and costs of racial divisions differently than do Wanda and Ethan or Kristie and Burton, who each waded through census data and surveyed neighborhood streets to find attractive, racially mixed neighborhoods, the emotional energies that Black lesbians like Onika and Monique expend in order to navigate a segregated queer landscape are also a form of racework. Deciding whether and how to discuss this issue with their partners, figuring out how to describe and justify their desire for Black queer spaces, and then visiting such spaces and making connections that their partners cannot be a part of are all social practices that constitute racework.

Conclusion

In this chapter, I have explored the intimate geographies of segregated neighborhoods and racially homogeneous social spaces. My main concern was not to uncover new patterns of segregation and separation but to show why racial separation is particularly onerous for interracial partners and families. Couples who are able to agree on what constitutes a comfortable racial mix and find such a neighborhood may be able to avoid some of the race fatigue I have described, though this is likely to be true more for White than for Black partners. Race fatigue is a commonplace experience for African Americans, especially middle-class partners who work in majority-White environments. But for the majority of partners in my sample, who live in fairly homogeneous neighborhoods or who must negotiate the dynamics of racially separate spaces, dealing with these everyday stresses requires racework. The work I have described here involves some of the emotional practices I discuss in detail in chapter 4. The emotional labor covered in this chapter arose from the challenge of being interracial in racially separate social environments.

I have shown that African Americans engage in the majority of race-work that is associated with navigating racially homogeneous spaces. African American partners sometimes do the double work of negotiating racial difference when they are in the numerical minority in White social spaces and when they are in the numerical majority, as in Black lesbian bars. Although White partners do experience fatigue from feeling racially conspicuous, they have much less emotional conflict over bringing their partners into majority-White spaces.

Analyzing how racial difference manifests in racially segregated and separated spaces shows that intimacy does not dissolve the social inequalities between partners. The relationship that one's racial group has to decades of racial privilege or exclusion shapes how the individual is perceived in and experiences public places. We think of intimacy, marriage, and family as relationships defined by cooperation and not competition. But even two people who are in an essentially cooperative venture—a romantic relationship—must navigate social structures that privilege one of them over the other, that give special allowances to one partner's group over the other partner's group.

Racial divisions are only part of the challenge that public spaces represent for interracial partners, however. Dealing with the prejudice and judgments attached to interracial intimacy and the possibility of harassment brings forth another set of issues. How Black/White partners anticipate and respond to these issues is the focus of the next chapter.

CHAPTER 3 | Public Interraciality:
          | Managing Visibility

I think, it's really sad, but I think that people think it's so unusual for
people of different races to have any kind of intimate relationship,
even a friendship, that people don't consider it, you know. And like
that's why depending on where we are, I feel like Sylvia's work-
friend, that people are like, "Oh, who's this random White woman
that's with you?" Like it doesn't occur to people that we could be
close—even if we weren't lovers—that we could be important to
each other in that way that you might want to say hello to both of
us. ... A lot of times I feel invisible and particularly with men who
will walk—if we're together—they'll walk straight up to her on the
street and start talking to her without even making any eye contact or
looking at me in any way. So I feel like when men pick her out like
I'm invisible completely. Which is really gross, it's a gross feeling.

SHARING THESE THOUGHTS, Leslie Cobbs (introduced in the previous
chapter) draws attention to a social reality not commonly associated with
interracial relationships: invisibility. Her perception that on the streets of
her Brooklyn neighborhood, she becomes "a random White woman" in
relation to her Black partner, Sylvia Chabot, is at odds with most social
research on how racial difference is perceived in public spaces. Qualitative research on interracial intimacy has shown that because Black/White
couples are both visually conspicuous and heavily stigmatized, they commonly face negative reactions in public. The force, form, and frequency of
these reactions have changed over time. When St. Clair Drake and Horace
Cayton conducted their infamous study of Black life on Chicago's South
Side in the early to mid-1900s, persons in Black/White relationships had

difficulties holding a job, securing a place to live, and avoiding social ostracism.[1] Researchers who study social life at the turn of the twenty-first century encounter interracial partners who lead lives that differ vastly from those of their historical counterparts. Contemporary couples live in an era in which colorblindness is the dominant racial logic.[2] On college campuses and within families, the influence of colorblind logic is evident in the veiling of opposition to interracial intimacy.[3] In public spaces, negative reactions are generally nonviolent and subtle. They take the form of curious glances, under-the-breath comments, expressions of disbelief, or verbal intimidation.[4] Yet learning to deal with these less overt forms of public harassment may be crucial to successfully maintaining an interracial relationship.[5]

Leslie's account of feeling invisible sheds light on how lesbian and gay Black/White partners experience interraciality in public differently from their heterosexual counterparts. The ways in which the sexual status of lesbian and gay partners shape strangers' perceptions of their racial difference have been neglected in research that has been focused exclusively on heterosexual couples.[6] Sexuality plays a crucial role in mediating the prejudice that interracial couples face. To analyze the intersection of sexuality and interraciality in public experiences of prejudice, I draw on Erving Goffman's work on stigma management.

Racial Prejudice, Homophobia, and the Concept of Stigma Management

In chapter 2, I showed that interracial partners use racework to navigate racial homogeneity within public spaces. But racial divisions are not the only challenges present in public spaces. In these domains, interracial couples are also vulnerable to racial prejudice and, in some cases, to homophobia. It is worth repeating that racial prejudice against interracial couples has different origins, depending on whether it comes from White or Black communities. As I explained in chapter 1, White communities historically imposed social and legal penalties on interracial couples because they deemed Blacks to be inferior and did not want Black men to father children with White women. In Black communities, racial judgments against interracial couples originated from a fierce distrust of Whites and a deep suspicion of the motives of individual Whites who intermarried with Blacks. Both sets of attitudes are forms of racial prejudice, although their effects have not been commensurate. Blacks have had far less access to institutional resources with which to marginalize Black/White couples. Moreover, Black communities have a long history of being more accepting of interracial couples than White communities.

In this chapter, I analyze how interracial couples anticipate and protect themselves against racial prejudice and homophobia. I draw on Goffman's notions of stigma and stigma management. His analysis of stigma as "an attribute that is deeply discrediting" directs attention to the small acts and maneuvers by which those who bear social stigma navigate social interactions. His lens is therefore quite useful for examining the microinteractions of public spaces.[7] Small gestures, like an arm around a partner's shoulders or a hand gently pressed on the small of a back, can have consequences of disproportionate magnitude when they reveal information that makes interracial partners vulnerable to harassment. Further, Goffman notes that stigmatized individuals are not passive objects of stigma but are instead actively engaged in processes of stigma management. Most germane to my study are Goffman's insights regarding the ways in which individuals monitor the amount and type of information they disclose about themselves in order to manage stigma. "The issue is not that of managing tension generated during social contacts, but rather that of managing *information*. ... To display or not to display; to tell or not to tell; to let on or not to let on; to lie or not to lie; and in each case, to whom, how, when, and where."[8] As I explain below, strategic decision-making of this sort can also be thought of as a form of racework.

There are some shortcomings in Goffman's conceptualization that should be acknowledged. First, he attributes stigma to *individuals*. When he does consider how stigma manifests in small groups or partnerships, he generally assumes that one partner possesses the social stigma and the accompanying partner must manage the consequences of being associated with the stigmatized person.[9] My reading of the marginalization of interracial couples is slightly different. Though in the context of entrenched racism, African Americans are visually marked by their Blackness, interracial stigmas are not placed solely on Black partners. Instead, when racial difference between two people is stigmatized, it is the interaction, the connection itself between two partners that is the primary object of stigma, not a mark exclusively embodied by one or the other person as individuals. The same is true for gay and lesbian sexuality. It is the same-sex relationship itself—deemed immoral or perverse—that is stigmatized. For this reason, managing interracial or same-sex stigma does not involve masking or displaying individual attributes; rather, it is about concealing or revealing intimacy itself. Second, Goffman tends to see stigma as an embodied mark or blemish. He emphasizes stigma as a characteristic *of* or *within* a person, instead of as part of a relationship between an attribute and a social system that devalues that attribute.[10] Goffman gives as an example a woman born without a nose. She would experience this lack as a stigma, and Goffman would call it such. But if we speak only of her stigma and the ways in which she is discredited by others, we risk naturalizing that process. Only in a social setting where full-featured faces are normative and visual and olfactory modalities are privileged over other senses (like hearing and touch) would a missing nose be marked as a stigma. So too, in the context of my study, if we identify racial difference and same-sex attraction as the physical markers of stigma, we risk naturalizing the systems of racism and homophobia that make them so. Being racially different from your partner is only a stigma in a social environment that expects and privileges same-race relationships. Likewise, homosexuality is only a stigma in a society that assumes and rewards heterosexuality. For this reason, I prefer the terms "racial prejudice" and "homophobia" to "stigma." These terms direct our focus back to the systems of White supremacy and heterosexism that privilege some forms of intimacy above others. I use the term "stigma" sparingly, as a way to acknowledge the value of Goffman's concept for understanding the microdynamics of interracial life.

Many interracial partners attempt to reduce their vulnerability to racial prejudice and homophobia in public by managing the visibility of their intimacy.[11] Managing visibility is a form of racework that includes two sets of seemingly disparate strategies. It includes the practices by which interracial partners interpret social cues from their environments and modify their actions in public to avoid possible confrontation. It also includes the choices that couples sometimes make to overtly signal their relationships to unknown others. Although these strategies may seem contradictory, both are ways of trying to control a situation in which being interracial or lesbian/gay (or both) may expose a couple to harassment. Whether couples avoid conflict by minimizing public displays of affection or confront potential conflict by using public displays of affection to assert an intimate status, they are attempting to manage how much people know about their relationship. In this study, same-sex interracial couples engaged in these social practices more often than did their heterosexual counterparts.

Conceptualizing visibility management as *work* advances the critical analysis of interracial intimacy. Although other qualitative researchers have examined the curious looks, long stares, and public harassment that interracial partners experience, they have paid less attention to the anticipation and forethought with which some partners try to either sidestep public conflict or meet it head-on. These researchers describe couples' awareness but do not emphasize the routine strategies conditioned by that awareness. By conceiving of partners' responses as a type of work, I highlight the dynamic nature of public spaces and argue that visibility and invisibility are not static states of being. They are statuses that require ongoing management.

In the first half of this chapter, I examine the public experiences of interracial partners specifically in light of their sexuality, a perspective absent in past research. Heterosexual couples report feeling their racial difference as being particularly salient in social spaces, although they intermittently experience moments when their racial difference makes them less, not more, visible. For same-sex partners, especially lesbians, racial difference increases the experience of invisibility. There is also evidence in these narratives that racial difference may sharpen the homophobia directed at couples when they are recognized as intimate partners. In the second half of the chapter, I examine the racework that interracial partners use to manage visibility and discuss why same-sex interracial partners engage in certain social practices more often than heterosexual partners.

Public Experiences of Interraciality

Heterosexual Interracial Intimacy

In public spaces, heterosexual Black/White couples experience their racial difference in two contrasting forms—hypervisibility and invisibility. *Hypervisibility* refers to the ways in which these couples feel especially conspicuous as the objects of strangers' attention. Straight couples sometimes feel that their racial difference draws them together: It is the first thing that others observe. *Invisibility* includes the moments when heterosexual interracial partners feel that others cannot see them as a couple: Their intimacy is unrecognizable. In these instances, their racial difference makes them seem farther apart. The public experiences of heterosexual partners in my study were more often characterized by hypervisibility than by invisibility.

Hypervisibility

The heterosexual interracial partners I interviewed often felt strangers' attention—curious, hostile, or affirmative—in public spaces. Feeling conspicuous in public reinforces heterosexual couples' awareness that their interraciality is a public identity. It is a symbol from which strangers draw a host of social, cultural, or historic meanings. Interracial partners may not always be able to discern precisely how strangers read their intimacy, but they often know that something about their relationship intrigues, offends, or confuses others. Christopher Tomlinson explains how he interprets others' reactions. Christopher is a twenty-five-year-old heterosexual African American man whose two-year relationship with his twenty-nine-year-old White partner, Lana Keyes, has strained many of his close friendships. He speaks to me quietly, but his body language seems to reflect the strain he describes. With his elbows at his sides, he crosses his arms as if he is hugging himself. He bends over a little as he speaks.

> In relationship to my outlook or perception in society, it's weakened my thought process of America in relationship to race and acceptance. … Most statistics say that Black and White people in interracial relationships are accepted. But in reality, my whole experience has been wild, because the whole accepting thing is an issue on all levels, not just stereotyping [or] the KKK. It's the everyday focus—people's actions or attitudes, no matter how subtle.

Other interracial partners also feel noticed. Myron Tanner, a fifty-year-old Black man, explains that he often feels conspicuous when he is out with Norma Tanner, his forty-five-year-old White wife. Norma has straight blond hair that reaches her shoulders and a contagious laugh. Myron is tall with a medium build, round eyeglasses, and black hair peppered with a little grey. As a pair, they are easily noticed. "It comes up all the time. I mean, there's a striking contrast between Norma and I, you know? I'm taller than her. She's short. I'm Black. [She's] White and blond. … I'm always conscious about that."

Strangers' attention is a constant for heterosexual Black/White couples in which the woman is White and the man is Black. These relationships may receive more attention in part because they are a larger demographic group—75 percent of all Black/White marriages are between Black men and White women.[12] But their hypervisibility may also be seen as evidence that longstanding anxieties about Black men having sexual relationships with White women are still very much alive. Kalvin Oster's experiences seem to confirm that. Kalvin (introduced in chapter 2) has been with his White thirty-three-year-old wife, Vera Oster, for five-and-a-half years. Kalvin is about five feet, seven inches tall, with broad shoulders and a shaved head. He likes to tell jokes and has a wry sense of humor. When I ask him whether he and Vera attract attention as an interracial couple, he dryly explains strangers' stares: "I think they are more star-struck because I am an incredibly handsome man and my wife is remarkably beautiful. That's the way I look at things. You have to kind of hypnotize yourself to believe why those people are staring at you." This reference to hypnosis reflects the constancy of the looks and stares he and Vera receive when they go out, whether to a restaurant, shopping mall, or baseball game.

Beneath Kalvin's sarcasm is a palpable contempt for the way strangers in public sometimes react to Black men who are with White female partners. He directs some of this resentment toward African American women, from whom he often senses overt disapproval.

> In my opinion, the Black race is more vocal. The Black women are upset because this White woman came and took one of their men, one of their "good brothers." ... You'll see the dirty looks from some of the Black women, who are sitting in a group of Black women [mimics an exaggerated sigh]. You'll see them stare you up and down, and I'll grab my wife and kiss her or something. I'll give them a show if they want. It doesn't matter to me.

Other Black men and some of their White female partners describe a similar frustration with Black women's reactions to their relationships. Social scientists have noted the anger and fear that many African American women have about the lack of Black "marriageable men" due to high levels of incarceration and poverty and low levels of education.[13] Kalvin does not appear to be sympathetic to the broader social forces that may underlie the anger directed at him. Instead, he confronts Black women's frustration by making a public display of his affection for Vera, an act that signifies his own frustration with and retaliation against others' expectations.

Although not as conspicuous as Black men with White women, Black women and their White male partners also experience subtle negative reactions in public. Consider the experiences of Brianna Simmons, a heterosexual Black woman in her mid-twenties. She lives in Philadelphia with her White husband, Kurt Simmons, and their two young daughters. Brianna and Kurt have been married four years. They moved from Boston to Philadelphia a year ago so that Kurt could pursue a professional degree at a nearby university. She works in the alumni development office at the same school. Brianna's experiences with Kurt and their daughters in their neighborhood and around the city make her want to move back to Boston. Although universities are often characterized as sites of progressive thinking and tolerance, this has not been her experience. "I can walk down [the university's main walkway] and have professors and students both stare at us in the most unwavering gaze. It's invasive. … One time I was [on campus], this has happened a couple times, but most recently last week, when Kurt and I were having lunch together, which we do when we're both on campus. I had kissed Kurt [on the main walkway]. You could have heard a pin drop. It was surprising, and it's hard to deal with." Continuing, she explains: "It's not only been from Whites, it's been from Asians, and it's also been from Blacks." The cumulative effects of these occurrences leave Brianna weary.

Sometimes, Black women in relationships with White men are antagonized more directly. Warren Geiger lives in Brooklyn with his Black wife, Nakia Geiger. Both are in their twenties. Now a filmmaker, Warren met Nakia while he was working as a production crew member at an outdoor summer theater. They have been together for eight years and married for two. Negative reactions from strangers used to upset Warren, but he is growing accustomed to them. He describes a fairly typical interaction. "[We've had] problems as an interracial couple. … We would get a lot of troubled comments from a lot of Black men. … They'd be like, 'Whoa, sister what are you doing with this guy?' I mean it was never—on occasion once or twice— was it Black women. At least not outspoken, it wasn't White people." These interactions are memorable for Warren. He is able to recount a few of them. That he does not feel disapproval from other Whites when he is with Nakia in his racially mixed neighborhood could reflect a greater tolerance of interracial relationships by the young, artsy White urbanites in his neighborhood, although national polling data show that Blacks are more likely than Whites to approve of interracial relationships.[14] A lack of direct confrontation from other Whites may also point to the social power embodied in White masculinity. Historically, White men from the middle or upper classes have been able to engage in interracial sexual relations or marriage with less dire repercussions than those experienced by other racial/gender groups.

The public attention that heterosexual interracial partners in my study receive is often negative, but it rarely escalates to overt aggression. This is consistent with the findings of other qualitative researchers in this area.[15] Violent opposition to heterosexual Black/White intimacy is much less frequent today than it was in the early to mid-twentieth century and before.[16] Yet, these instances still occur. Scott Patterson, a thirty-two-year-old Black man, was attacked by five "neo-Nazi skinheads" in Greece while walking with a White girlfriend. The attackers chased them through crowded streets and eventually nearly beat Scott to death with railroad ties. Scott prides himself on not living in fear of another attack. Still, he remains vigilant and hyperaware in public settings. Kalvin Oster recalls that as teenagers, he and a White female classmate were the victims of an attempted assault by White men as the two adolescents sat together in a car stopped at a red light. Yelling "Nigger lover!" the men spat at Kalvin and his classmate and grabbed at the car doors. Kalvin refers to this incident as both "ridiculous" and "gut-wrenching." Notably, he points out that he and the young woman were not even dating—they were just friends. The presumption of heterosexuality in public spaces was so strong that Kalvin and his friend were assumed to be in a romantic relationship simply because they were sitting together in the same car.[17]

Less often, heterosexual partners experienced ostensibly positive social recognition. These encounters reflect the emergent popularity of a multiracial ethic in which interracial intimacy is assumed to embody the potential for racial transformation. From this perspective, interraciality represents "love's revolution."[18] In these interactions, interraciality is read not as deviant or disruptive, but rather as progressive and righteous, a promise of a more cohesive racial future. Ethan Smolen, a White heterosexual man introduced in chapter 2, relates the variety of public reactions he and Wanda Maxwell, his Black partner, receive in their Philadelphia neighborhood and its environs:

> People are screwy. You had the people that would see Wanda wearing dreadlocks walking down the streets with a White man and have to make a comment about her being a traitor. Or you would have even more frustrating—or not frustrating but annoying—would be the people that would be like, "It's so good what you're doing." Like we're doing a community service project to promote racial harmony. "Oh, that's good. That must be so hard here in America."

Ethan's observations and those of many heterosexual partners in my study make clear that, whether the reaction they elicit from strangers is antagonistic or affirmative, their intimacy most often carries a comprehensible social meaning. Bradley Tyson, a heterosexual Black man in his mid-forties, makes a similar assessment when I ask him whether he and his White wife, Julianna Tyson (introduced in chapter 2), receive looks or stares in public. He says, "Yeah, we do. ... And we know it. But I don't think those looks are all hostile looks. They're just curious or congratulations. [They] go, 'Wish we saw more people like that.'" In a similar vein, Brianna Simmons, whose negative public experiences in Philadelphia make her long to return to Boston, recalls a much happier moment there. She says, "One time in [a Boston city park], a young guy who was my age, came up and said, 'I'm really encouraged by what you and your husband are doing because you remind me of my mom and dad so much and we need so much more of that.'" Brianna and her husband Kurt, like Bradley and Julianna and Ethan and Wanda, are read as intimate partners. As heterosexual couples, they inhabit a sexual status that—whether or not it is deemed problematic—is legible to others. Their stories demonstrate that heterosexual interraciality is a meaningful social category that strangers use as the basis for making assumptions.

Invisibility

Between the more usual moments of hypervisibility are instances in which heterosexual interracial intimacy fades from view. In these situations, heterosexual Black/White partners feel the lack of social recognition that, as I will show, profoundly affects lesbian and gay couples. Despite the dramatic differences between hypervisibility and invisibility, both experiences derive from being racially different in a social context where such difference is both marginalized and infrequent. Other qualitative researchers have uncovered a similar pattern.[19] For heterosexual interracial partners in my study, this experience occurs most frequently in public places like restaurants, where many people are waiting together and the host must visually assess who is next in line or who is with which party. In these quick judgments, interracial intimacy can become invisible because assumptions of monoraciality prevail. If partners are not holding hands or being physically affectionate, the quick glances of strangers may assess them as unrelated.

The significance of these instances to the couples themselves varies from indifference to annoyance and anger. For instance, Vera Oster, Kalvin's White wife, has a twelve-year-old White daughter, Becky, from a previous marriage and a six-month-old daughter, Kaya. Vera relates her frustration at not being recognized as a family:

> We'll be next to each other [in line] and the clerk will say, "Can I help you, sir?" or something like that. Just assuming we are not together, even though we all may be standing there together and it may be all four of us standing there together. The people just assume that you're not with this person because he is not White.

Warren, the heterosexual White man described earlier, voiced his resentment at the persistent inability of strangers to see him and his wife Nakia as a couple:

> For instance [we're] waiting in line for a deli and she pays, and they're like, "Can I help you?" I'm like, "I'm with her. Don't you get that?" Why would

I stand so close to her? People look at you, like you're not [together]. It happens all the time. ... It pisses me off. I mean small things ... a small thing
like that pisses me off. I don't understand the ignorance, but maybe I would
react the same way. Because you never know who is with who or what. So
maybe I'm the one that is oversensitive.

It bears repeating that Black/White interracial relationships—both same-
sex and heterosexual—are numerically unusual. Fewer than one in every
hundred couples in the United States has one Black and one White partner. In a society where neighborhoods, schools, and churches tend to be
racially segregated, the infrequency of interracial intimacy may seem to
render strangers' misreadings understandable. Persons in same-race relationships undoubtedly experience such misunderstandings once in a while.
But when interracial partners are unrecognized, it is not only because there
are so few of them, but because their racial difference—and for some,
their lesbian or gay sexuality—does not fit within the dominant image of
romantic intimacy. They are not same-race heterosexual couples. These
seemingly benign misunderstandings underscore the normative status of
same-race intimacy and the invisibility of closeness across racial lines.
Their persistence and cumulative nature make them meaningful.

Moments of invisibility during which heterosexual couples' racial status denies them the privilege of social recognition are useful reminders of
the significance of race. We might assume that an important element of
heterosexual privilege is that a man and a woman can comfortably express
affection in almost any social setting, even a gay one, without wondering
whether kissing or holding hands will make them targets of violence.[20] But
not all heterosexuals have equal access to heterosexual privileges. In fact,
the experiences of interracial couples show us that there are racial prerequisites to fundamental heterosexual privileges, like kissing and hugging
in public without worry.[21] For interracial couples, intimacy is sometimes
unrecognized, or it is met with animosity and intolerance. Neither reaction
is typically associated with same-race heterosexual intimacy.

Lesbian and Gay Interracial Intimacy

Although heterosexual partners occasionally encounter a lack of social recognition, many lesbian and gay Black/White couples experience a much
deeper, more profound sense of invisibility. Many assume that unless they
are holding hands or being physically demonstrative, strangers will not
recognize their partnership. Unlike heterosexual partners, who may be

assumed to be romantically involved simply because they are interact-ing socially or—as in Kalvin's case—sharing the front seat of the same car, some same-sex couples feel that their intimacy is largely invisible. This assessment derives from numerous quotidian experiences. Maureen Wiley, a thirty-year-old White woman who lives in Washington, D.C. with her thirty-one-year-old Black partner, Terrina Nissar, describes a typical occurrence:

> We have this thing that we always laugh about. We'll be in a crowded space—like a bus or a movie—[and] people always cut in between us. Cause if you see a couple, you don't cut in between them. You know what I mean? But people just cut right in between us. . . . I think [Terrina] gets more annoyed at it. I think it's hysterical. I'm like, "Hello? [We're] together." Um, I'm sure I've cut off people that I haven't seen were together either, whether they're together intimately or just together hanging out. I have my own assumptions of who knows who.

Though Maureen and Terrina interpret this type of experience differently, its repetitive nature reinforces a shared sense that they inhabit a marginal intimacy unrecognizable to others.

Thad Thompson is a forty-six-year-old White man whose Black partner, Lucas Tatum, is twenty-eight. When I ask Thad whether he thinks people recognize them as a couple, he pauses and takes a deep breath. "You know, I don't really think about that a lot. But if I do think about it, I would assume, no. I would think that they wouldn't. I would think they would look at us and go, 'What are those guys doing together?'" Thad is often conscious of the age difference between him and Lucas, a factor that may compound their racial difference. He tells me that as an individual he often feels very conspicuous in the predominantly Black neighborhood where he and Lucas live. Having lived in this neighborhood, which is undergoing gentrification, since before he met Lucas seven years ago, Thad experi-ences a race fatigue similar to that of the Whites I described in chapter 2. Yet even as his Whiteness makes him stand out, he feels that when he is with Lucas, their relationship is something that goes unrecognized.

For Maureen and Thad, as for other partners in lesbian and gay relation-ships, it is unclear how much of this lack of social recognition is shaped by their same-sex status and how much by their interraciality. Does being a Black/White couple make them less visible or more so? Some partners think that their racial difference makes the invisibility of their intimate relationship more acute. Jessica Merriam feels this way. Jessica is a tall, light-skinned Black lesbian in her early twenties who recently graduated from college. When I meet her, she is working as a grant writer at a non-profit community organization. She describes herself as "femme," reflecting her identification with traditionally feminine expressions of gender. Her partner of three years, Bryce Cook, has a more masculine, or "butch," presentation of self. Bryce is a twenty-two-year-old White woman. She is five feet, six inches tall and has short, dirty-blond hair and pale white skin. Because of her boyish looks, Bryce is more frequently read in public as an adolescent boy than as a young woman, and she is comfortable with this. Jessica references the intersection between interraciality and queerness directly. She tells me about men's forward gestures when she and Bryce walk down the street holding hands:

> Bryce and I were talking about this last night, or a couple nights ago, about why we think people don't recognize us as a couple ... or why men hit on me when she's with me. And so she was like, "You know what? They wouldn't do that if I were a Black man." And I was like, "You're right ... and if you were a Black dyke, they would probably still hit on me, but not as much." But because of who she is, they do hit on me. ... I'm talking about Black men hitting on me, because that's usually who hits on me. Um, so, I guess that's like the way that they interact with us differently because we're interracial—the fact that they don't read us as a couple or that they don't respect that even if they do read us as a couple.

Jessica's continual experience of being approached by Black men in front of her White lesbian partner exemplifies the two important ways that queer interracial relationships become invisible in certain public spaces. Like Leslie Cobbs, whose reflections are quoted at the start of this chapter, Bryce is completely ignored when men approach Jessica. Jessica's assertion that men would not approach her if Bryce were a Black man reflects her sense that same-race heterosexuality is seen as a legitimate type of romantic union. Her suggestion that if Bryce were a Black lesbian, she might still be "hit on," but "not as much" reflects her belief that even when queer intimacy is acknowledged, it is easily disregarded.

The racial difference between Jessica and Bryce makes their relationship seem unrecognizable in other kinds of situations too. Bryce's non-normative gender presentation plays an implicit role in these interactions. She tells me that people have assumed that Jessica is her babysitter or have asked if Bryce is Jessica's son or little brother. These various imaginings of their relationship affirm to Bryce that many people are unable to recognize queer interracial intimacy. "Each time it's like just, 'You're going out of your way to not see us as a couple.' ... Like maybe that pattern is easier for certain people to see than as a lesbian relationship. ... I'm still kind of figuring out how other people perceive us." Bryce explains that she and Jessica hold hands in public and are affectionate in their body language or in how close they stand. In these situations, the intimacy between them is not invisible. It is indecipherable. Strangers may recognize a connection, but they attach a host of other meanings to it before they consider Bryce and Jessica to be a romantic couple.

Gender can shape the interplay among racial difference, sexuality, and visibility in other ways. When both lesbian partners project a gendered self that others recognize as traditionally feminine, they are often assumed to be heterosexual, making their intimacy hard for others to see. In other words, when lesbians are stereotypically defined as short-haired, aggressive, androgynous women who flout social conventions and always wear pants, then lesbians who take on a more "feminine" gender presentation become invisible.[22] When very feminine-looking lesbians move through non-queer public spaces without their female partner, they often pass for straight. Leslie refers to this phenomenon when she describes her experiences with invisibility. With straight, reddish-brown hair that is just long enough to tuck behind her ears, Leslie looks as if she is in her mid-twenties. Only at the occasional angle when the tiny crinkles around her eyes are revealed do her thirty-seven years become apparent. Her twenty-nine-year-old Black partner, Sylvia, is tall and lean, with stylish tortoiseshell eyeglasses and long dreadlocks that are tinted reddish-brown. When she and Sylvia first met, Leslie wore her hair much shorter. She believes this aesthetic difference influences assumptions that people make about her sexuality and, by extension, her relationship:

> I think if I was more butch, say, people might be more likely to perceive us as a couple and that could be both good and bad. ... It could mean I wouldn't feel as invisible at times, but it could also mean that we would get more shit, you know? 'Cause people don't necessarily read either one of us alone as lesbian, um, which some days is irritating to me and other days is fine.

Unless they were holding hands or kissing, when both lesbian partners expressed a stereotypically feminine style—in dress, hairstyle, use (or no use) of makeup, and/or physical bearing—they felt invisible as romantic partners. Leslie's words also capture the ambivalence other lesbian and gay couples expressed around visibility. Feeling visible carries the privilege of recognition but also the danger of harassment.[23]

Not all gay and lesbian interracial partners feel a constant lack of social recognition. Some same-sex partners in the study were surprised when others did not identify them as a couple. They assumed that people would recognize intimacy in their comfortable exchanges or in the closeness of the space they shared. This expectation more closely characterizes the experiences of gay men in my study, some of whom were confident that "you can just tell" they are a couple. Kirk Belton-Davis, a White gay man whose Black partner Walter's thoughts I quote at the beginning of this book, explains his own assumptions: "I think most people probably figure it out because we are very much like a couple. How we talk here is how we talk everywhere. I think it's fairly obvious, but some people are fairly dense."

Social location may explain why gay partners in my study were more likely to feel that their relationship was visible in public. The joint workings of sexism, racism, and heteronormativity privilege certain bodies and marginalize others. Or the explanation may lie in which groupings of people are assumed to be friends. One interracial partner suggested that gay intimacy may be generally more visible than lesbian intimacy because interracial pairs or groups of women are more likely to be read as friends, whereas a Black man and a White man are unlikely to be socializing on a city street or in a restaurant unless they are doing business.[24] Nelson Ingles, a fifty-six-year-old Black gay man, echoes this sentiment: "You rarely see a Black man and White man out together at night. When you do, you just sort of assume that they're gay. So I just assume that everybody else is assuming that we're gay, that we're together." His expectation that strangers would assume that he and his White partner, Edmond Springer, are lovers is likely also influenced by the fact that the two men live in downtown Philadelphia, only a few blocks from the neighborhood where most of Philadelphia's gay and lesbian restaurants, bars, and nightclubs are located.

If racial difference intensifies the invisibility that some couples experience, for others it may heighten the vulnerability associated with recognition. Some narratives seem to suggest that racial difference can draw additional attention to same-sex intimacy. Katrina ("Trina") Stevens is a Black lesbian who is frequently perplexed by these intersections. Trina, who works as a case manager in a social service agency in the Bronx, is a tall woman with closely cropped hair. Her voice is raspy from too many cigarettes; this makes her seem older than her forty-two years. Trina's self-presentation is decidedly masculine—when I meet her she is wearing a dark grey, loose-fitting sweatshirt, baggy blue jeans, and work boots. Her knit Yankees cap is turned to the right so that the logo faces off to the side. Trina details a particular experience she and her White partner, thirty-one-year-old Pamela Donato, had in the New York subway. They were riding the A train toward Manhattan from Brooklyn, talking and holding hands, when they noticed that the people around them were staring. For Trina, recounting these details rekindles some of the frustration she felt in the original interaction.

> It felt like everybody in the subway car was staring at us. I got so mad. ... [Pam's] like, "What's going on?" "I don't know but they're stupid and they better stop staring. I feel like saying, 'What the fuck you all staring at?'" She said, "No, no, no." ... People were laughing. It was just kind of fucked-up. ... Even Pam was getting mad and she's not one to get upset about stuff like that. ... The point of the story was we weren't sure what it was. We weren't sure if it was because we were two women or because we were Black and White. And that's always our confusion. I guess that's our main question across the board. ... We're not sure.

Although Trina and Pam do not fit the normative vision of romantic intimacy—a same-race heterosexual couple—in this moment and in many others like it, they cannot decipher which transgression draws others' attention, their sexuality or their racial difference. When I talk with Pam, she brings up this same experience but also says that she is often not sure if people read Trina as a woman or a man: "I never really know what is in their head, if they are seeing us as straight or gay. I don't know. There is no way for me to know. We could be getting a dirty look from someone. ... I don't know if they think we are gay, or if they see that we are interracial, or if it is both." A possible interpretation is that racial difference between same-sex partners is what first draws others' attention, which then increases the chances that their romantic intimacy will be noted, which in turn would render these couples more vulnerable. I introduced this notion earlier, in the context of the history of Black/White intimacy (see chapter 1). More contemporary research finds that being interracial makes same-sex couples more identifiable than two women or two men of the same racial/ethnic group. Increased recognition then heightens their experience of homophobia.[25]

Trina and Pam may have a difficult time understanding the attention they receive in public places, but for other partners, this intersection is not at all murky. They state firmly that it is their racial difference that draws attention to their romantic intimacy and makes them more vulnerable. Dionna Yates, a Black lesbian in her early twenties, met her White partner, Lindsey Michaels, in college. The two have been together four years. Dionna is conscious of reactions to both their sexual status and racial difference when they are in public places in Philadelphia.

> I think people are quicker to look at any mixed-race group of people faster than they would a group of people of the same race and then would say "hey," if they're looking over [here]. "Oh, they're both girls." You know? And then I feel like that puts us at a greater sort of risk for any kind of assault than, say, a same-race couple.

Although racial difference may make more acute the invisibility that some couples feel in movie theaters and on city streets, Dionna's comment suggests that racial difference may also heighten the risk of homophobia for same-sex partners, should their intimacy become apparent. Lindsey notes that lesbian and gay partners who are both White may experience forms of racial privilege unavailable to interracial partners:

> We don't often hold hands in public. I think neither of us are into PDA [public displays of affection]. Dionna grew up in the South and is I think much more sensitive than most of our other friends to the fear of being harassed for either being an interracial couple or a queer couple. I have noticed especially with our White [lesbian] friends ... they are much more likely to have PDA in public. And I don't know if that is a racial issue. ... And I was just like, "Um, you realize like, that's your privilege." And there also—there is the one couple in particular—they are very like girlie-girl, so guys would be really into that, watching them make out in public and stuff. But like if we had done that, that would have been a problem.

Lindsey's explanation makes it clear that she sees a number of factors—not just racial difference—at play in how strangers perceive her and Dionna in public. Like Dionna, she thinks racial judgments and homophobia may work together, each aggravating the effects of the other. But how each woman performs gender may also influence these situations. Lindsey has curly brown hair and a serious demeanor; Dionna wears sturdy-looking black-framed glasses and has closely cropped hair. Because Dionna has a more masculine or butch presentation of self, while Lindsey's persona is more feminine, she does not expect that their intimate gestures would titillate others in the same way as two "girlie-girls" kissing.

These gay and lesbian interracial narratives are qualitatively different from the stories told by most heterosexual interracial partners. Straight Black/White couples' intimacy is generally visible to strangers. Whether this recognition registers as affirmation, curiosity, or hostility, straight interracial couples bear the marker of interraciality as an intelligible cultural symbol with established historical, social, and political meanings. In contrast, many of the gay and lesbian partners in this study perceived their intimacy to be unrecognizable in most public places and did not interpret their interraciality as having any public identity. As I began to explore in the previous chapter, only in spaces that were self-consciously marked as lesbian, gay, or queer did these couples perceive their interraciality to be a meaningful marker.

So far in this chapter, my goal has been to describe public experiences of interraciality by foregrounding sexuality. This puts normative assumptions about romantic intimacy (namely, that it is heterosexual and same-race) into sharp relief and reveals that certain forms of intimate connection are more easily recognized than others. It also shows that if we assume that racial difference always makes intimacy hypervisible, we see only part of the picture. In the next section, I draw from these public experiences to examine how interracial partners navigate public spaces and why these practices are best conceptualized as racework.

Managing Visibility

The narratives in this chapter present a complicated portrait of marginalization and recognition. Racial prejudice and homophobia create subjects that are alternately invisible and hypervisible. Invisibility may be frustrating or exhausting, but being recognized as sexual partners can expose interracial couples to harassment or physical harm. To exert control over these two contrasting public modes, some interracial partners modify their behavior to either conceal their intimacy or clearly signal its presence. By avoiding recognition or confronting it, same-sex interracial partners, and some heterosexual interracial partners, act to reduce their vulnerability in public. These social practices constitute visibility management, a form of racework through which partners respond to the racial difference in their relationship and also, for lesbians and gays, to their shared marginality as same-sex partners. Because it is difficult to parse the influences of racial difference and homophobia in the marginalization of gay and lesbian partners, the work they do to manage both must be analyzed within the context of racework.

Monitoring Public Displays of Affection

Not every couple wants to hug or kiss in public. Whether heterosexual, lesbian, or gay, some partners explained that public displays of affection (PDA) were not their "style" or that they have "never done that." Evan Cody, a Black gay man in his twenties, makes this point when he tells me, "I don't necessarily want to see anyone gay or straight or whatever, you know, displaying that in public." Brent Isley, a White heterosexual man (introduced in chapter 2) speaks for his Black partner, Velena Julien, as well as himself, asserting that "neither of us are big on [it]. Our private space is private and our public space is public. We keep them fairly separate and I think that's how we both are." Kristie Kelley (also introduced in chapter 2) feels the same way. Kristie is reluctant to position herself as the object of others' scrutiny, but being in an interracial relationship adds to that ingrained reluctance. She explains, "I am not the type of person, even if Burton was Black, that I would be holding hands and kissing in public. I don't do that kind of stuff, that's me. But being in an interracial relationship, I definitely wouldn't do that, you know? I would not do anything to purposely call attention to myself more than I would have to."

However, even romantic partners who are comfortable expressing affection in public may regulate that behavior so as not to draw unwelcome attention. They may, for instance, refrain from hand-holding, hugging, or kissing when they believe such displays of affection might elicit negative reactions from others. In order to avoid not only public recognition but also the public harassment that can accompany it, some interracial partners pay particular attention to social context.[26] They read the social geography of urban and suburban landscapes, identifying and interpreting cues about the safety of engaging in PDA. Both this evaluation of social environments and the purposeful containment of affection itself involve a particular kind of racework—visibility management.

Heterosexual partners self-monitor their PDA occasionally. Aware of the social stigmas attached to interracial intimacy, they sometimes read contextual cues before engaging in behavior that could create conflict. Warren provides an example. The negative attention that he and Nakia sometimes attract has made him cautious and more attuned to the racial geographies of individual New York neighborhoods. He reads these cues when deciding whether holding hands would be a good idea.

Yeah, I think 80 percent of the city we feel comfortable in, especially Manhattan, even all the way to Washington Heights, which is Harlem. There are certain parts where you might feel a bit more uncomfortable. I think a place like this [Brooklyn neighborhood] is just perfect. … It's kind of what you would look for because people are nice, people are open. You're just a regular old couple, there is no interracial in the couple; you're just a couple and people look at you like that. It's not like, "Oh, they're different. That's interesting." … What I'm saying is that you just kind of blend in. … I think maybe if we go to Harlem and go to 105th [street] and walk around hand in hand, we're not just a couple; we're suddenly becoming an interracial couple. We can go to certain parts in Brooklyn that are either predominately White or Jewish Orthodox, or predominately Black—you suddenly become this interracial couple again. It's because the environment changes, not because you change.

His own neighborhood, which he describes as a "hipster town" that contains a mix of people, a "good New York soup," includes enough other interracial couples that he does not feel particularly conspicuous walking hand in hand with Nakia. In other neighborhoods, however, he and his wife "become" an interracial couple. Warren's own sense of visibility and the social practices by which he manages it are intricately tied to the social geography of the city. Warren and Nakia are only two of a small group of heterosexual partners in my study who described taking these sorts of precautions.[27]

Same-sex partners were much more likely than their heterosexual counterparts to assess their environment for cues before engaging in PDA. About half of same-sex partners but less than one-fifth of heterosexual partners in my study engaged in this form of racework. The gay and lesbian partners are attuned to both the racial and the sexual geography of social spaces, and they sometimes also use social class as a proxy for sexual tolerance. Most gay or lesbian partners expressed feelings of cautious restraint in spaces they did not perceive to be accepting of nonheterosexual identities. Many, but not all, related an increased sense of comfort and safety, and a greater inclination to be physically affectionate, in lesbian or gay spaces. As discussed in the previous chapter, however, the racial divisions within these communities mean that both partners may not feel comfortable in the same lesbian or gay space. Lucas Tatum explains his stance on being affectionate with his White partner, Thad Thompson, in public places:

We have a lot of PDA but not overt, not, not loud PDA. It's very quiet. For example … we'll walk and one of us will rub the other on the back. Or if we hold hands, it's sort of brief, very brief. If I had my arm around him it won't last long. … I'm definitely more comfortable doing it, uh, you know, under the cover of night, when it's dark out versus when it's light out. When there are, when I know for a fact that there are other gay people around, I'm definitely more comfortable than if there's, if I don't know there are gay people around.

Similarly, Evan Cody reads his social environment for cues when he is in public with his twenty-four-year-old White partner, Vance Dalton. "I think occasionally [Vance and I] may hold hands. A lot of it also deals with security issues. I don't necessarily always feel safe ... especially if I don't know the area. If we're in the [gay neighborhood] I don't think twice, but if we're on the cusp or something." For Ulrich Drescher, a White gay man in his early forties, zones of tolerance can be demarcated block by block. Ulrich is tall and lanky, with short brown hair that shows only the slightest hint of grey. He lives in Philadelphia with his Black partner, Marvin Nelson, but he describes for me his experiences visiting Boystown, a historic gay neighborhood in Chicago:

> If you go out in certain quarters like in Chicago. ... It is amazing. It is this one street where Chicago basically put up the street lamps in the [gay] rainbow colors. I mean it is clearly, the city itself says like this is sort of "Boystown" or whatever you may call it. But you step there and you can hold hands and kiss or anything. ... And as you step up Halsted [Street], maybe a half a block from Halsted, you immediately let go.

For these gay men and for lesbians as well, there are valuable cues in the spatial environment that signal whether same-sex affection will be read as unremarkable or even celebrated, or whether it is likely to elicit negative reactions. Managing visibility involves scanning the surroundings for reassuring signs—other gay or lesbian couples, commercial establishments, rainbow symbols, even physical boundaries such as street signs. Until they identify symbols like these, some same-sex partners are less likely to be open with their affections, leading strangers to assume that the partners do not know each other or are simply friends.[28]

Some same-sex partners scan public places for other sorts of cues before holding hands or hugging and kissing goodbye. These partners observe the racial, ethnic, or social class composition or the gendered interactions in specific neighborhoods to make inferences about the level of sexual tolerance in these areas. For example, Tara Hilliard, introduced in chapter 2, says that she is not "that big on" PDA with her White partner, Kate Taurisano. Still, she asserts that, "if I feel like I want [Kate's] hand ... I'll just take it." Yet, almost as soon as these words are out of her mouth, Tara qualifies them. There are certain places where she would not "just take" Kate's hand:

> I mean, if I was like down in Flatbush or something, in Brooklyn, I might not do it. ... It's just a lot, it's like a predominantly Carib[bean] neighborhood living there. I mean, they're aggressive toward women to begin with, especially aggressive toward White women, and I just don't really want there to be problems. It's like, I lived there before in Flatbush, um, with my [last] girlfriend who was also White. ... I don't know, they're just, weird guys, you know? ... They don't have a, they don't think it's a problem to just like say stuff to you and like touch you, you know, and I think that's a problem. And like I just don't want to get caught up in something.

Tara's explanation shows that she sometimes uses observations about ethnicity and gender as a barometer of the sexual tolerance of her social environment. She attributes the aggressive masculinity she observes to the shared Caribbean origins of many neighborhood residents. She does not, however, make cultural distinctions between different groups, such as Haitians and Jamaicans. Gendered interactions in which men comment inappropriately on women's appearances or touch them inappropriately are evidence to Tara that PDA between two women would not go unnoticed.

Other same-sex couples mention taking similar precautions in certain neighborhoods. Terrina and Maureen, introduced earlier in this chapter, live in Washington, D.C. Terrina says that she is likely to raise her guard in "rougher" areas. She is wary of "the type of people that hang around on the street," especially in neighborhoods that are unfamiliar to her. She tells me that "in more affluent areas ... people [are] mainly in their houses," and she is less likely to be accosted by men who are "usually pretty drunk." Although she does not reference race, Terrina, like Tara, also considers the potential for street harassment by men before deciding whether to hold hands with her White partner.

Sometimes same-sex partners modify their behavior not because they fear homophobia, but rather because they fear racial judgments. For example, Maureen explains that the neighborhood she and Terrina live in is predominantly Black, but it is rapidly gentrifying. "This neighborhood even when we moved in, this square block here, there were, I think, four White people on this square block, and now there's like ten. And that was only since last winter." She adds that most of the White people who live on her block are also queer. In talking about her comfort level with PDA, Maureen tells me that she is more cautious with affectionate gestures toward Terrina in her own neighborhood than in other areas of the city:

> Yeah, I don't hold her hand in this neighborhood. I noticed that the other day. And I actually think it's more a race thing here than it is a gay thing. ... Like I don't want anyone to think I'm stealing a good Black person. You know that whole thing. ... Kind of like [with] White and Black straight women. "There's so few out there. Why are you taking one?" ... And I will hold her hand. And it's not like a big thing, I don't want you to think that I think about that all the time, but I have noticed that I don't, don't hold her hand, don't kiss her goodbye at [this] bus stop.

The noticeable presence of other gays and lesbians in her neighborhood may make Maureen less worried about homophobia, or she may just be particularly focused on people's negative perceptions of interracial intimacy. But, as she notes, her stance on PDA is not fixed. Part of the visibility management that Maureen does involves making judgments about when it is appropriate to hold Terrina's hand and when it is not. She modifies her actions on the blocks outside her apartment by taking into account the racial dynamics of the neighborhood space.

Monique Gilliam, introduced with her White partner, Barbara DiBacco, in chapter 2, reads the racial dynamics of public spaces because she is more sensitive to homophobic stares and comments in Black neighborhoods than in White neighborhoods. She and Barbara are one of three couples in my sample who do not live together. Monique describes the demographics of her Brooklyn neighborhood this way: "This neighborhood I think, well particularly this block ... is predominately African American, middle class, and there are some wealthy African Americans. But [it is] predominately middle class, upper middle class and there are some African Americans who are working class like on the fringes ... going further, deeper into Brooklyn." In this neighborhood, she sometimes is publicly affectionate with Barbara. "We might walk arm and arm like this. We usually just walk side by side. On this block, she's kissed me in front of my house. And that was prompted or initiated by her because she's much more affectionate than I am." But Monique is much more cautious in Black neighborhoods where she senses strains of homophobia:

> If we're in a, for *me*, if we're in a predominately Black neighborhood and if I know the neighborhood—meaning that I know that there is a threat or that there are people who are anti-lesbian or anti-gay—I'm not holding her arm.

I'm not going to even touch her because my thing is if someone says some-thing to me or gets in my face, I'm going to have to fight and I'm not fight-ing. 'Cause I can't do that anymore. If we're in a place that's predominately White, which is not very often, but if we're in a place that is predominantly White and heterosexual, I'll say, "Sure" [to holding Barbara's arm]. 'Cause White people don't scare me when it comes to like anti-queer stuff. They don't scare me.

Monique's explanation that she is more intimidated by homophobia in Black communities than in White ones may reflect her greater social investment in Black spaces. She and Barbara rarely frequent predominantly White social spaces, unless they are gay or lesbian settings. Homophobia in Black neighborhoods may "scare" her more because she knows that she will engage any potential harassers, escalating the situation beyond a level with which she is comfortable. Her noninvestment in White heterosexual social spaces may make it easier to dismiss any homophobia she encoun-ters there.

The narratives presented in this section describe a particular form of racework that partners use to deal with racial prejudice and homophobia in public places. These partners show a willingness to modify their behavior in order to avoid harassment. Heterosexual partners engage in these moni-toring practices because they anticipate prejudice directed toward both their racial difference and the perceived sexual and gender transgressions of choosing a partner of another race. Same-sex partners monitor their vis-ibility management as a means of navigating racial and homophobic preju-dices and, sometimes, others' discomfort with their non-normative gender presentations as well. It is impossible to parse these as discrete influences, though some same-sex partners interpret their racial difference as increas-ing their vulnerability to the effects of homophobia. This form of racework is therefore a response not only to how these racial differences manifest in public places, but also to the widespread existence of homophobia. As we have seen, making visibility-related decisions can involve reading the racial, sexual, gender, and social class dynamics inherent in local geogra-phies; but there are additional ways to manage visibility. The next section examines some interracial partners' attempts to preempt prejudice by con-fronting it head-on.

Asserting Presence

In *Weaving a Family*, an autoethnography about another sort of interracial intimacy, Barbara Katz Rothman explains that as a White mother of an adopted Black daughter, she consciously performs numerous small acts by which she attempts to make her connection to Victoria, her Black daughter, obvious to others.[29] Rothman uses subtle gestures, such as putting an arm around her daughter's shoulders or purposefully using the words "my daughter," to indicate to others that she is indeed the mother of this child. The situations in which she signals her attachment are ordinary ones—purchasing rocket pops on the street from the ice cream truck or meeting a violin teacher for the first time—yet they are moments in which Rothman is concerned that strangers' inability to perceive the parent-child bond may be hurtful to Victoria, or to Rothman herself. Using common gestures and phrases that people in same-race families take for granted, she hopes to make her connection to Victoria legible for strangers.

Some interracial partners make similarly conscious decisions to make their intimacy obvious. Rather than intentionally modifying or censoring their PDA, they demand public recognition.[30] Their efforts, although very different from those preferred by the partners described in the previous section, represent the same type of racework—visibility management. I encountered a particularly dramatic version of this racework as practiced by Tommy Smith-Donnell and his partner, Brian Smith-Donnell. Tommy is a fifty-four-year-old Black gay man who wears big round glasses and has a warm gregarious personality. He and Brian, who is a sixty-year-old White man, have been together for twelve years and live in a racially mixed working-class community in Philadelphia. They each hold leadership positions in an organization that brings gay men of different races together for social events and to talk about racial issues. When I meet Tommy, he is wearing dark jeans, a yellow long-sleeve cotton shirt, brown leather loafers, and a small black pin with the words "Smash Racism" in white letters. Upon meeting Brian that same day, I immediately notice his attire. He is wearing an outfit that looks *exactly* the same as Tommy's—dark jeans, yellow long-sleeve shirt, brown loafers, and a "Smash Racism" pin.[31] The image of two men over fifty dressed in identical clothing is striking. It is impossible *not* to notice that they go together. Tommy explains that this is precisely why they have been dressing in identical attire every day for the past several years. He tells me that by combining this strategy with an open display of their mutual affection, they demand social recognition. He speaks excitedly as he tries to help me understand:

> We do everything a straight couple can do—hold hands, kiss in public, be close, laugh, whatever! Wear each other's clothes. ... That's one reason why we dress alike. ... Everywhere we go, we'll dress alike. It proves, it proves

the point. ... It says to society that this is possible. "You say it's impossible. It *is* possible." There's a lot of [gay] people around here who [are] together and don't dress alike, but they're still together, okay? We're, we're speaking for them too, in our own little way. ... We're not gonna wear a sign; we don't have to hit you in your face about it. We're just there, you know. To prove the point.

When I talk with Brian, he echoes Tommy's sentiments and points out that being physically affectionate in public may initially create conflict, but in the long run it will diminish negative attitudes toward lesbian and gay intimacy:

We wanna be an out couple, and so, I mean, if we see a couple in the grocery store, you know, a heterosexual couple in the grocery store getting all lovey-dovey, I'll get lovey-dovey. I wanna let them know that we are in love and we are a male-male couple. I want people, other people, and I think it's important to me because it, I think when you put a face to an issue, it makes it difficult to, you know, to be against it.

Tommy and Brian's decision to counter invisibility by dressing identically is a unique strategy for confronting prejudice. But their purposeful use of public affection to overtly signal their gay interracial relationship to others is a form of racework that other partners use as well. Partners with this outlook willingly endure the curious or hostile stares of others.

Nancy Taylor, introduced in chapter 2, shares a similar impulse to interrupt the invisibility of her relationship. Nancy is a White lesbian in her late thirties. She and her Black partner, Nadine Allen, who is ten years older, live in Washington, D.C. When Nancy and I meet, she is between jobs and is working temporarily as a consultant to an international health organization. She tells me that she and Nadine "don't really kiss a lot in public," but that there are certain circumstances that seem to demand it:

Yesterday we were on the Metro ... and I noticed a couple, like a female and a male couple, kissing all over each other on the Metro. And I was just like, "Oh, God." And nobody was raising an eye and so we're like walking out of the train I just said, "I just need to kiss you to make a political statement, just kiss back." I used to feel very, very hesitant and I was afraid or whatever, you know? Then I finally just said, "You know what? This is who I am." This is how I feel and if I feel like kissing my girlfriend in the middle of the street, then I will and I did on the Metro platform.

Trina Stevens, whose experiences with overt rudeness from fellow A-train riders were recounted earlier in this chapter, vented some of her frustrations that day, like Nancy, by intentionally adopting a more confrontational form of visibility management. She gave the staring riders the finger and then kissed Pam.

Same-sex partners in this study engaged in this type of racework with some frequency. Heterosexual interracial partners did so occasionally. Recall, for example, Kalvin Oster, the heterosexual Black man who described being annoyed with Black women who censure him for having a White wife. He makes a show of kissing Vera when he notices Black women staring at them. This intentional display reflects his disregard for the women's judgments. His impulse to confront conflict is similar to Nancy's. Nancy feels the sting of invisibility; Trina and Kalvin feel the burn of disapproving stares. Each resists the prejudice attached to their relationship by signaling its resilience. Each fights back with a kiss.

Engaging in racework defensively by monitoring PDA or, instead, proactively asserting intimacy account for the public experiences of many interracial partners, but not all. Some kiss and hug in public neither out of defiance nor to resist prejudice, but simply because they are comfortable doing so. These practices are not racework. For example, although Trina used public affection to confront the conflict that seemed to be brewing in the New York subway car,. her everyday intimate practices are far less intentional. She explains, "We hug and kiss everywhere we go. In front of anybody, we don't even care. ... It's not even part of my thinking. ... We'll stop right in the middle of the street and just stand there and hug each other, it doesn't matter to us. ... We're oblivious to all that bullshit." Similarly, Kayla Carson, a Black lesbian, tells me that her public affection with her White partner, Laurie Lewis, is a constant. "It's obvious. We don't hold back in any way. ... It doesn't matter where we are, if we're in [this town] or downtown [Washington, D.C.] or at a restaurant, or at a bar, straight or whatever. We hold hands. When I walk out the door in the morning or she goes to pick up the paper, I give her a kiss. We really don't care." Some might doubt whether it is possible for gays and lesbians to express affection unselfconsciously in public spaces, given that even at the beginning of the twenty-first century, homophobia is still widespread. Yet, the confidence with which these individuals discuss their PDA suggests that these intimate practices are not microconfrontations with prejudice.

The majority of heterosexual partners in my study are comfortable expressing affection in public places. Thus, for this group too, public intimacy does not usually constitute racework. Consider these examples.

Marie Thomas tells me that she and her Black husband Frank are effusive enough so that their friends sometimes tell them, "You make us sick." Scott Patterson's fiancée, Tamara Stills, is a thirty-year-old White woman. Tamara confesses that she and Scott are "probably like the disgusting couple, everyone's like, 'Oh, jeez already, get a room,' or whatever. We're very lovey-dovey." According to Ethan Smolen, he and Wanda are "very affectionate in public, yeah, but not like sticking our tongues down each other's throats or anything like that … but we definitely hold hands all the time." There is no evidence in these quotes or in the broader conversations of which they are a part to suggest that these simple gestures of affection are enacted with any intention of resisting prejudice. Though each of these partners makes clear to me in other parts of our conversation that they are mindful of how interracial intimacy is marginalized, they make no connection between this marginalization and their own public expressions of intimacy. It would be a mistake, I believe, to conceptualize these gestures as a form of work. They are the pleasures of privilege.

Conclusion

Even at the beginning of the twenty-first century, public spaces present particular challenges to interracial couples. In the previous chapter, I discussed the ways in which Black/White couples navigate racially homogeneous neighborhoods and social spaces. Racial prejudice and homophobia create additional layers of complexity in public spaces. Depending on their sexuality and gender, interracial partners experience marginalization through strangers' overt stares, sighs, or comments, or through the inability of others to recognize their relationship. In other words, prejudice can visually connect two people, making their marginalized identity hypervisible, or it can dislocate partners, rendering their intimacy invisible. To navigate public spaces safely and comfortably, some interracial partners attempt to sidestep prejudice by controlling their self-presentation. They do so by either refraining from PDA in order to conceal their intimate status or overtly signaling their romantic status to others. Though seemingly divergent, both strategies help partners control how they are perceived by others. Both are forms of racework practiced in public places.

Both the heterosexual and same-sex interracial partners in this study are conscious of how their relationships are marginalized. The lesbian and gay partners, however, are more likely to manage their visibility. The heterosexual partners demonstrate a curious pattern. They experience a more consistently elevated level of attention—whether or not they are being physically affectionate—and yet expend much less energy managing this higher level of visibility. Returning to Goffman's theories about stigma management might help us understand this pattern. He distinguishes between the plight of the already *discredited* (those who assume that their differentness is plainly known or is "evident on the spot") and the plight of the *discreditable* (those who assume that their differentness is neither known by others nor immediately apparent to them).[32] What I have shown in this chapter is that heterosexual interracial partners feel themselves to be in the former category, among the already discredited. In my study, most of these couples, especially Black men and White women, assume that other people recognize them as a couple, and they know that this may diminish their social standing in the eyes of others. I have argued that this assumption of recognition is a privilege of being heterosexual in a heteronormative social world. Though their racial difference sometimes precludes them from enjoying the full privileges of their sexual status—for example, showing affection without harassment—most of these couples do experience the confidence of embodying a normative status. Because they feel their interracial status to be self-evident, they are less likely than same-sex partners to modify their actions in an attempt to control others' impressions.

Lesbian and gay interracial partners, on the other hand, largely count themselves among the discreditable. Because they are often unsure whether strangers can perceive the intimate connection between them, and because recognition of intimacy may unleash homophobia, as well as racial prejudice, they are more likely to manage their visibility in public spaces. In a heteronormative social context, gay and lesbian partners "out" themselves with every intimate gesture. In uncertain environments, significant social costs may be attached to seemingly minute social gestures. For this reason, gay and lesbian partners are more likely to manage visibility.

In this chapter and the previous one, I have examined how interracial partners navigate public spaces that are generally racially divided and in which they may feel vulnerable to harassment. But public spaces are not the only places where couples experience the significance of being racially different in a racially stratified society. These moments also arise in "private" spaces, ones that are too often assumed to be racially neutral. In the next chapter, I examine how partners negotiate racial difference as it arises between them.

CHAPTER 4 | Intimate Interactions: Racework as Emotional Labor

I said to [Nancy] because I don't think she had been with a Black woman before ... I said, "You know, you have to think about this—being in a relationship with a Black person. When we go to restaurants, you get slightly different treatment. Sometimes people may take a long time to seat us or we might get sat in a particular corner. Or we don't get really good service because they make assumptions that we're not going to give them a good tip." ... Because she hasn't always had this experience, she hasn't had to devise a strategy for keeping her psyche intact. So in some ways that can be, that sort of makes me tired in a way. ... You have only so much energy, so I'm frequently thinking about how to replenish my energy. ... Not only [to] support myself but to support my relationship and help my partner along in being in a relationship that's not acceptable by the larger society. And sometimes that gets a little challenging. ... It's one thing to deal with the race issue alone but it's another thing to deal [with it] with another person.

THIS DESCRIPTION OF HOW race works in Nadine's relationship makes visible a set of interactions that go largely unseen in studies of interracial intimacy. Nadine Allen's account of everyday racism begins in public spaces, but her narrative quickly moves to another level—the intimate sphere. At forty-seven, Nadine has had decades to establish the daily habits by which she maintains her energy and steels herself against racial animus. By contrast, Nancy Taylor's Whiteness has exempted her from the need to develop similar habitual actions and accommodations. Before this relationship with Nadine, Nancy rarely noticed racial prejudice and had a less personal investment in challenging racial discrimination. This is one of the privileges of being a White person in the United States. Partnering with Nadine has created a new reality for Nancy in which she is the direct and indirect object of racism. Not surprisingly, given their contrasting experiences with racial stratification, Nadine and Nancy have different racial frameworks for understanding it. Their separate—and unequal—racialized statuses indelibly shape how the world sees each of them, and how they each see the world. Their racial difference thus has consequences not only in public places, but in their personal interactions as well. To mediate conflict between themselves, partners employ the form of racework that I term *emotional labor.*

Because social researchers rarely acknowledge the potential for or the presence of racial conflict within intimate relationships, previous analyses of interracial intimacy have offered very few conceptual tools with which to interpret how race works inside these relationships. Researchers' tendency to overlook the possibility of racial conflict between partners stems largely from two sources: the assimilation paradigm, whose dominance during the early-to-mid-twentieth century powerfully shaped the way sociologists comprehend group differences, and the strength of love myths in American culture.[1] Assimilation theory suggests that marriage is the ultimate site for blending racial and ethnic groups—through both the reproduction of "mixed" children and the sheer closeness of social contact.[2] This notion that marriage can dissolve or erase group differences has had a powerful and durable effect on how Americans think about interracial unions. Contemporary love myths come to a similar conclusion by positioning love as an unpredictable and irrational force, but one that has the power to unite individuals across social divides.

In this chapter, I turn the lens from public spaces to the inner workings of relationships in order to look more closely at how interracial partners interpret and negotiate racial difference in everyday life. I introduce the concept of racial habitus developed by Eduardo Bonilla-Silva to explain how these differences emerge in routine interactions. I then identify emotional labor as the form of racework that individuals use to manage race and racism. I show how this type of racework permits interracial partners to negotiate differences in their racial habitus. I also discuss the minority of partners whose racework is best characterized as racial silence. I have two goals in this chapter: to make clear the ways in which racial difference infiltrates intimate relationships, and to show how interracial partners go about directly and indirectly managing this difference.

Habitus as a Racial Orientation

Social scientists have a strong tendency to conceptualize racial difference as static or determinate, perhaps because this results in significant analytical advantages. It makes it possible to establish discrete groups for empirical study and to observe racial differences in, for example, wealth, school quality, and health.[3] Yet acknowledging that racial differences also include subjective gulfs in attitudes and orientations provides a fuller, more nuanced way to think about stratification. I treat racial difference itself as a social product, created through everyday interaction and shaped by the constraints of social structure.

Pierre Bourdieu's concept of habitus provides a useful framework for understanding how social differences emerge in intimate relationships. Habitus refers to the orientations and predispositions that individuals develop as a result of their social position. This "schemata of perceptions, thought, and action" is acquired through experience.[4] A habitus, or "socially constituted nature," affects how people perceive and classify their worlds.[5] Although individual experiences of social life are distinctive, those who share the same social position possess similar dispositions that make them recognizable—to researchers and to each other—as a coherent group. Habitus does not determine individual action; rather, it provides socially situated dispositions that people use routinely to understand reality and act in the world. Consider street fighting, for example. Young women and men who grow up in poor or working-class neighborhoods where crime rates are high and violence is common learn that fighting is a fact of life. Whether to defend one's reputation or to assert dominance over others, physical aggression is acceptable and normative. In this context, people learn to carefully read subtle body movements and assess verbal barbs to anticipate whether an ordinary altercation will cross the line into physical violence. This sort of socially situated disposition—the learned readiness to fight and the cultivated awareness for sensing situations that will become violent—is an example of habitus. This protective stance is often internalized early, as the result of prior direct or indirect experiences with physical violence. Importantly, experiences that form dispositions are fundamentally shaped by people's social position. If the young people in this scenario had grown up in more stable and less impoverished communities, it is likely they would not have had the experiences that establish the disposition to fight. Developing this habitus does not mean that each person in the neighborhood will react to potential altercations in exactly the same way, or that every verbal slight will result in a physical fight. But possessing this kind of habitus does mean that people who grow up in this environment will share a common set of perceptions and attitudes that orient their actions toward others.

Eduardo Bonilla-Silva broadens Bourdieu's concept of habitus by exploring its racialized character.[6] Bourdieu was concerned with the way in which individuals' social class "orients action." Bonilla-Silva, focusing on Whites who grow up in racially segregated environs and thus have little social contact with other racial groups, suggests that race too provides a set of orienting processes. He defines White habitus as "a racialized uninterrupted socialization process that conditions and creates Whites' racial tastes, perceptions, feelings, and emotions and their views on racial matters."[7] When Whites grow up exclusively around other Whites, the homogeneity of their surroundings normalizes everyone else's Whiteness, making it seem natural and therefore invisible. This racial sameness also promotes in-group solidarity and negative views about non-Whites. Bonilla-Silva argues that White habitus spatially and psychologically limits Whites' chances of developing meaningful relationships with African Americans and other minorities.

Although many White narratives in this study reflect the perceptions, appreciations, and actions of a segregated upbringing, the narratives of African American partners reflect a markedly different orientation toward racial stratification—a Black racial habitus. Like White partners, Black partners do not share a uniform or homogeneous racial perspective. Nevertheless, they possess a common racial orientation, a strategic anticipation developed out of necessity. W. E. B. Du Bois terms this orientation "double-consciousness." Writing at the turn of the twentieth century, Du Bois explored sight as a metaphor of racial understanding.[8] African Americans see Whites, he contended, as if through a veil from which they can observe, but behind which they themselves remain shadowed and unseen. Whites view Blacks through the clouded lens of prejudice and thus do not see them clearly. Extending this metaphor, Du Bois argues that as a condition of survival, Blacks in the United States have developed a double-consciousness. Blacks are able to see themselves not only as agential subjects, acting on the world, but also to see themselves through the racial gaze of Whites, as racialized objects. For a contemporary example of double-consciousness, we may consider the experience of a hypothetical African American youth who walks into a bookstore, intent on finding the science-fiction section amid seemingly endless aisles of shelves. She may be aware that her Blackness will make her highly visible to White sales associates, who may assume she is a potential shoplifter or troublemaker.

As she shops, her mind contains two simultaneous visions of herself. She is a subject acting upon the world—a shopper, perhaps an avid reader of Octavia Butler—but at the same time, she is a racialized object—a Black teenager who may be seen by others as up to no good. This dual awareness is what Du Bois means by double-consciousness. It is both a burden and a gift. It creates a painful psychological duality, but it also represents a form of power—the power that comes from being able to see yourself as you appear to others.

Understanding the disjuncture between a Black and a White racial habitus provides insight into the daily racial conflicts experienced by partners in my study. Race-based differences in viewpoints often emerged in very ordinary settings. Scott Patterson's account of an experience with Tamara Stills, his White fiancée, provides an example. Scott (who was introduced in chapter 3) grew up in a predominantly Black neighborhood in Davis, a small town just outside Philadelphia.[9] He and I meet on a spring afternoon in the row house that was his childhood home. Scott was raised by his mother, who was an actress, and by his grandmother, who was the principal of the public high school in Davis. He describes growing up feeling like he was a member of "Davis royalty" because his grandmother was so highly respected in the town. Scott's own experiences, including attending private schools, were more privileged than those of many in his working-class Black community, and he has likely experienced more upward mobility. Scott has traveled extensively. He works as a paralegal, but his real love is music. He is a guitar player who used to play gigs in New York City and Philadelphia.

When asked about his experiences with Tamara, Scott explains that race is not "too much" of an issue. Yet differences in their racial perspectives sometimes emerge in ordinary circumstances. A few nights before our interview, a short piece on television inspired a conversation between Scott and Tamara about Bessie Smith, a famous jazz singer who died in 1937 after a car accident. Many believe that she died as a result of being refused admittance to a nearby "Whites-only" hospital. Scott realized, as they talked, that Tamara had never heard this story. What he emphasizes as he recounts their conversation is Tamara's reaction to the tragedy:

[That] has happened to so many historical Black figures as well as nonhistorical Black figures and I think that information, though she knows that consciously because she lives in this world and knows that in a previous time [Black] people were treated openly in a certain kind of way, she said really earnestly, "God, that's really horrible." And when I hear that I think, and I said, "Yea', the world can be a horrible place," sort of cynically to her. ... I don't want it to come off like I'm not giving her enough credit because that's absolutely wrong, but I think just in general Tamara's very ... she'd have a really earnest reaction of, "Oh my God," which actually I really love about her. But sometimes I'm like, "What do you mean, 'Oh my God?'" Like, like I'm almost cynical enough that I'm past the "Oh my God" stage, where she's not. She's not cynical at all. Sometimes I feel like I've reacted to that earnestness, with my sort of, a little too much cynicism. And that sort of happened the other night, of like, "Yeah, the world's a hard place," you know?

Scott describes their different racial lenses—his ingrained awareness and Tamara's surprise—as not simply a reflection of individual temperaments but as a product of how stratification has shaped their orientations. He and Tamara both inhabit "this world," but their different racial habitus provides one, and not the other, with the ability to anticipate racism. These conflicting perspectives derive from the cumulative nature of the racial experiences that shape habitus. Despite having grown up with many social class privileges, Scott's experience of anti-Black racism from a particular intersection of race and gender (i.e., Black masculinity) has shaped his worldview. Similarly, Tamara's experiences as a White woman have influenced her racial lens. The daughter of a minister, she grew up in a small town in Maryland that she describes as "mostly White." In high school, she was friends with many international exchange students and developed a keen interest in other cultures. She says that she is "in love with difference in people."

Scott interprets Tamara's "earnest" reaction as a manifestation of her Whiteness, of the privilege of not being continually confronted with the pervasiveness of anti-Black racism. He suggests that Tamara's ignorance reflects a type of innocence long lost to him. "She's legitimately shocked, which she should be. It's almost like I've lost that, for a million reasons, starting with my grandmother telling me over and over again about Emmett Till."[10] Scott believes that because Tamara grew up White in an almost exclusively White town, she lacked opportunities to be exposed to another vantage point that might have refocused her privileged racial lens:

Unless it's a White person that has been very much around Black people—I mean like around Black people as much as a Black person would be around Black people—there is still a learning curve there. ... You tell a White person that [kind of story] and they're like, "What?!" Which is the reaction they should have, unless they've grown up around Black people all their lives and they're just used to how badly Black people have been treated [so] they're just not surprised. ... [But] if you're Black or just cynical, and you see somebody having an earnest reaction like that you're like, "Pff." ... So I think there's a little bit of that dynamic [with us] sometimes.

Perhaps because Scott interprets the sincerity of Tamara's shock as an inevitable product of her embodied Whiteness and her segregated White environment, he does not blame her for her inexperience. Nor does he suggest that she participates willingly in this "not-knowing."

The impact of racial habitus on everyday intimacy is also visible for Lucas Tatum and Thad Thompson (introduced in chapter 3). The men live in New York City in a segregated Black neighborhood. Each mentions to me that the nearly twenty-year difference in their ages adds to the challenges posed by their racial difference. Lucas says that the relationship has created some tension between him and his friends. Some have accused Lucas of being "kept" by Thad; others dismiss Thad as "some older White guy" who is not fun to be around. But Lucas and Thad have much in common. They share an interest in music—Thad is a composer and Lucas is a musician—and have a similar dry sense of humor characterized by a mutual loathing for what they each identify as "political correctness." When it comes to race, though, they have very different ways of seeing the world. Lucas, like Scott, often cloaks his skepticism with humor. He characterizes the difference of racial perspectives in his relationship this way:

I actually have more of a sense of humor about it. ... When things are bad racially in the world or in the neighborhood or in the city, Thad can have a tendency to get more angry and more down about it than I can. ... I can see the ebb and flow of things. I think that he, I don't know if it's part of his personality that takes things on a little bit more earnestly ... [but] he can get angrier and get sadder about, you know, things that are happening in the world.

Lucas, remarking that this difference in viewpoints happens "so often," offers as an example an account of Thad's reaction to a recent police shooting. At one o'clock in the morning, a nineteen-year-old Black man was with some friends, crossing from the roof of one building in a Brooklyn project to the roof of an adjoining building. Just as this young man approached the doorway to the stairwell leading into the apartment building, a White police officer on patrol was coming out of the stairwell and pushed the door open. Startled, the officer drew his gun and shot the unarmed Black youth, killing him. In a city plagued by police violence against African Americans, the case soon took on racial overtones.[11] Thad reacted with outrage; Lucas tried "to make a joke out of a horrible situation."[12]

Like Scott, Lucas grew up with many class privileges, including private schools, but he did not escape the blows of everyday racism. He learned to practice a constant vigilance in order to anticipate and deflect racism. Putting this learned caution in context, Lucas explains:

> I can get very angry about a cop, a White cop who's patrolling the neighborhood, [and shoots someone] who wasn't doing anything wrong. I think part of this is ... that it happens so often and so much that, you know, my skin has become a little bit more thicker. Like Thad can get outraged about that, but I can say, you know, "Yup, shouldn't have been on the roof." You know, but not completely—and not mean it all, but you know just have that be the way I deal with that problem. It's easier for me to make a joke out of a horrible situation, racially at least.

As with the differences between Scott's and Tamara's reactions, Thad's tendency to "get outraged" and Lucas's "thicker" skin could reflect differences in these partners' individual temperaments rather than responses that are shaped by their membership in particular racial groups.[13] But the repetition of these types of stories in Black partners' narratives suggests that these emotional reactions reflect the pervasive nature of racial habitus. Thad's upbringing in a predominately White environment in small-town Michigan did little to encourage him to notice, let alone understand, the ubiquitous nature of anti-Black racism. Even now, thirty years later, his life experiences, which include having had other Black partners, have not convinced Thad of the ubiquity of racism. His earnest anger therefore reflects an element of surprise, an initial disbelief that this type of "accident" could cost a young Black man his life. Reacting to racial incidents with surprise is part of a broader worldview that sees racism as irrational, as an aberration in the usual workings of everyday life, instead of as usual or commonplace, just part of how society works.

As Black men, Lucas and Scott have developed perceptions, interpretations, and emotions regarding racial matters that differ markedly from those of their White partners. Sometimes they react to the privilege embodied in their partners' perspectives with impatience or annoyance. Ultimately, though, each accepts these differences in orientation because they are so deeply rooted. A meaningful divergence in Scott's and Lucas's reactions to

White habitus is that Lucas is not so quick to attribute Thad's not-knowing to racial innocence. He makes a point of distinguishing between thinking about race "intellectually" and in the "real world." "When the tire hits the road ... [Thad] does need to be brought up to speed sort of sometimes." When asked why that is, Lucas says, "It's easier and more pleasant to, you know, not think that that's what's going on." This is an important distinction. Whereas Scott suggests that Tamara *cannot* see racism, Lucas suggests that Thad *does not want* to see it. He does not push himself to develop perceptions that challenge his White racial habitus. By suggesting that it is convenient to possess this type of racial ignorance, Lucas identifies in Thad a complicit acceptance of the privileges and blinders of Whiteness.

The perspectives expressed by Scott and Lucas, and by Nadine at the start of the chapter, are similar, and they are consistent with those of other Black men and women in this study who experience double-consciousness as fundamentally at odds with White habitus. Whites have not needed to develop a fragmented consciousness. Indeed, one of the privileges of Whiteness is not having to consider oneself a racial object or wonder how one appears to people of color. This disjuncture is at the root of many everyday conflicts in interracial relationships. The middle-class African Americans in this study grew up understanding and anticipating how they might be seen by Whites. Their middle-class White partners (with some exceptions) grew up with no analogous insights into how their Whiteness might be perceived by African Americans. Whites are often unable or unwilling to develop the critical consciousness that would make them more reflective about the pervasive nature of anti-Black prejudice and the everyday manifestations of White privilege. Racial habitus provides a valuable conceptual framework for understanding these interactions, because it points to the influence of social location and the subjective orientation that emerges from that position.

Racial stratification affects all African Americans, but it does not create homogeneous racial subjects. As individuals, Blacks experience racism differently, depending on their gender, social class, and sexuality. Not surprisingly then, they have a wide range of perspectives on how race influences their daily lives and how best to address anti-Black racism. Similarly, although Whiteness confers racial privilege, it does not create a uniform racial perspective among Whites. Many, but not all, Whites consider Whiteness to be invisible, a nonrace. In short, social location does not dictate individual racial perspectives, and not all interracial partners experience deeply situated conflicts of habitus. Some partners share very similar racial orientations.

This is the case with Lindsey Michaels and Dionna Yates, a lesbian couple introduced in chapter 3. Lindsey is the director of youth outreach at a local community center. Dionna works as a drug counselor in a social service agency. They have encountered resistance to their relationship from Dionna's family members, who live in the Deep South and dislike the fact that Dionna is a lesbian and in a relationship with a White woman. In long car rides back to their home in Philadelphia after holiday visits, Lindsey and Dionna counsel each other about how to deal with these family dynamics. "We're usually on a very, very similar page," Lindsey tells me. She continues:

> I really feel like I can say anything, anything to her. I mean I can express opinions to Dionna that I would feel nervous about saying to other people. ... I feel totally, totally comfortable and safe talking about racial issues with her. It's never felt scary or awkward for me. I think that from really early on it's always felt okay.

Even apart from periodic tensions with in-laws, Lindsey explains that she and Dionna talk about race daily. The topic surfaces readily in conversations about current events or in debriefings about work. Seemingly casual discussions about how race plays out in pop culture—like the media analysis of the O. J. Simpson trial or of Black celebrities more generally—invoke complex and serious racial issues.

> We talk about White privilege ... and we talk about racism from White people and some of the disapproval of queer communities of color for dating White people. We always talk, I mean these are hard things to talk about. I can't think of stuff we don't talk about.

Dionna tells me that Lindsey's ideas on race are "amazing," and she and Lindsey sometimes work together to decode unsettling public interactions:

> I mean sometimes it's like something is weird and then we'll talk it out and like figure out maybe she saw something [that] I didn't see. Maybe I saw something [that] she didn't see and we come to a conclusion. ... I guess she can probably better perceive when White people have problems with race and what that looks like in expressions and gestures and I can perceive what that'd look like in a mostly African American [setting].

Dionna and Lindsey's interactions are instructive because they show that racial difference is variable. Unlike Scott and Tamara or Lucas and Thad,

Dionna and Lindsey share a critical stance on race. Both believe that racial stereotypes pervade mainstream media and culture, and that racial discrimination is a common practice in everyday life. The similarity in their perspectives derives in part from the fact that Lindsey has cultivated a critical racial lens. She not only has learned to understand the pervasive nature of anti-Black racism, she has also come to understand that her Whiteness confers symbolic and material advantages.

Racework as Emotional Labor

I use the concept of emotional labor to describe the numerous ways in which interracial partners negotiate differences in racial habitus. They adjust behaviors, conceal emotions, translate racial perspectives, decide whether and how to discuss racial matters, critically examine their own racial status, and attempt to understand their partner's racial disposition. This form of racework is somewhat routinized by its repetitive nature. Nevertheless, the practices involved in emotional labor represent creative adaptations to the complexity and uniqueness of social interactions. Importantly, they also exact an emotional cost.[14]

In talking about their relationship, gay partners Vance Dalton and Evan Cody (introduced in chapter 3) describe their individual and joint emotion work around racial difference. "I think he's uber-sensitive to it," Vance reasons as he explains how his partner experiences race in public spaces. He and Evan have been dating for a year and a half. Both men work in downtown Philadelphia, Vance as a city planner and Evan as a school psychologist. Vance tells me that they live in a city neighborhood with "a large population of Caucasian people." But as a White gay man in his twenties, this demographic is not something he generally thinks about. "I don't know how to say it. I don't mean to be like I don't even pay attention, but I don't even notice it." For Vance, and many other Whites in this study, the Whiteness of majority-White spaces is comfortable; it feels normal. Vance grew up in what he describes as "an old 1940s suburb" with sidewalks, tree-lined streets, and "neighbors that you talk to." His high school was "very stereotypical white-bread, upper-middle class," and though he admits his childhood environment was very homogeneous, he recalls it fondly. "I think it was the best place for me to grow up."

The tendency to see White homogeneity as natural—and therefore race-neutral—is a consequence of Whites' own spatial segregation. It is also one of the fundamental characteristics of White racial habitus.[15] Because Vance does not perceive the dominant Whiteness of his Philadelphia neighbor-hood as a racial phenomenon, it is difficult for him to understand why Evan exhibits a "very high level of sensitivity" in heavily White spaces. Evan may interpret being the target of a prolonged look in a local retail store as a sign of suspicion or hostility; Vance believes Evan attracts notice because he is handsome and has a very "polished look." Evan is always aware of his membership in a particular social category—Black males. Vance sees Evan only in individual terms. When Evan expresses concern that he is being racially profiled, Vance insists he is being "uber-sensitive."

Evan is twenty-nine years old. Like Vance, he grew up in a majority-White, upper-middle-class environment. His father was a professional baseball player. Evan estimates that he was one of about sixteen African Americans in a high school of two thousand in his affluent Southern suburb.[16] High school involved him in a tricky set of social negotiations, bouncing between his White friends and his Black friends, and dating a few young women even as he grew increasingly aware of also being attracted to men. This complex matrix of social positions affected the way Evan came to think about his own racial identity. His family's class location buffered some of Whites' negative response to his Black masculinity, but it did not prevent its occurrence. As an adult, he continues to contend with everyday experiences of anti-Black racism. Thus, although Evan and Vance both grew up in similarly segregated, White upper-middle-class environments, their different social positions resulted in different racial lenses.

Philadelphia feels to Evan much more tolerant than the suburb where he grew up. Still he is constantly aware of people's reactions to Black mas-culinity. For instance, as a jogger who runs along city streets, he notes the reactions of Whites, and some Blacks, with whom he crosses paths: "[It's an] 'Oh my god, a Black man's running towards me' kind of thing." Grow-ing up Black, male, and American, Evan has learned to anticipate these judgments and to consider his response. Years of experience do not make dealing with racism and homophobia much easier.[17] Anger, fear, frustra-tion, shame, confusion, and sadness are all feelings that are part of the experience of oppression. Managing these emotions can be complicated and exhausting for Evan. Taking on this work in the context of his relation-ship with Vance only adds complexity:

I feel as though he doesn't understand what it's like to be [Black]. . . . So there are times when I feel as though I can't make the comment about—I may say something and it's totally obvious to me [that what] happened was because I was Black. . . . He thinks, "No, that can't be the reason." Because in his mind, people don't think like that. And I feel as if every once in a while I have to remind him [that] people *do* think like that and race is a very divisive issue, especially in this country. And, you know, you need to take these things into consideration if you're going to be in a relationship with a Black person.

The ways in which Evan calls Vance's attention to racial incidents or the decisions he sometimes makes to censor his social observations or experiences with anti-Black racism are examples of emotional labor. Wanting to discuss his experiences and find validation, Evan weighs the benefits of possible affirmation with the frustration of having the reality of his experience denied. The decision to initiate talk and the talk itself require emotional effort and a willingness to be vulnerable. Sometimes he does initiate conversations with Vance about "understanding race and understanding what it's like to be the other person." In these instances, Evan occasionally feels that he has an "unfair advantage" over Vance. This is because, having grown up in a socially isolated and racially segregated White community, Evan has experienced some aspects of White habitus.[18] He "knows what it's like to be White." Evan possesses a dual perspective; Vance knows *only* what it is like to be White.

Talking about racism can be difficult for Vance as well. In opening himself up to Evan's perspective, Vance must consider his own racial prejudices, an act that requires that he too engage in emotional labor. For example, Vance explains that when he admitted to Evan that he was afraid of being attacked if he walked through Black neighborhoods in North Philadelphia to reach a job site, "I felt like I was totally in the wrong, I felt like I shouldn't be saying it to him. ... He's Black, and I'm talking to him about Black people. And I felt like I would be offending him." When emotional labor results in a dialogue, both partners have something to lose, as well as to gain.

For another gay couple in the study, Shawn Tarwick and Daniel Embry, it is parenthood that occasions this form of racework. Shawn is a forty-nine-year-old White man with curly brown hair and grey-blue eyes. As we sit chatting at his cluttered kitchen table, he sometimes talks loudly to be heard over the fussy whines of his sixteen-month-old son, Chester, to whom he is desperately trying to feed dinner. Shawn and Daniel are the only gay couple in the study who are raising a family together. Shawn tells me that Chester, whom they adopted, has one biological parent who is White and Jewish, like himself, and one who is African American, like Daniel. Their other adopted son, a nine-month-old, has biological parents who are both African American. Although Daniel and Shawn have been together for eighteen years, their more recent experiences parenting these children have made it evident that the two men read race and racism differently.

Most of Shawn's early social interactions were with other Whites. He grew up outside of Philadelphia in a neighborhood that formed the borderline between a Black community and a White community. Shawn lived in very close physical proximity to African American families but had few friendships with the Black children in his area. "Most of my friends were kids like me—upper-lower-class Jewish kids." The public high school he attended had a very small percentage of African American students. Daniel, who is forty-nine, grew up in the Bronx and attended a private, majority-White high school (he estimates that about 10 percent of the students were Black). He has dated White men in the past. His chief concern, however, was not their race but whether these men were completely out of the closet.

For Shawn, being a journalist for an African American newspaper has led to the development of meaningful social ties with Blacks. Daniel explains that he immediately noticed a quality in Shawn that set him apart. Other Whites Daniel has known seem to try too hard to let him know that they "get the Black experience in America," or they pepper him with queries about how it feels to be Black:

> Part of it may or may not have to do with again his being at an African American newspaper—a newspaper where so many of his coworkers are African American—but there wasn't, there weren't a lot of questions ... from him about being Black, or identity, or culture. ... There wasn't like a "Oh, oh well, what's it like?" You know? There wasn't any of that. ... It's never, nothing's been mysterious to him.

Daniel credits the fact that as an adult, Shawn had had other meaningful interracial relationships—even though they were not necessarily romantic—as facilitating a certain ease between them that he appreciates. He describes their intimacy as generally "really easy."

Yet even with this zone of comfort between them, Shawn and Daniel still read race differently and have disparate definitions of racism itself. Though neither of their sons is old enough for kindergarten, the men have begun to discuss where to send the children to school and what kind of real-world experiences their children might have. Shawn describes the divergence in perspectives that these extended conversations have revealed:

> I accuse him of being an alarmist about the kids and their welfare as Black citizens. ... We both share the same basic political views; the only, the only

big difference, and it's not really, it's more of a philosophical conversation than a real fight, is that he tends to subscribe to a kind of conspiracy theory that White America has banded together to exclude Black America. And I don't see it as being, I see the racism, but I don't see it as being organized in the same way. Because I'm White and nobody ever came to me and said, "Hey, let's get together and do this thing to the Black people." So that's a difference of philosophy in terms of things like redlining and mortgage rates. He sees it as institutionalized and I see it just as kind of widespread.

Shawn delineates his own racial philosophy by suggesting that Daniel's racial logic is "alarmist" and extreme. He accepts the existence of racism but explicitly questions whether it is systemic. Shawn sees racism as an aberrant but common affliction of an otherwise sensible, or at least neutral, system. Daniel sees it as "institutional," as an organizing principle of our social world. Their debate is not a matter of semantics. The two perspectives are similar in some ways, but they generate quite different strategies for dealing with race in everyday life.

Daniel's awareness of pervasive anti-Black racism involves anticipating racial incidents in order to deflect or ameliorate their effects. Shawn, though also deeply concerned, is less likely to proactively combat the racism his sons might experience at school because he thinks of racism as a failure of the educational system, instead of as an inherent part of its design. Daniel explains that the conversation usually leads to the same impasse:

A big part of it is, I mean as far as I'm concerned Shawn has to see something before he'll really. … If he doesn't believe it in his heart, he's got to see it. He won't take my word for it. … He thinks that I am like, looking for trouble. I said, "I'm not looking for it, but I want to be aware, I want to not be, I don't want to be asleep when that stuff happens. I don't want it to have been going on for half a semester before I know that something's going on." And that's really what I just say to him. It's about, you know, being aware of it … so that if something doesn't feel quite right, then we'll look a little further, you know what I mean? As opposed to his going, "Oh, it'll work itself out."

Daniel attributes the difference in their strategies to Shawn's having grown up with White racial privilege. "Of course not being raised Black, he doesn't expect that kind of behavior, and it's hard [for him] to believe that in fact that can happen. Shawn still doesn't believe, just doesn't believe that … a teacher would look at an eight-year-old and actually treat one eight-year-old differently from another eight-year-old simply because ... of the color of their skin." Throughout the interview, Daniel gives Shawn much credit for being sensitive and astute in racial matters. In this moment, however, he suggests that there are inevitable limitations to a White subjectivity—that White privilege ultimately constricts his partner's racial vision. Shawn has never developed the double-consciousness that defines Daniel's racial habitus. Yet because both men are deeply invested in protecting their sons from racism, neither feels he can afford to yield ground in this debate. The clash of philosophies is ongoing.

For Shawn and Daniel, as with many of the gay and lesbian partners in this study, sexuality plays a limited role in shaping how partners use emotional labor to deal with racial differences. But there are exceptions. In some instances, the shared marginalization that gay and lesbian couples face facilitates a willingness to explore racial issues. For example, Evan, whose partner sometimes finds him "uber-sensitive," gets frustrated with the differences in their racial orientations. Yet Evan also acknowledges that Vance's sexual identity enables him to use his own experiences with homophobia to relate to Evan's encounters with racism:

> I feel as although in a lot of ways he can relate because being gay is being a minority. And I guess you can say that about any gay person involved in an interracial relationship, but I feel like he takes it a step further, and he knows. I can say something to him about what I feel and he won't negate what I feel. He'll try to understand it a little bit better.

A gay identity does not automatically equip Vance with a heightened awareness of other social inequalities. But these conversations do provide him with the opportunity to make connections between different forms of subordination. Through emotional labor, he utilizes his familiarity with homophobia to try to understand the racism that he is unable to perceive with his own eyes.

The Value of Emotional Labor

For partners in my study, sharing racial perspectives and experiences through talk is a way to seek validation. Acknowledging differences in racial perspectives does not make them disappear, nor does it guarantee that they will not re-emerge. Sometimes the purpose of talking about race is not so much to resolve conflict as to temporarily neutralize it. Benjamin Walters and his White partner, Helen Rutkowski (introduced in chapter 2), make this function of emotion work clear as they independently describe a difficult episode in their life as a couple. Ben grew up in the South; this is his first interracial relationship. Helen grew up in a Pennsylvania suburb, but she has been living in Philadelphia for the past fifteen years. Ben and Helen met when they rented apartments in the same four-story building; they have been together for three-and-a-half years. They are not married. Ben tells me that what people might think of him and Helen as they negotiate their predominantly Black neighborhood, located a dozen blocks from downtown Philadelphia, is a "dead issue." Still, these public moments do sometimes insinuate themselves into his relationship with Helen, as a story he relates shows.

Ben's voice has a low timbre that bears more than a few traces of his South Carolina roots. He speaks slowly and carefully, periodically taking long pauses to assemble his thoughts, as he recounts a Saturday afternoon walk that he and Helen took along train tracks that parallel the banks of Philadelphia's Schuylkill River. He explains that as a hobby, he creates simple woodwind instruments from bamboo. That Saturday, he and Helen were looking for wild bamboo growing along the riverbanks. Ben carried a small handsaw to cut the reeds. As they walked along a concrete path, they neared a construction area and noticed a White security officer who appeared to be monitoring the work site. While Ben and Helen were waiting for a freight train to pass so they could cross the tracks and continue along the river, the security guard drove by in a Jeep, slowing down before passing the couple. The guard did not speak to either of them, but according to Ben, he made eye contact with Helen, beckoning for a signal that nothing was wrong. "[The guard] looked at Helen and he said with his eyes, 'Are you alright?'" After she greeted him casually, the security officer drove on. Once the Jeep was gone, Ben urgently wanted to discuss this interaction with Helen.

> I wanted, only wanted from Helen, did she see that? She couldn't respond. She was really put off by [the security guard] inquiring into her. But that's the norm for America. ... She couldn't talk about it. That was a problem for me. And where I didn't label this guy anything negative, I only wanted confirmation on the action.

In Ben's view, the security officer interpreted Ben's Black masculinity as a threat to Helen, a White woman whom the officer may have considered vulnerable.

Helen would not discuss the interaction at the time it happened or in the days that followed, leaving Ben with mounting anxiety and frustration. He questioned whether the relationship could last. "It was hard. . . . While she was making up her mind, I was busting loose inside. We don't have to fix things, but I'll be damned, we've got to see 'em. . . . I was let down so much. She don't know this, [but] I was torn to pieces." Ben does not hold Helen responsible for the security officer reading him as dangerous and implicitly offering her protection. What he needs and expects is for her to acknowledge the significance of that glance. Her silence makes him wonder whether he is with "another female who can't see." After two weeks, Helen begins to talk about the encounter, and Ben's anxiety dissipates. He empathizes with her. "I think what it is, she had never been placed in that situation before, and also there was a reality that she had never encountered. This guy came into our space. He wasn't asked to, there was no evidence of anything, but he came in anyway."

When Helen and I talk, she brings up this same event independently. Her description reveals that she too was struggling with how to talk about the difficulty of the interaction. She worried over the extent to which she might have acquiesced in the officer's attempt to protect her from Ben. Recounting the day, she says,

> A cop came by and he checked out me and he checked out Ben. The way he checked us out was like he was waiting for me to say I was okay. . . . I just said, "Hi, how you doin'?" Or something like that. . . . Ben just zoomed into that and he totally knew what was going on. Saw what was going on. He got angry over what was going on. It was just a big thing. . . . Oh, God, yeah. We end up having this argument because I felt like I didn't want to talk about it. "Okay, we both know that happened. But I don't feel like talking about that now, because here we are walking along the river, it's all nice, let's just put it aside." But I didn't say that, I just acted like it didn't happen. Like I just kind of ignored it. He got angry at me because I ignored it. Like I was saying that it didn't happen or he wasn't seeing it correctly.

Clearly, Helen sensed that heightened moment when Ben's Black masculinity may have marked him as suspect and her as vulnerable. It is unclear whether her unwillingness to directly engage this situation reflects a reluctance to talk about racial issues specifically, or whether she prefers to dodge conflict in general. In either case, as Ben's intimate partner, Helen's refusal to acknowledge how she and he were each racialized in this moment seriously strained their relationship.

In the days following their encounter with the security officer, Ben and Helen each engaged in emotional labor—first separately and then together. Ben had wanted Helen to immediately acknowledge the racial assumptions embedded in the interaction. He did not need her to "fix" it, only to "see" it, to validate his perception of what had occurred. For Ben, Helen's two-week-long failure to meet his expectations invoked issues of faith, trust, and the possibility of betrayal. He wondered about his intimate partner's ability to understand race and racism and her commitment (or lack of) to engage him in a dialogue about these issues. He struggled to maintain intimacy across the space of structural inequality.

When I ask Ben whether this type of difference in perspective still arises, he says, "Sure it happens. Sure it happens." But he tells me that he and Helen are committed to working through these things. After a long pause, he explains their approach like this: "Helen is not callous [showing me his hands]. These are calluses and they have no feeling. Helen is not callous. Ben is not callous towards Helen. So in an event … where there are differences, then over time we go at them. Sometimes willingly, sometimes unwillingly. We've got so many people to support our relationship." For Ben, racework includes the willingness and patience to share his perspective with Helen and to describe his experiences in a way she will understand. "Sometimes in my approach in getting Helen to see another side, or to look at it differently, I might be coming at it at an angle that she can't digest. I'll stop and I'll back up. And I do it in other ways … [chuckling]. I've been so successful at it, she's thought it was her idea. That's how successful I've been."

Helen's emotional labor to resolve the crisis in the relationship took a very different form. She was aware of Ben's frustration and anger, but she did not want to directly address their interaction with the security officer. She wanted to just "put it aside" and move on. Helen knows that racial prejudice exists and that Ben experiences its constant barbs. At times, however, she prefers not to dwell on it. "[Ben's anger] is all valid. But I choose sometimes not to stay there, where he tends to look a little harder. … It's not like I'm not aware of it. But Ben gives it more priority than I do, because it's him, not me." She understands that as a Black male, Ben is vulnerable to prejudice and discrimination. What she does not see is where her own location as a White woman positions her. She sees how racism hurts Ben, but not how it advantages her.

That ultimately Ben and Helen were able to discuss this situation may have saved their relationship. Their mutual willingness—despite their frustration and fear—to talk about the presence of everyday racism reflects a commitment to the emotional labor of racework.

Some partners perceive talking about race as a type of emotional labor that is inevitable in interracial relationships, and they consider a willingness to engage in this work as a prerequisite to any type of intimate relationship. Monique Gilliam (introduced, along with her White partner, Barbara DiBacco, in chapter 2) is quick to explain her stance on this matter. To avoid misunderstandings with a possible future partner, she tries to get a sense of their racial perspective:

> I do the work because I refuse to be in pain. ... I refuse to be in love with someone who can't see me or only sees parts of me or sees me as only this racial being. I've been there, done that, don't like it. So I just have my own little screen and I'm very serious. ... If I'm dating someone who is a different ethnicity you know, race and/or ethnicity, and we can't talk about race or ethnicity, we can't date. 'Cause my thing is, this is New York City, this is the United States, this is the world, these things are huge. ... People interact with me based on what they see and what they assume because of my skin. [To a prospective partner] I'm like, "No, we need to have a conversation. ... "

For Monique, the relational work involved with interraciality begins when two people are getting to know each other and continues as a routine emotional practice. Because race is a salient element of social life in the United States, it will always be a part of Monique's intimate relationships. She cannot fathom an intimacy that does not include discussions of race, because Blackness is such a focal point of her own identity and racism so much a facet of her everyday life. "If I'm having this experience, you need to know [about it] if you're going to be with me. ... My stuff impacts you and vice versa." Having a partner who can understand and affirm her perspective is crucial. Talking about race allows Monique to "feel validated. I'm not crazy—it's not just me."

Establishing an intimate relationship does not diminish the salience of racial difference for Monique or for Barbara. Instead, it represents a commitment to the emotional practices of dealing with racial stratification. Barbara moved to the United States from Italy eight years ago. She is still learning what race means in America. In the two years they have been together, Barbara has persistently tried to understand how race affects her partner. Monique explains, "We may spend more time talking about my stuff around race than us being 'an interracial couple.'" Yet the process or the context of this talk is framed by how each is positioned in relation to White supremacy in the United States.

For Monique and Barbara, racework includes the talk itself—conversation about looks, comments, and interactions that are or may be of a racial nature—but it also encompasses more. The emotional labor of racework involves deciding when and how to talk, how to explain the inner workings of a racial system to someone who is becoming newly familiar with its mechanics, and how to understand a set of racial meanings and interactions that are foreign to one's own experience. Finding the language to talk about race across racial boundaries in the United States is inherently complicated. For Monique and Barbara, the cultural differences that arise from being African American and Italian make these racial translations even more complex.

Emotional Labor through Humor

The conversations that interracial partners have about race are often serious—and sometimes angry. Yet for many partners, humor has a place too. Jokes and laughter about racial issues provide a seemingly safe cover from which to acknowledge racial or cultural differences, to express anxieties, to recognize everyday racism, or even to play with racial meanings by "performing" or "doing" race.

Neil Chambers (introduced, along with his family, in chapter 2) uses humor for exactly these reasons. Neil and his wife, Mary, have been together for nearly ten years. The racial difference between Neil and the Black middle-class community in which he and his family live makes him feel anxious. Assuming that others feel a similar discomfort with him, he refers to himself as "Whitey" when he describes his interactions with African Americans in neighborhood stores and parks. The issue of racially segregated spaces also influences Neil's feelings about the school the children attend. He would prefer a more integrated setting, but in their area, that environment is available only in a private school, which would be expensive. Mary, on the other hand, is comfortable with the predominantly Black neighborhood school.

Still, Neil insists that he enjoys the racial difference between himself and Mary and notes that humor allows him to highlight this element of their relationship:

Well for us, I mean, I think it's a source of pleasure. Because we kind of joke about it, you know, it can be, you know, we just have fun with it. ... I don't look at her physically, at the fact that physically she's a Black woman, as anything but positive, 'cause I like that. And just who she is as a person is cool, and whatever differences we have we can joke about it. ... And it gets into like stereotypes of Blacks and Whites, and you can just joke about it. We have these types of little jokes. Like I'll say to her, "You know, I went to the gym today and I was doing some squats and how does my ass look?" and she'll say, "What ass?" ... You know, just joking with it. Having a good time with it, really just makin' light of it, cause it is what it is. It's cool. Between us, it's kind of a fun thing.

For Neil and Mary, laughing about stereotypical differences between Black and White bodies—specifically her Black *female* body and his White *male* body—is part of an ongoing practice of joking not only about race, but about gender, sexuality, and attraction. This kind of banter is, for Neil, an exotification of racial difference. There is pleasure and play in these exchanges, but they also serve as a welcome counterpoint to more serious and difficult conversations about racial and cultural differences. The couple contends with strained relations between Neil and Mary's parents, who are both Jamaican, about whether to remain in their Black middle-class neighborhood and where to send the children to school. In this broader context, playful exchanges represent a type of emotional labor because they create a space for talking about race irreverently.

Onika Marsh and her White partner, Margaret Otterlei, also rely on humor in their relationship. This couple (introduced in chapter 2) has been together for two years. Like Neil and Mary, Onika and Margaret sometimes poke fun at the racial difference between them. But they also address racial issues directly, and sometimes the line between joking and earnest conversation grows blurry. At such times, using humor becomes risky. Onika explains:

We're relatively able to be humorous about it and like sort of crack jokes with each other in recognition of the difference and the challenges, which helps. I mean, it can be slightly dangerous, because on occasion it's like, "I'm not joking anymore. You are." You know? And so that can be a problem. But for the most part, we'll like crack, you know, make little jokes about stuff. ... I don't know if that was like an explicit decision on either of our parts, but ... I think that I had said ... we can't operate [as] if [race] is a nonissue. But it's like a way to kind of keep it an issue and keep our presence and reality of it without it being like, "Okay, this is something that we need to fight about or this is something that needs to be really serious all the time, or needs to be straining all the time."

As this quote shows, although Onika and Margaret value humor as a tool for managing racial difference, their overall approach is much different from Neil and Mary's. Onika and Margaret perceive their relationship as embedded within, not separate from, broader systems of stratification. They directly engage the racial dynamics between them—including how Margaret's Whiteness privileges her. Still, both of these couples, as well as others in the study, strategically use humor to try to create a safer way to talk about race.

Avoidance as Emotional Labor

Where there are marked differences in racial habitus, such as exist in the relationships I described in the previous section, the divergence in racial perspectives creates the necessity and the context for racework. In these relationships, racial difference is best managed through reconceptualizing racial meanings, which involves emotional labor in the form of intensive communication. In other relationships, racial difference is best managed by not addressing it. These partners deliberately engage in a form of emotional labor that I term *strategic avoidance*.

During the twenty-six years that Burton Connell and Kristie Kelley have been married, each has depended on strategic avoidance to manage the racial differences in their relationship. Burton, who is White, grew up in the Northeast, less than a hundred miles from the affluent New York City suburb where he and his family now live. He has not had previous interracial relationships. When I ask him about his experiences with interraciality, he answers my questions in a soft-spoken, deliberate way, explaining that an interracial relationship is a challenge that requires some "added understanding." Elaborating, he tells me that he and Kristie each interpret racial matters in a way "that makes us different, and [that] I cannot understand completely. It's just the way it is." He has, over time, come to simply accept this disconnect:

> I think we talk about it some and resolve some things but probably more of the things we just lump in the category of this is something we don't share. Kristie needs her time to do her quilting; Kristie may need some time to, um, it's been a while, I think there have been some [Black professional organizations] she was involved in. It's kind of just like, "Well, we're different. Give her time for that. I'm not going to understand it. Just let it [be], you know." ... There's all these other things we share, so let's

just, you know, probably more just kind of agreeing to disagree or just not going there. And there are some times where we have these kind of heart-to-heart talks about what it's like for her as a Black person, what's it like for me being with her relatives, but it tends to be more of not getting into it too deeply. ... I don't know whether she doesn't go into it, or I don't ask, in letting some of this lie.

Burton's words suggest that he thinks of Kristie's racial perspective in terms of activities and interactions that are unknowable to him. Burton is generally more comfortable avoiding race than discussing it with Kristie. He describes his circle of friends as "entirely White" and notes that there is "not much overlap" between his friends and Kristie's. Importantly, he describes her Blackness but not his Whiteness as an element of racial distance between them. He does not consider whether his Whiteness and her willingness or ability to understand *its* inner workings are also glossed over when racial dynamics are not discussed; nor does he consider whether gender shapes the racial difference between them.

Kristie and I talk while seated in the family's bright, sun-filled living room. The walls are decorated with Kristie's quilts; they showcase her talent. I begin by asking Kristie how she thinks of herself, what characteristics best describe her. Her response emphasizes her race and gender: "I would say that I'm a Black woman. I think that's how I see myself first. Although I am a spouse and a mother, I don't think of myself like that. ... I am those things but they don't define who I am. ... I see myself as a Black woman. I see myself as a quilter." Kristie comes to strategic avoidance from a different path than Burton. She is not averse to talking about racial issues, but says that there are certain "cultural things" that she does not bring up with Burton because she knows he will not understand them. She tells me that early in their relationship she and Burton separated for about a year. During that time, she dated a Black man with whom she had discussions that she and Burton would never have. She also points out that gender would remain an issue if she were with a Black man. "I would be talking one thing and that other [Black] person would be talking something else."

When I ask Kristie what kinds of things she would be more likely to talk about with a Black male partner, she says,

Issues related to race and work [real estate law], or when those things come up at work, [with] other Black employees and we might get into a discussion about that. It's not something I'd talk about with Burton. ... Because I think, um, because I think for me the purpose of the conversation is to get the perspective of someone who might be in a similar situation and since that's not going to be the case. Although you could say to somebody—if I run the whole scenario out—you could say ... like therapy, "Just because someone's not the same race as you doesn't mean that they can't follow the line." But I think I would be looking for a more personal, um, experience with that, or someone to call upon personal experience. ... I mean I could get your opinion, but I'm not necessarily looking for your opinion. I'm looking for your personal resonance with this, so I wouldn't have that conversation [with him].

Kristie's racial habitus is quite different from Burton's. She has an acute sense of herself as a Black woman, and she is alert to the social consequences of this identity. In debriefing about race, she would be looking for empathy, not sympathy or "opinions." Burton, by virtue of his social position, cannot provide that. "His racial identity and his gender don't have particular consequences, you know? I mean being male and White—that is *the* world, that is your world. The world is yours." Kristie's and Burton's narratives each indicate that racial differences (and for Kristie, gender differences as well) create a status and power differential not easily traversed.

Kristie and Burton are unusual among the couples I interviewed in their routine reliance on avoidance as a way to deal with racial issues. Other couples employed this strategy only in particularly difficult moments or especially volatile situations. Further, racial difference was not always the most salient social difference for interracial partners. Gender or class differences were more stressful for some couples. For instance, lesbian partners Bryce Cook and Jessica Merriam (introduced in chapter 3) find that social class differences create the most friction in their relationship. Jessica describes Bryce's family as "very WASPy and upper class" and her own as "very working class, like working poor." These differences create major challenges for the couple. Jessica explains:

Sometimes when we talk about, not like class in the abstract, but if I'm like stressing out about ... having all these student loans or like having credit card debt and then she wants to talk to me about it ... I'm like, "I can't talk to you about it." Because I feel like it's—she's great, she has wonderful politics, but like she can never understand what it's like to be me when it comes to class.

Though she and Bryce have a constant dialogue about race, when it comes to issues of money and social class, Jessica strategically avoids them. Bryce offers a similar assessment of this tension in their relationship:

> The ways that class has shaped our relationship—it's like, um, like so deep, and like almost causing us to break up. Whereas like [I] think about ways that race has shaped our relationship, that like there have definitely been like challenges. ... In our particular relationship, [race] hasn't brought us to the edge.

When partners intentionally dodge the emotional minefields of social differences, they practice a form of emotional labor—strategic avoidance. Although these practices are characterized by evasion and omission, and not by the explanations and contestations that mark most racework, partners who use this strategy do acknowledge that when they are "letting some of this lie," they are making conscious decisions to do so. In contrast, other couples do not engage in this emotional labor because race is not especially salient for either partner, and the racial difference between them is rarely explicitly acknowledged. These relationships are best characterized by the absence of racework.

Racial Silence

Many of the stories in this chapter describe partners who engage in racework because they think about race differently. I have traced these disparate orientations to differences in the partners' habitus. Sometimes, however, people with conflicting habitus arrive at a similar way of interpreting their social world. When both partners have racial lenses that are similarly critical, political, or even radical—as do Bryce and Jessica, Onika and Margaret—they still engage in emotion work around racial difference. This is because race is such a salient part of their individual worldviews. Racial silence, however, is the absence of racework between partners for whom racial difference is *not* a salient aspect of their intimate relationship. The couple discussed below exemplifies this approach.

Keith Fischer is a sixty-five-year-old White man. He lives in downtown Philadelphia with his forty-nine-year-old Black partner of twenty-eight years, Zachary King. Before he retired, Keith was an executive in his family's business. He and Zachary eat out almost every night, travel extensively, and live in a quiet, predominantly White neighborhood a few blocks from a main avenue of Philadelphia nightlife. Keith remains very active and is passionate about music—he spends a few nights almost every week at the symphony. He has a historical, academic interest in race. For instance, he is likely to watch civil rights documentaries on public television. He says, "I tend to be more sort of liberal on [racial] issues than Zachary [is], so, it wasn't like he felt he had to educate me about the Black issues because he doesn't tend to focus on them. I tend to focus on them more than he does." Keith's analysis of race and racism in everyday life, however, is more conservative than liberal. He differentiates between the social injuries of everyday prejudice and more "serious incidents" of racism. He is dismissive of African Americans and "a good number of women" who focus on everyday "ignorant slights" and are prone to what he calls a "victim complex." He explains that Zachary does not fall into this category; his partner does not "find things to constantly complain about." So, when Zachary comments about ill treatment, Keith knows to take him seriously.

Zachary is a financial analyst, a job he describes as "very stressful." He tells me that he is very comfortable in his and Keith's majority-White neighborhood and at their private swim club, where "you can count the Black members on one hand." This kind of racial imbalance is a longstanding characteristic of his social world. "It's something that I've dealt with all my life. It's a situation that I've always been in, where I'm the only Black person in the crowd. So for me, it's not an uncommon situation at all." In contrast, in predominantly Black settings, like family weddings, he feels more awkward. "To tell you the truth, that's kind of like new for me. It's not something that I'm really used to at this point. Other than being with my family or friends of my family … it's really rare for me to be in a mostly Black situation." This is not to say that Zachary does not experience, recognize, or anticipate racism. Drawing examples from trips abroad with Keith, he describes the cool treatment he received at a hotel in London and the open stares he endured on the streets of Acapulco. But these public experiences do not creep into the inner dynamics of his relationship. Racial difference does not appear to be a salient element in his life with Keith. Neither of their narratives contains examples of the emotional labor of racework.

In partnerships like Zachary and Keith's, racial difference is not a site of negotiation. Neither partner perceives racism as noticeably influencing their everyday lives, so there is little need for emotional labor in their relationship. Although other couples *reported* race as insignificant in their relationship, they often went on to describe conversations, strategies, and actions involving the emotional labor of racework. Keith and Zachary are in the minority of couples who did not show any signs of engaging in the intimate labor of negotiating racial difference.

Conclusion

The assimilation paradigm and popular notions of romantic love view interracial intimacy as a resolution for group differences. The narratives I have presented in this chapter portray a more complicated story about race and intimacy. That macrolevel inequalities shape microlevel interactions is not so surprising. Scholars of gender and the family have long considered heterosexual marriage a "locus of struggle" whereby women and men express competing interests over time, resources, and labor.[19] But scholars have been much more adept at understanding how gender inequalities play out inside the family than they have been at exploring how racial hierarchies manifest in this realm. The interracial narratives I have drawn on in this chapter demonstrate that when intimate partners occupy different positions on the racial hierarchy, they generally also have different racial orientations, or racial habitus. Habitus provides "a feel for the game," a way for individuals to interpret the world around them.[20] Racial habitus is rooted in social location and acquired through "deeply cultural conditioning"—it does not vanish with the formation of intimate bonds.[21] Racial conflict is not limited to public spaces; it arises inside kitchens and living rooms, often prompted by commonplace occurrences, such as watching television or discussing local news. Further, what may begin as a discussion about external events can quickly develop into a more personal, fundamental conflict over how to understand racial stratification.

To negotiate differences in racial habitus, most interracial partners in this study engaged in racework involving forms of emotional labor. These practices include the ways in which interracial partners evaluate how and when to initiate discussions of race, interpret and translate their perspectives, critically evaluate their own racial positions, conceal their emotions, or introduce humor. The practice of racework, whether in public space or within an intimate relationship, is an ongoing process, not a one-time accomplishment, because each partner's racial habitus is rooted in a lifetime of experiences. Many couples deliberately engage and confront their differential access to racial privileges and their differential vulnerability to discrimination, because addressing these issues relieves tension, not because communication itself resolves these inequalities.

Using racework as the conceptual thread, I have examined the texture of everyday interracial life through its public and intimate spheres. There is one important realm left to consider—interracial identities. Issues of identity are the focus of the next two chapters. In chapter 5, I look at how interracial partners construct positive identities for themselves, their partners, and their relationships in contrast to longstanding negative images of interracial intimacy. In chapter 6, I investigate White racial identities in more detail to analyze how interracial intimacy shapes partners' experience of Whiteness.

CHAPTER 5 | Interracial Identities: Racework as Boundary Work

I think that some White people have a very stereotypical view of
what interracial couples are, you know? White women who can't get
anybody else, with no teeth. And Black guys that take advantage of
them and don't work and live off them—stereotypical. As to whether
that's the real truth, I don't think so. Maybe in some places, in some
areas. And you do still see it, where both Norman and I will look
at 'em going, "You give interracial couples a bad name. You are
so stereotypical. You are what people hate. And fear." ... [People]
don't think about [interracial couples] making good money, college
educations, being together, having a family.

WITH THESE WORDS, Trudy Crenshaw, who is White, describes a powerful
stigma attached to interracial intimacy in the United States. This pejorative
account is not at all how she sees her own relationship, however. Referring to
her Black husband, Norman Crenshaw, Trudy says, "He loves me and I love
him. He's a pain in the neck sometimes, but he's a good person, and he has a
good heart." Trudy and Norman relate to each other with the ease and comfort of old friends—teasing and correcting each other's inaccuracies as they
recount old memories. But when they describe themselves as a couple, they
inevitably bump up against persistent images like the one Trudy describes.
Whether interracial couples accept these stereotypes as true or not, they
encounter them frequently in everyday life. In this chapter, I explore how
both heterosexual and same-sex interracial partners interpret characterizations of interraciality. I also show how they use the last of the four types of
racework—*boundary work*—to create interracial identities that allow them
to separate themselves from others' perceptions of them as deviant.

Conventional Images of Interracial Intimacy

Black/White partners in this study encounter opposition to interracial intimacy from both Black and White communities. As I have explained in previous chapters, opposition from these two groups differs in both its magnitude and origin. Historically, Blacks have been less uniformly hostile to interracial couples—in the early-to-mid-twentieth century, interracial couples generally lived in Black neighborhoods.

Objections to interracial intimacy have long depended on particular images, or stereotypes, of interracial partners and their motivations for engaging in mixed-race relationships. White hostility toward these relationships rested upon a set of sexualized gender and racial meanings created in the late nineteenth century. These meanings were part of an ideological apparatus through which elite Whites in the United States aimed to discourage interracial sex and marriage ("miscegenation"). Although the Supreme Court abolished all remaining legal barriers to heterosexual interracial intimacy in 1967, nineteenth-century images of interraciality linger, even today. White women who enter into sexual relationships with Black men have been construed as dirty, promiscuous, immoral, or psychologically ill.[1] These stereotypes rely heavily on assumptions about social class. They suggest that only "low class" White women have sexual relationships with Black men.[2] Stereotypes about Black men who sleep with White women are harder to disentangle from racist images of Black masculinity more broadly. They involve associations that link Black men with hypersexuality, aggression, and violence. They also allude to another kind of threat, that of a Black man who has gotten ahead of himself, who seeks to prove himself as being outside the confines of his social status. White communities have portrayed Black men dating White women as a breach of social contract, a direct confrontation with White patriarchal authority.[3]

For Whites, the pairing of White women with Black men is the archetypal image that has sustained fears of miscegenation. Its complement—White men with Black women—has not evoked the same anxiety. White communities have generally positioned White men as upstanding or as unwilling victims of Black women's voracious sexuality.[4] These stereotypes reproduce controlling images of Black women as jezebels—lascivious, overly fertile, and domineering.[5] Such images also divert attention from the ways in which African Americans have historically felt terrorized by Whiteness.[6] Notably, although images of heterosexual Black/White pairs—Black men with White women and much less visibly, White men

with Black women—were the images that fueled antimiscegenation sentiment and legislation, race-mixing between women and between men, as I
discussed in chapter 1, continued to be looked down upon by Whites.

The images that fuel Black opposition to interracial intimacy are quite
different. These stereotypes rest on the assumption that there is a set of
cultural practices and values that inhere to Blackness and Whiteness, and
that these can be dangerously muddled by Black/White romantic relationships. Love relationships between Black women and Black men are seen
as fundamental to the formation of healthy families and the reproduction
of strong Black communities.[7] Romantic relationships outside of one's race
signal a devalued or "inauthentic" racial self and a betrayal of the Black
community. In addition to one's romantic partner and friends, Black racial
authenticity is also demonstrated through such cultural practices as dress,
music, language, and aspects of physical appearance such as hairstyle. In
the post-civil rights era, middle-class African Americans have achieved
greater access to White neighborhoods and to predominantly White institutions, such as universities and businesses. Thus for Blacks today, cultural
politics are an important marker of a Black racial identity.[8]

Some ideas about interracial intimacy circulate in both White and Black
communities. Interracial intimacy has been constructed as a site in which
individuals indulge sexual desires heightened by the exoticism of racial difference. These stereotypes cast interraciality as purely and primarily sexual,
with little depth of feeling beneath the excitement of illicit eroticism. Relationships established on such a faulty premise are presumed to be doomed
to failure.[9] These assumptions may be less widespread than they once were,
but they have not fully disappeared. They coexist with our era's colorblind
racial ideology, which finds race to be an increasingly irrelevant category.[10]
From this contemporary perspective, interracial partners are racial mavericks who have already managed to "get beyond" race. Interracial intimacy
thus now occupies an ambivalent cultural space: Older stereotypes render
it deviant; newer logics find it at worst irrelevant and at best transformative.
This jumble of racial logics is the result of the changing political, social,
and historical forces that mold racial meanings. Interracial partners anticipate and avoid these stereotypes through boundary work.

Racework as Boundary Work

Social scientists and historians have traced the emergence of conventional
images of interraciality, but they offer little empirical evidence about
how interracial partners create identities apart from these stereotypes.

To address this omission, I examine *boundary work*. The concept of boundary work emerges from the idea that social actors draw symbolic boundaries to categorize people, relationships, social practices, and objects.[11] On a large scale, boundaries legitimize stratification by establishing social distinctions and justifying inequalities. For example, at the end of the 1800s, social scientists and public health professionals argued that there were important biological distinctions between Whites of different social classes. Poor Whites were biologically degenerate. They could be distinguished from other Whites on the basis of a distinctive skin color, a vagabond way of life, a promiscuous nature (especially among women), and a tendency toward violence. By drawing these boundaries, middle-class professionals elevated their own social standing and positioned this status as a natural reflection of genetic superiority.[12] On a smaller scale, individuals erect or affirm symbolic boundaries to distinguish themselves from members of other social groups or from members of their own social groups with whom they do not want to be associated. As prospective homebuyers, for example, middle-class African Americans may consciously project recognizable signs of their middle-class status when meeting with a real estate agent. Anticipating racial stereotypes that may mark them as poor or unsophisticated, they may wear clothing that signals affluence, use language that reflects their education, and display a knowledgeable competence about the housing market.[13]

Boundary work helps individuals reshape the meanings of social identities, especially when these identities are subordinated.[14] As Trudy makes clear at the outset of this chapter, the interracial couples in my study are aware of the negative images associated with interraciality. To affirm a positive view of their own relationships, they must distance themselves from these negative stereotypes. Two forms of boundary work, *exclusionary* and *inclusionary,* accomplish this goal.[15] Through exclusionary boundary work, interracial partners erect symbolic boundaries against a group of stereotypes connected to interracial intimacy. Exclusionary boundary work is most readily apparent when interracial partners describe their relationship in colorblind language in order to emphasize its normalcy, their middle-class status, or their racial pride. Interracial partners are engaged in inclusionary boundary work when they downplay or attempt to blur distinctions between themselves and same-race couples. Assertions such as "we're just a man and a woman in love," or we are "just a regular couple," are examples of inclusive phrasing that highlights the ordinary quality of interracial partners' relationships.

I begin by examining the boundary work that interracial partners use to separate themselves as individuals from particular interracial stereotypes. I then shift the analysis to the "couple identity" to explore more broadly how partners construct interracial intimacy. I explain how study participants frame the significance of race in their own relationships. Their perspectives range from colorblind to race-conscious, with an intermediate stance that incorporates elements of each. These frameworks facilitate exclusionary boundary work that allows partners to erect symbolic boundaries to distance themselves from notions of deviance. The last section of the chapter considers how sexuality affects interpretations of interracial intimacy. I discuss how heterosexuality functions as a symbolic resource for straight couples, allowing them to deflect stereotypes of deviance and to practice inclusionary boundary work by blurring boundaries between themselves and same-race couples, whose relationships are generally regarded as positive, healthy, and legitimate. Lesbian and gay Black/White couples, on the other hand, experience sexuality not as a resource, but as an identity that intersects with interraciality in multiple, sometimes contradictory, ways.

Boundary Work and the Construction of Individual Identities

Navigating White Racial Identities

Not *That Kind* of White Person

White partners often erect exclusionary boundaries to separate themselves from negative images of interracial intimacy. In my study, White heterosexual women were the most likely to emphatically assert their individuality, distancing themselves from the stereotype that a White woman who has sexual relationships with a Black man is "trashy" or promiscuous. Marie Thomas (introduced in chapter 2) is a case in point. Although she is now a manager at a high-end clothing boutique in downtown Philadelphia, a few years earlier she had worked in Manhattan at the company's regional offices. She looks back on that as her "dream" job. She transferred to a lower-level position so she could accompany her then-fiancé, a White man named David, who was moving to Philadelphia. When that relationship ended abruptly, she began an "on-and-off fling" with a middle-class African American man who projected a "bad boy" persona. "Of course he had a regular job," Marie explains, "but it was very, you know, that whole thuggish appearance.... Sexually, it was very fulfilling. It was what I needed—just a fling.... We were both using each other." Their sexual relationship lasted for about a year. It ended in part because this man, whom Marie does not name, did not want it to become serious. He was "totally against interracial relationships." As an educated, professional Black man, he believed he should be dating Black women, and eventually he did marry a Black woman. Over a year later, Marie met Frank. She describes him as "overwhelmingly kind," "funny," and "wonderful." Comparing her relationship with Frank to her previous "fling," she notes, "the sex is good, but it's not about the fascination or whatever about why we got together."

Marie is critical of those who replicate the image of the "slutty" White woman. She tells me, "I think there [are] some White women that perpetrate the stereotype. You go to these basketball games and see all these slutty White women standing outside the [locker] room, waiting for their prize. Or Black men that do the same—have all the White sluts, then marry a Black woman. It's clearly about race, not love or a relationship." Even though she exotified Blackness and eroticized racial difference in her previous relationship with a Black man, Marie shuns this stereotype. She does not consider herself to be "slutty." She constructs symbolic boundaries to differentiate herself from the image of the low-class, promiscuous White woman who has sex with Black men.[16] One way she deflects this perception is by asserting her middle-class credentials. Alluding to a career in which she works with affluent clients, manages a small staff, and engages in extensive international business travel, Marie remarks, "I think we're professional people, so I'm speaking from that strata." Because the "White slut" stereotype connects social class to constructions of femininity, Marie also deliberately projects a conservative, less overtly sexual femininity when she and Frank go to Black clubs. "I have a more classy style of dressing and it would never come to that [being mistaken for a slut]. ... I'm also very aware that I don't want to come off as a stereotype, so I may make provisions that I wouldn't [otherwise]." She admits that if she went to a club without a Black man as her escort, she probably would dress "a little more provocatively," because she would be less vulnerable to this pejorative label. By choosing clothing that she believes confirms her status as a respectable, middle-class woman, Marie is doing boundary work. She attempts to distance herself from an image that simultaneously implicates her social class, gender, race, and sexuality.

White partners in interracial relationships also contend with the notion that sexual relationships with Blacks are part of a broader move to appropriate African American cultural practices, to "act Black." Vera Oster (introduced in chapter 3) and her Black husband, Kalvin Oster (introduced in chapter 2), have been together for nearly six years and have two children. When they first met, they both worked for an insurance company. Kalvin, who is in upper management, remains at the company; Vera manages the daycare center that the couple owns. This is her first romantic interracial relationship, although she went to a predominantly Black high school and had many African American friends as she was growing up. Vera tells me that she does not think she and Kalvin fit the "typical stereotype." She says, "I don't think I am a typical White woman with a Black man ... I don't act the part. It's just not me." When I ask her what she means by "the part," she clarifies: "A typical, Black stereotype—[the] dress, the hair, the nails, the talk, the slang. I don't talk slang. Sometimes I feel like do I need to do that ... in a club, in that type of atmosphere ... [I think,] 'Do I need to act the part?' But I can't." For Vera, "acting the part" of a White woman in an interracial relationship involves engaging in African American cultural practices, including language, style, and dress. Like Marie, Vera erects exclusionary boundaries.

The "acting Black" stereotype resonates with the notion that interraciality represents a blurring of racial essences that results in dangerously amorphous identities—not quite Black and not quite White. Unlike the Black partners I discuss in the following section, White interracial partners rarely framed this issue as a matter of White racial authenticity. This is not surprising, as many Whites are not conscious of having a race. When Whiteness is invisible, the notion of an "authentic" White identity is neither relevant nor meaningful. Instead, White partners interpret the acquisition of cultural practices and styles of interaction associated with African Americans as "acting Black."

Among White partners in my study, heterosexual women feel most marked by interracial stereotypes. Heterosexual White men do not describe social practices with which they signal to others that they are not *that type* of White man. This sort of direct defense of their White identity is rarely necessary, because in White communities, White masculinity has not been marred by heterosexual interracial sexual relations. The "trashy" or "slutty" White woman has no analogous male counterpart. When it is presumed to be heterosexual, White masculinity embodies extraordinary privilege, especially among middle-class or affluent men. Thus, White men's interracial sexual encounters have largely been accorded privacy and protection, whereas those of White women have been publicly demeaned. Some White gay men, however, do feel negatively labeled by their interracial relationships. They recoil at being labeled a "dinge queen," a White man who seeks sexual relationships only with Black men. "It's a little disgusting," says Shawn Tarwick, the White gay man who, along with his partner, Daniel Embry, is raising a family (see chapter 4). "It's real objectification of people," he explains.

Finding the Black Exception

Some White women and men in my study construct symbolic boundaries in order to reconcile what may seem like contradictory feelings about their partner and their partner's racial group. They portray their partner as atypical or exceptional. Because such descriptions simultaneously describe one's partner and oneself, these rhetorical gestures constitute an indirect form of exclusionary boundary work. Before meeting his wife, Mary, Neil Chambers had never dated a Black woman. Still, he tells me that if their relationship should ever end, he would probably seek out relationships with other Black women. He believes that they are more "receptive" to average guys like him. At his school, he meets many "educated Black women on a consistent basis who are not married, who are—to an extent—disrespected by Black males." He feels that those women would be more amenable to dating someone who is "halfway decent looking" and "halfway intelligent," if that person "show[s] them respect." Even so, Neil is adamant that Mary is an exception to "typical" Black femininity. "So you got my wife who is, in a way, not a typical girl of African-American descent. I mean she's … not someone who would curse or, you know, say anything that's inappropriate or off color. Not that she's a saint but … she has a certain background. … She's not offensive to you. She's very pleasant." This description of Mary is superficially positive. But, in positing her good traits as *atypical* of African American women, Neil presents a fundamentally demeaning image of Black femininity. If Mary is exceptional because she is pleasant, inoffensive, and avoids using inappropriate language, Neil's opinions of Black women as a group are very low.[17]

Neil's intimate relationship with Mary has not eroded the negative stereotypes he has of African Americans in general. This kind of contradiction is not necessarily unusual. One of the subtexts of the narratives in this study is that, even while deeply loving and caring about their own partner, people in Black/White relationships sometimes hold racial judgments and prejudices about their partner's racial group.[18] This simple fact is notable because it casts doubt on the assumption that interracial partners are racial mavericks who live without prejudice. This is simply not so. Sometimes interracial partners retain racial prejudices but position their own mate as an exception to the rule. Social psychologists explain this tendency as a common response to the cognitive dilemma that arises when a person develops positive feelings toward a member of a social group that they generally devalue, dislike, or fear.[19] Seeing one's partner as an exception to his or her social group relieves some of the resulting emotional conflict. The alternative is to recast one's feelings for the entire group of which one's partner is a member.

Trudy Crenshaw, the White woman whose words open this chapter, also differentiates between "typical" and "atypical" African Americans. Trudy is in her mid-fifties; she trains customer service representatives for the local gas company. We talk about the past twenty-six years she has been with her Black husband, Norman, who is a structural ironworker. I ask her about introducing him to her family. Explaining that Norman is "not ghetto by any means," she says, "Everybody loves him. I think they love him more than they love me."

> Norman is not so typical of what some people fear and look at as a Black man. He's kind and he's giving and he wouldn't hurt you. And you know, he's not carrying a gun, he's not dealing drugs, and he's not carousing with women, and he's not stealing [laughs], you know, he's not a murderer. And you know, there's a lot of people that define Blacks that way; and that's pretty sad because that's, [there's] such a small, small percentage of any race that's bad.

It is unclear whether Trudy accepts these stereotypes of Black masculinity or is simply enumerating them, but she returns to this point several times during the interview. In describing Norman's relationship with her friends, she tells me, "I've had actually women friends say how easy it is to be around him. He's not, um, he's not threatening, you know? Like you're around some guys and you always feel like they're always, they got the dog thing going on. But Norman, he's not like that." Together, Trudy's statements suggest that she feels she must explain why she has forged a relationship with a Black man. In constructing a positive picture of Norman, she is also constructing her own identity, as well as a favorable characterization of her marriage. As with Neil's descriptions of Mary, when Trudy constructs an exclusionary boundary that positions Norman as exceptional—as not your "typical" Black person—her own identity is also inevitably at stake.

Whether partners such as Neil and Trudy accept the stereotypical images they reference as true, or are just describing them, is debatable. Either way, however, part of the narratives' significance lies in the fact that the speakers feel it necessary to tell these stories. How people talk about their partners and relationships is intrinsically connected to definitions of the self.[20] When White partners construct symbolic boundaries that distance them from far-reaching interracial stereotypes, they protect elements of their core selves, including their Whiteness. By establishing that their partners are exceptions—Norman is not a "ghetto, drug-dealing thief" and Mary is not an "offensive," profane, or unpleasant person—Trudy and Neil simultaneously establish themselves as not "trash." They do not fit the stereotype of low-class Whites who have sexual relationships with Blacks.[21] Engaging in this form of racework allows them to verbally protect their class and—for Trudy—their gender status. Neil and Trudy situate their own Whiteness in relation to their partners' Blackness, showing not only that their Black partners are not *that kind* of African American, but also that they are not *that kind* of White person.

Navigating Black Racial Identities

Not *That Kind* of Black Person

Like their White counterparts, some African American partners engage in deliberate boundary work to separate themselves from widespread stereotypes about Blacks in interracial relationships. They reject the notion that their relationship with their White partner reflects a lack of cultural pride or racial authenticity. Keenly aware that their interracial intimacy may be seen as "selling out," they draw exclusionary boundaries to separate themselves from the "traitors, Uncle Toms, Oreos," and others who are defined as disconnected from their "true" Black selves.

My conversations with Myron Tanner (introduced in chapter 3) provide clear examples of this kind of boundary work. Myron owns a construction company in a small city in the New York metropolitan area. He is very aware that owning a business in a Black community elevates his status and earns him special respect. He takes pride in this. He and his White wife, Norma Tanner, met fourteen years ago. They have been married for five years. For a few years, Myron tried to "keep personal life and business life separate" so that his clients, whom he anticipated might negatively judge his interracial relationship, would be unaware that his wife is White. He presents himself as having made this decision for a highly practical reason: He knows how people think. "A lot of times when you have a Black man who dates a White woman, they automatically think that he's a Black guy who's [trying] to be White. ... That's their immediate assumption. ... A lot of people are surprised I'm married to a White woman because I'm so pro-Black. I'm not anti-White, I'm just pro-Black. Everything about me is Black." As we continue talking, Myron explains his own racial self in greater detail. He locates his racial pride in his Southern upbringing:

> I think people ... down South—because they've been there such a long
> time you know—they have a stronger sense of themselves as Black folks ...
> they feel comfortable being Black and they don't feel like they need to

kowtow. Where I figure folks up here have only been here since like maybe the '40s and they came up here … probably during World War II. … What a lot of them here for [are] jobs. So they came up here, probably some of the ones that weren't as educated … and they were more or less used to being second-class citizens, and you can still see some of that today. … So as a result of that, you don't have a sense of Black pride, you don't have a sense of like, "We belong here." It's a tad bit different so, as a result of that, I didn't find a woman, a Black woman that I relate to that much.

In these two exchanges, Myron very clearly sets himself apart from African Americans in the North, whom he does not perceive as having a strong racial identity. By explaining that he is unable to "relate to" the Black women he knows because they do not "have a sense of Black pride," he stands a common interracial stereotype about cultural politics on its head. He dated and is now married to a White woman not because he *lacks* racial pride, but because he has *so much more* racial pride than the Black women in his northeastern city. Further, Myron has a healthy self-esteem. He is proud of his accomplishments and his standing in the community, so he separates himself from Blacks who, he believes, still consider themselves "second-class citizens." By explicitly affirming that "everything about me is Black," Myron constructs symbolic boundaries that separate him from Blacks who "[try] to be White." This form of racework allows him to express his obvious racial pride.

Jessica Merriam (introduced, along with her partner, Bryce Cook, in chapter 3) also engages in a direct form of exclusionary boundary work when she talks about interracial intimacy. Explaining her racial identity, she tells me that she is "biracial … but I identify as Black." Before meeting Bryce, Jessica had been in a relationship with a Latina for a year and a half. They had "very similar politics," which Jessica feels is an important foundation for intimacy. "I always said that I don't ever want to have to explain myself or, like, to explain what racism is or, you know, my experiences." She had not intended to date a White woman. Bryce is the first. Jessica describes the reversal of her position as "one of the best decisions I've ever made." Nonetheless, this interracial relationship places her dangerously close to a stereotype from which she intentionally seeks distance. Like Myron, she recognizes that people make negative assumptions about African Americans who date Whites. Jessica accepts these same generalizations:

I think that there are people of color who have some issues about being a person of color, who maybe never had a community of color, who had a lot of internalized racism—who seek out to date White people as a status symbol or whatever. Or because, "Oh, we find White people attractive." ... Maybe they grew up more around White people. ... Like I would say most people of color who I know ... who mainly date White people ... don't have the same race politics as me. My race politics are much more intense and much more radical. ...

Jessica and Myron articulate similar assumptions about the cultural politics of Blacks who date Whites. Neither directly challenges the validity of these assumptions. Jessica suggests that for most African Americans, dating Whites is an expression of self-loathing, of their own "internalized racism." In contrast, she lays claim to an authentic Black self by referencing her critical, politicized identity. No matter what derogatory traits people (including her) might attribute to African Americans who date Whites, Jessica's radical racial politics establish a boundary that separates and protects her from this negative portrayal. From her perspective, these stereotypes accurately describe most Blacks who date Whites, but they do not describe her.

Finding the White Exception

Black partners also use indirect methods to exclude themselves from stereotypes about cultural politics when they describe their White partners as exceptionally astute about race and racism. For example, when Marvin Nelson met his White partner, Ulrich Drescher (introduced in chapter 3), seven years ago, Marvin had already had several unsuccessful relationships with White men. A Black man in his early forties, Marvin is dean of students at a small liberal arts college in New England (he returns home to Philadelphia each weekend). He feels that White men are threatened by his intellect and financial stability. This has not been his experience with his current partner, however. When Marvin talks about Ulrich, his tone changes. "It's just been so equal ... where other relationships I've been in, it didn't feel equal. The love wasn't equal. The expectations were not equal. The understanding wasn't equal. The trust level wasn't equal. And so with Ulrich, it's been so equal and so balanced ... that's been really good for me." He attributes part of this difference to the fact that Ulrich did not grow up in the United States. He was born and raised in a small city near Stuttgart, Germany.[22] Before he met Ulrich, Marvin had decided not to pursue any more relationships with White men. "At one point, I told my friends I'm not dating any more White boys," and then I met Ulrich and said, "Okay, no more White *American* boys. It was different and it continues to be."

Although he is less direct than Myron and Jessica, Marvin too distances himself from negative assumptions about the cultural politics of Blacks who date Whites. He emphasizes that they maintain discrete and separate racial identities—he is still Black and Ulrich is still White. He is wary of White gay men in interracial relationships who try to "act Black." He explains, "Some [Black] guys will tell you, 'I don't want my White boyfriend trying to act like a Black guy, try[ing] to say things that he thinks Black guys are going to find cool.' And then they get into an environment and they realize what this guy does. It's a little late, and then of course, we're all like, 'Whoa, [sarcastically] nice boyfriend.'" Marvin hopes to avoid a relationship with someone who would reflect negatively upon him and his own racial identity. Like White partners who portray their partners as exceptional, Marvin also knows that his own identity is implicated when people see his partner as a stereotype.

Boundary Work and the Construction of Intimacy

Interracial partners in this study use symbolic boundaries not only to reshape perceptions of the kind of individuals who enter into interracial relationships, but also to recast notions of interracial intimacy more broadly. They do so by drawing from a diverse repertoire of images and meanings. Many adopt a colorblind logic as a path away from stereotypes that portray interraciality as deviant. Colorblind language minimizes the importance of race and allows interracial partners to frame their relationship as positive and legitimate. Although colorblind discourse is the racial ideology that most of the study participants favor, it is not the only way in which race is interpreted. Some partners' views are adamantly race-conscious, and some favor an intermediate perspective.[23] In the sections below, I discuss how partners use these viewpoints to construct boundaries that differentiate them from negative images of interracial intimacy and blur the distinctions between them and same-race couples.

Colorblind Intimacy

When I ask Black and White partners about their experience of interracial intimacy, many eagerly explain that they did not go looking for an interracial relationship and that racial difference was not something they even noticed. They assert that their partner could have been purple, green, or any color. They do not "see" race. This use of colorblind language is a form of boundary work. Stereotypes of exoticism and illicit sex (in which

Blacks and Whites find erotic pleasure in racial difference) are frequently associated with interracial relationships. Partners thus are motivated to create more positive conceptions of interracial intimacy. One strategy is to describe racial difference as irrelevant or coincidental. This positions one's relationship firmly outside the reach of negative portrayals. It also avoids the challenges of trying to recognize race and racial difference without becoming mired in racial stereotypes. The lesbian/gay and heterosexual Black and White partners I discuss in this section use colorblindness to construct boundaries that affirm their relationships as healthy and positive.

Helen Rutkowski (first mentioned, along with her partner, Ben Walters, in chapter 2) describes her relationship using colorblind language, though she peppers it with direct references to race. Helen describes Ben as both serious and "very silly." His intelligence is what first attracted her, although she also tells me that she does find Black men "exotic." And, although she was once married to a White man and has two sons from that marriage, Helen says that she has long been attracted to strong Black men who are "committed to living life properly." Still, in describing her relationship with Ben, she stresses that she sees people—Black or White—as human. "It's really funny because me and Ben filled out a questionnaire … and when it came down to race, we both wrote 'human,' which is so weird because we both [did] it separately. I don't look at people as Black or White." Her explanation relies on the metaphor of colorblindness to convey a lack of racial prejudice and a frustration with the persistence of racial categories. Helen's account suggests perspectives that do not seem to go together—she is attracted to Black men and yet she claims not to see Blackness (or Whiteness). In other words, having racialized desires does not preclude Helen from identifying herself as someone who does not see color.

Ben is in recovery from a drug addiction and has been clean for eight years. The arduous path out of addiction has left him with a deep spirituality. He tells me over and over again that he has been through too much to sweat the small stuff—he has got to keep his eyes on the big picture. When Ben describes meeting Helen, he expresses a colorblind sentiment similar to hers: "I wasn't seeking a relationship, so I never saw Helen's skin. I saw the world jerking to establish her presence and her aura first." Ben's words convey the relative insignificance of Helen's skin color in comparison to the force of their connection.

Like Helen and Ben, Mary Chambers uses colorblind language to describe her relationship with Neil. Although she grew up in the United States, Mary's Jamaican heritage shapes how she sees her own racial/

ethnic identity. Like other Americans from West Indian families, when she talks about "Black Americans," she sometimes positions herself outside of this group.[24] Mary's parents, who live nearby, help with the children and are a constant presence in the family's everyday lives. The cultural and racial differences between her parents and her husband can cause problems. For instance, Neil gets frustrated with the deference Mary shows her parents and their friends; and Mary's parents are sometimes quick to attribute Neil's shortcomings to his Whiteness. Mary intervenes, assuming the role of peacemaker. She seems reluctant to identify racial difference as a dynamic in these situations. "I suppose it's there," she admits hesitantly. "It's obviously—it's there. But really, it's just about who you are as a person and how you've been raised and where you're coming from. ... I don't see Neil as black or white or green or purple or anything. He's just who he is." She laughs.

Interracial partners also use colorblindness to minimize the relevance of race in their relationship when they position race as a happenstance. This strategy is clear in comments Norman Crenshaw makes about his wife. When I meet Norman, he is about to turn fifty. He and Trudy have been living in the Philadelphia metropolitan area since they met, nearly three decades ago. Norman was married once before, also to a White woman. When I ask him whether being in an interracial relationship is a salient part of his identity, he starts with a familiar metaphor: "I don't really see color. ... I just, I met Trudy, I fell in love with her, she just happened to be White. ... I wasn't out looking for a White woman or anything like that." Here, Norman downplays the importance of race in two ways. He emphasizes that he is colorblind (he does not "see color"), but he also positions his wife's race as happenstance—Trudy "happened to be White." Although there is a self-evident truth to this statement—the color of one's skin is an accident of birth—there is a deeper meaning for interracial partners. Statements like these neutralize certain stereotypes about interraciality: that interracial partners are marginal characters, that they eroticize racial difference, and that their relationships are destined to fail. In addition, such statements minimize the extent to which race structures inequality and shapes everyday life. As social science research has repeatedly shown, race fundamentally affects our life chances, from where we live to the schools we attend, the people in our social networks, and the amount of wealth our family possesses.[25] That Norman and others posit race as a matter of chance reveals the tendency for both White and Black study participants to blur distinctions between themselves and same-race couples by minimizing the influence of race within their intimate relationships.

The use of a colorblind ideology is not limited to interracial partners, but it provides them with a simple way to explain interracial intimacy in a race-neutral manner. This perspective allows partners to de-emphasize their membership in specific racial groups and reposition their relationship as a pairing of two individuals who "happen to be" in love. Put differently, the notions of free choice and individual autonomy that are embedded in colorblind racism enable interracial partners to see their relationship as a coincidence of skin color instead of as a union shaped by social and historical forces. Trudy may happen to be White, but it is not mere happenstance that Norman chose to marry a White person.

There is one more layer of meaning in Norman's words that merits analysis. Like some other Black interracial partners, he conceives of romantic love as a uniquely raceless space within a broadly racialized society. The colorblind language he uses to describe his marriage might seem to suggest that he does not see race at play in other parts of his life. This is not the case. As we talk, Norman brings up numerous examples of prejudice and discrimination. He recounts instances of everyday racism he experiences as a foreman on construction sites; he also mentions more extreme encounters, such as a visit from a local member of the Ku Klux Klan while he and Trudy were spending time at their summer home in Maryland. Norman does not contest the existence of racism. What he rejects is the notion that race permeates the innermost sanctum of his social world—his marriage. Although he and Trudy talk about racial encounters that occur at work, Norman finds that race rarely shapes the interactions between them.[26]

The race-neutral language many partners adopt when discussing interracial intimacy in the abstract sometimes fades as the conversation turns to the specific realities of their day-to-day lives. We see this with Helen, for example, who asserts that she does not "look at people as Black or White," but who also tells me that she has always been attracted to strong Black men. Mary notes that racial difference sometimes strains her marriage to Neil, yet she also minimizes the relevance of race. Other narratives, recounted by gay, lesbian, and heterosexual partners, reveal similar contradictions. The seeming inconsistency in how intimacy is constructed in the abstract versus how it is described through day-to-day occurrences is important because it prompts us to examine why individuals employ particular racial logics in specific circumstances. For partners who utilize a colorblind logic, their romantic union is the relationship that is, above all the other interactions of daily life, the most important to construct as a raceless space.

Race-conscious Interraciality

Faced with the same stereotypes about interracial deviance, other partners in the study use a different racial framework to create alternative notions of interracial intimacy. These partners prefer a race-conscious perspective, a view that considers racial dynamics to be at play in all spheres of social life, including intimate spaces. Race-conscious partners' perspectives are also deliberately critical or politicized. Notions that cast interraciality as deviant are rooted in the assumption that persons who seek out interracial relationships use racial difference instrumentally, as a form of erotic pleasure. In contrast, those with a race-conscious view of intimacy position themselves as people who understand race and have a critical analysis of racism. These assertions permit race-conscious partners to draw boundaries that separate them not only from historic interracial stereotypes, but also from more recently popular colorblind viewpoints.

Ethan Smolen, who is White, grew up in a "relatively affluent" suburb of Cleveland. He and his wife, Wanda Maxwell, who is Black, live in Philadelphia (both partners were introduced in chapter 2). Ethan has no patience with colorblind notions. Describing the experience of being in an interracial relationship, as opposed to a same-race relationship, Ethan says,

> It's going to be different, it's different from the first second you meet somebody. Like Black or White—it's just such a part of who someone is. It's like saying, "Would it be different to date a fat person than a skinny person?" Of course. It's an integral part of who they are. ... It's just a given. ... To me it's not like a person's race only comes into play where there's a Confederate flag on something. Every interaction is influenced by every part of us. And race, especially in America, is such a big part of it. So from the moment I met her [Wanda], it was different than other interactions that I'm going to have with someone who's White or Asian or something like that.

Ethan views race as significant to his relationship because race matters to him and Wanda as individuals. Her Blackness and his Whiteness have consequences in all of their interactions, with each other and with other people in their lives. Their relationship is embedded in "race ... in America," not shielded from it. Ethan is adamant that being interracial is "not oppressive ... it's just life," yet he sees colorblindness as an absolute impossibility. "What kind of world would it be if everyone was colorblind—it would be a world of stupid frigging people. It's not a realistic expectation."

Maureen Wiley (introduced, along with her Black partner, Terrina Nissar, in chapter 3) also rejects the notion that romantic intimacy is a raceless space. Maureen was raised in Virginia. She is a longtime social justice activist who currently works as a fundraiser for a women's health organization. She and Terrina have been a couple for four years. Describing herself, Maureen says she "… used to be radical, now I would say liberal to radical. … But definitely political." Having educated herself regarding race and racism, and especially about White privilege, she is critical of the notion of colorblindness.

> It's not like the race is just gonna go away. It's not like she's gonna suddenly wake up White or I'll suddenly wake up Black, or suddenly we'll live in a world that doesn't see one as supreme and the other—you know, like where there's not White privilege anymore. I mean, I'd like to wake up in a world where there isn't White privilege, but that's not gonna happen. There's always gonna, there's always gonna be power issues. There's always some privilege I have that she doesn't, because of race.

Like Ethan, Maureen views race as relevant in her relationship because she understands race as relevant in every other aspect of her life. By highlighting this awareness, she constructs symbolic boundaries that separate her and Terrina from other interracial couples who have a different stance. "I do know a lot of couples who are kind of like, [speaking in a mocking, high voice] 'Oh, we don't see color. And I'm so happy. And I wish everyone could just see us as who we are.' [returning to a regular voice] It's like, 'No.' We are—she's Black, I'm White. It has stuff that comes with it just like being two girls has stuff that comes with it." Maureen sees no distinction between how race works in the outside world and how it works inside her apartment. This does not mean that she believes racial oppression is being reproduced in her home or in her relationship, only that domestic spaces are not immune to the ways in which race shapes identities and interactions.

An important reason why Maureen and Ethan have come to see race as an inevitable part of their respective relationships is because they are acutely aware of Whiteness and its privileges. They recognize that White people have a race. Unlike many White partners, for whom interracial intimacy involves feeling racially marked for the first time in their lives, partners like Maureen and Ethan were reflective about their racial identity before becoming involved in an interracial relationship. They believe that being White means being "racialized" in a way that involves attributing characteristics, such as authority, honesty, good intentions, civility, and humanity, to people based on their Whiteness. Over time, each has developed what I describe in the next chapter as "racial literacy."

Onika Marsh (introduced in chapter 2, along with her White partner, Margaret Otterlei) is another interracial partner who is quite conscious of the racial dynamics in her intimate relationship. She identifies racism as a salient element of American life, and she has a history of noticing how racial dynamics shape friendships and peer networks. Recalling her experiences at a majority-White boarding school in Vermont, Onika explains that she "often felt this tension, that I should have more of a connection with the, like, Black student group. It wasn't necessarily more uncomfortable, but it never … I always felt …, I never felt unwelcome … [but] I didn't necessarily feel like it offered me something, or that I often felt like I didn't fit in that any more than I did in with a lot of the White students." Not surprisingly, she also identifies race as a dynamic at play between her and Margaret. For Onika, interracial intimacy is a space that is inherently racialized—from the inside as well as from the outside.

> With Margaret, and as the relationship was developing … I remember at first being like, you know, we'd talk about stuff racially on sort of like broader, theoretical terms. And I remember being like, "Oh, this is gonna be fine," like, you know? She has a really kind of smart, but also personal kind of like race analysis, and she's gonna fit with mine and this is fine and blah, blah, blah. And then as things kind of developed, and you know, the conversations and issues became more personal and particular and how we saw each other and interacted, it became harder. And there have definitely been things that have like, that have come up that are challenging. … But I can't interact with somebody where we're just gonna like pretend that things don't exist or that they don't affect us in different ways and stuff like that. So, that's been … I guess that was what I had sort of expected would always be the thing [in an interracial relationship] and that's sort of met my expectations.

Like Ethan and Maureen, Onika is unequivocal about the fact that personal relationships are not immune to racial tensions. These partners practice boundary work by constructing a notion of intimate relationships as a site where partners acknowledge and negotiate the complexities of racial stratification. They define the influence of race on their own terms and separate themselves from those whom they perceive as misunderstanding the implications of racial difference.

Between Colorblind and Color Conscious: Racial Ambivalence

Meryl Agassi Ivers inhabits an intermediate position. She is critical of colorblindness, but she is much more ambivalent than Maureen and Ethan. Meryl, who is White, and her husband, Lionel, who is Black, were introduced in chapter 2. Meryl was born in Washington, D.C., and proudly describes herself as a fourth-generation Washingtonian, although she moved to New Hampshire when she was six, after her parents divorced. The area where she grew up was "artsy" and "cultured"—a "very old, blueblood" town. Now thirty-five, she is again living in Washington, where she works as a high school guidance counselor. Unlike Ben or Mary, Meryl does not claim to be colorblind. She is, however, more consciously aware of Lionel's Blackness than she is of her own Whiteness. "Here's this beautiful Black man in front of me. I glory in that. And I don't mean that I'm always seeing him as a Black person. I just see how beautiful he is. It's always present, in a sense. I guess it's back and forth." In this way she stands apart from those who do not "see" race. Yet unlike Ethan and Maureen, she does not view race in terms of privilege or power, but as an aesthetic property. Meryl is skeptical of colorblindness, though she is unsure about how to talk about race without objectifying Lionel.

> Well, first of all, you got to remember that we've been together now almost seven years. ... It's like this: Do you ever look at a beautiful car driving by and you're like, "Wow, it's so gorgeous!" ... And you get inside those cars, and you're just going somewhere. It literally doesn't feel an ounce different from any other car. It's just your being ... that's what it's like for us. That from the outside I'm sure it looks much more *something*, and from the inside, we are just being. We are just living every day. I don't like the idea either of this colorblind[ness]. I understand that that's a false notion and there's nothing wrong with his color and blah, blah, blah. But there is something to it, in the sense that, when you're living in it, I'm just not constantly just seeing him as that. Because that objectifies him, and he's not an object to me. We're in the moment together. He's not a thing that I'm looking at.

Like many other White interracial partners in the study, Meryl struggles to find a way to describe the presence of race in her relationship. She sees Lionel's Blackness as beautiful, but she does not want to group herself with those who exoticize racial difference. Lionel's Blackness is neither the only nor the most important thing she sees. For Meryl, the boundaries seem difficult. She hesitates to position herself as colorblind, but she wants me to understand that her relationship with Lionel works like any other.

She subtly acknowledges interracial prejudice "from the outside" that casts her and Lionel as different or unusual. But she argues that this misrepresents the fact that she and Lionel are "just being … just living every day." Being interracial is part of her partnered identity, what she calls her and Lionel's "we" identity: "It's a reality but not a driving force by any means." Her relationship feels normative and regular, though enduring interracial stereotypes and contemporary colorblind logic make it difficult to express this sentiment without discounting race altogether.

How Sexuality Shapes Interracial Identity

In chapter 3, I used examples of invisibility to show that some of the benefits of heterosexuality are diminished by interraciality. Heterosexual interracial pairs are particularly vulnerable to negative images associated with miscegenation. Yet even as heterosexuality affixes this burden, it simultaneously provides significant symbolic resources with which to lessen its weight. Their "normal" sexual status enables these interracial partners to blur the boundaries that separate them from same-race heterosexual couples. The situation is different for gay and lesbian interracial partners. Their sexual intimacy does not tap into the same historical anxieties about race-mixing. Instead, same-sex interracial partners experience racial difference amid another form of social exclusion—heterosexism. Heterosexism limits the symbolic resources available to gay and lesbian partners for the boundary work they undertake. Looking more closely at these intersections of sexuality with race and gender reveals important ways in which sexuality shapes constructions of interracial life.

Constructing a Straight Interracial Identity: Colorblind Heterosexuality

In the previous section, I traced the ways in which interracial partners use colorblind language to differentiate themselves from stereotypical interracial couples. Here, I shift the focus to sexuality to show that heterosexual couples engage in inclusionary boundary work on this front as well. By asserting that they are "just a couple" and by stressing the normalcy of their intimate bond, these interracial partners downplay differences between themselves and same-race heterosexual couples. Claims of colorblind intimacy mesh easily with the "natural" legitimacy of heteronormativity to shape how heterosexual partners construct their relationship.

The effects of merging potent ideologies about race and sex are evident when Warren Geiger, a White man introduced in chapter 3, recounts the evolution of his relationship with his African American wife, Nakia Geiger. Warren is Swiss by birth. He met Nakia when he came to New York City as a twenty-year-old. He implicitly highlights the social value of his heterosexuality as he recounts how, during the eight years that he and Nakia have been together, he has become increasingly comfortable holding hands with her in public spaces.

> If you're really aware of [being interracial], you send out those signals and your environment sort of picks up on those signals. ... If you do walk down the street and are constantly aware that [you're] holding a Black woman's hand, "Oh, she's different. She's dark. She's brown. She's not like me," I think people pick that up. If you walk down a street and it's like, "This is my wife and she just happens to be Black," that's just how it is.

Here Warren contrasts two interpretations of the visible racial difference between him and Nakia. (Note that in both cases, her black skin is the site onto which he codes difference. His Whiteness remains an unremarkable and invisible referent.) He first emphasizes his early public discomfort, suggesting that he is sometimes self-conscious of their intimacy as an erotic racial transgression. Although in other social contexts he experiences this transgression as "cool" and "exciting," in majority-Black public spaces he becomes anxious and self-conscious.

As Warren suggests, the passage of time has helped strengthen his confidence, and thus his sense of ease, in public places. An important change occurred during the years he and Nakia have been together: They married. Strangers may not notice the small metal band on his left hand, but for Warren, marriage is a source of confidence and affirmation. Same-race partners can also draw upon marriage as a form of symbolic power. For interracial partners, however, access to this resource is especially important because it allows them to erect symbolic boundaries that differentiate them from stereotypes of casual eroticism. When he describes Nakia's race as incidental—"she just happens to be Black"—Warren echoes narratives presented earlier in this chapter. In this second framing, he draws on the symbolic power of heterosexuality to gain the standing he needs to reject racial judgments and project self-assuredness in public spaces. In this shift, Warren lays claim to the form of romantic intimacy that U.S. society privileges above all others—heterosexual marriage. This sanctified status and its attendant social and legal rights remain limited to heterosexuals—same-race and interracial—in forty-four states.[27] When he alludes to marriage ("This is my wife"), Warren invokes a host of material resources, as well as symbolic ones.

As we continue our conversation, Warren rephrases his claim to the legitimacy of his and Nakia's relationship. In so doing, he suggests the seamless interweaving of heteronormative and colorblind logics. "We're just together," he says. "Just a man and a woman who love each other and it's comfortable. ... We're just two human beings." As I have shown, emphasizing one's general humanity over membership in a particular racial group is a common rhetorical strategy used to downplay the significance of race.[28] But Warren expands this claim. He asserts their shared humanity *and* their shared heterosexuality. He fends off negative judgments by positioning himself and Nakia as "a man and a woman who love each other." They inhabit a safe space protected by the institution of heterosexual marriage. Warren's ability to cast their intimacy as natural, even mundane, reflects the privilege of possessing a normative heterosexual identity. When he invokes this privilege, he engages in inclusionary boundary work that lessens any difference between him and Nakia and same-race couples and, at the same time, emphasizes the ordinary intimacy they share.

Norman uses a rhetorical strategy similar to Warren's, joining heterosexual privilege and colorblind logic as he describes his marriage to Trudy. He tells me, "I just don't perceive myself as in an interracial couple. It's just Norman and Trudy or Trudy and Norman." Here Norman engages in both exclusionary and inclusionary boundary work. Framing his relationship as a raceless space, he erects boundaries to distance it from interracial stereotypes. At the same time, this framing allows him to position his partnership with Trudy as very similar to that of same-race couples. He and his wife are "just" a couple. Both Warren and Norman want to make clear that they and their wives form pairs that are not out of the ordinary—they are just normal, just natural, just regular. Other heterosexual partners in the study also emphasize their normalcy this way: "When we're together I just feel like we're Evan and Wanda." "Frank and I are just Frank and I." "We're Brianna and Kurt. We're not Black and we're not White." These claims build on the logic of colorblindness, but they also reflect something more. They go beyond the notion that love sees no color, because they frame these claims within heteronormative notions of legitimate intimacy. Whether these statements, like Warren's, make reference specifically to romantic love between "a man and a woman," or whether they are framed as being "just a couple," they all rely on an abstract idea of a "couple" that is implicitly heterosexual.[29]

Constructing a Lesbian or Gay Interracial Identity

The colorblind claim of being "just a couple" seldom emerges within the gay and lesbian interracial narratives. This does not mean that the lesbian and gay partners in the study believe themselves to be abnormal or unnatural. Rather, it reflects the practical fact that making rhetorical allusions to ordinary intimacy is a bankrupt strategy in a sociopolitical context in which lesbians and gays are treated as far from ordinary. In more than twenty-five states, gay men and lesbians are denied the hospital visitation rights extended to heterosexual spouses, prohibited from jointly adopting children, and excluded from antidiscrimination protection in places of employment.[30] In this environment, homosexuality is considered at best an "alternative" lifestyle, and more often an immoral, unnatural, and unhealthy "choice." Put simply, gay and lesbian interracial partners are not "just couples" because, in the United States, even at the beginning of the twenty-first century, normative intimacy is heterosexual.

Although the heterosexual couples in the study rarely identify themselves as heterosexual, most of the gay and lesbian partners make direct references to their sexual identity and their experiences with homophobia. Chapter 3 examined how these interracial partners attempt to avoid homophobia through visibility management. Here I focus mainly on how inhabiting a marginalized, rather than a privileged, sexual position shapes interraciality in the context of a shared, couple identity. As the following narratives show, lesbian and gay sexuality compounds, eclipses, or diffuses the salience of racial difference in intimate relationships.

Sexuality Compounds Racial Identities

For some partners, sexuality and interraciality compound each other and complicate social interactions. Nadine Allen is a Black lesbian in a now two-year-long relationship with her White partner, Nancy Taylor (both women were introduced in chapter 2). The apartment they share in Washington, D.C., is crowded with books and artwork. Nadine works as a financial aid counselor at a nearby school. She tells me that her family has lived in Washington for three generations. She has been aware of her attraction to women since she was sixteen. Her sexual orientation has often caused conflict within her family—so much so that after high school, she chose to distance herself by moving to Los Angeles to attend community college instead of accepting the scholarship offered by the local, prestigious, historically Black university. When Nadine talks about being in an interracial lesbian relationship, she tells me that she has wondered if dealing with race—in their relationship and in the world more broadly—might be "too much" for Nancy. When I ask her what she means, she elaborates:

> Too much for Nancy as a person, as a White person—because I have said to her in the past, "Well, Nancy, you really have to think about whether or not you want to have this relationship. Because you know it's easier probably to be with a White woman where you don't have these things coming up, and I'm not the kind of person to be quiet about it. ... " It's complicated enough being in a same-sex relationship and then you throw in the race card. It can be exhausting. ... And I've said, "Are you ready for this?" And she pretty much says, "I love you, Nadine." That's what she says.

Nadine has been in several other relationships with White women, so these issues are not new to her. She has found that within intimate relationships, the considerable challenges of racism and homophobia amplify each other.

Other lesbian and gay partners also interpret issues of racial difference as compounded by sexual identity. For Vance Dalton, a White gay man introduced in chapter 3, visiting his partner Evan's family in Georgia brings up palpable tensions around both identities. Evan's family lives in an affluent suburb in a conservative, largely White community. His parents were initially uncomfortable with his sexuality, but both he and Vance agree that things have slowly gotten better. For instance, now, when Evan's mother calls, she sometimes asks to speak with Vance as well. Still, Vance characterizes the relationship between him and Evan's parents as strained. "I think for them it starts with us being gay, and it starts with us being two boys together. ... 'Okay, you're two boys.' That's really hard. And then you're going to be interracial, and that's really, really hard." Because his interpretation of what it means to be in a gay interracial relationship depends in part on social interactions with others, Vance, like Nadine, interprets both parts of his identity as shaping his relationship.

Sexuality Eclipses Racial Difference

Sexuality and interraciality do not represent equivalent or even comparable pressures for some lesbian and gay interracial partners. Instead, they suggest that the negative judgments attached to their sexual identity overwhelm the prejudice attached to being racially different. Based on cues they have picked up during social interactions in public places, these partners believe that if strangers recognize them as a couple, their non-normative sexuality elicits more attention than their racial difference. Or, as some partners succinctly put it, being gay or lesbian "trumps" being interracial. Both Black and White partners express this view. For Walter Belton-Davis and his White partner, Kirk Belton-Davis, who live just outside Philadelphia, "the interracial thing is really a back seat to the gay thing. The gay thing will always be more prevalent." Tara Hilliard, a Black lesbian living in Manhattan with her White partner, Kate Taurisano, would agree. "The fact that we're like, interracial … I don't think that's the most serious obstacle. … People would be like, 'Oh, they're gay,' [rather] than like 'Oh, she's White and she's Black.'" Shawn Tarwick also believes that when others recognize him and Daniel Embry as a couple, this identity eclipses all others. "I think the fact that we're gay and we are therefore outcasts … overshadows the fact that we're an interracial couple, and so they don't even get to that. It's like we're already *verboten*. … 'Pfft! They're gay.'"

Sexuality Diffuses Racial Difference

A smaller group of partners finds that possessing doubly marginalized identities—queer and interracial—makes it easier to form intimate connections. In describing intersections of race and sexuality, Sylvia Chabot (introduced in chapter 2) tells me that being socially excluded for being queer has its advantages. "There are ways I'm like it's totally normal, and in some ways more normal, to be an interracial queer couple [in the queer community]. … I don't know, but I think like in some ways when you feel outside of your community, it's easier to connect with someone." Maureen Wiley makes a similar assertion: "I actually think being queer might make [being interracial] easier. If you're queer, you're already fucked up. Like you're already weird. And so there's already something, there's something out of the ordinary that bonds you."

Although not all gay and lesbian partners experience intersections of sexuality and interraciality in the same manner, they are all marginalized in a social context that privileges heterosexuality, even interracial heterosexuality. Lesbian and gay respondents may disagree on the relative influence of sexuality and racial difference in shaping their experiences, but none of them draws on homosexuality as a symbolic resource. Unlike heterosexual partners, lesbian and gay partners in this study cannot tap into their sexual status to position themselves as normal, natural, or mundane. At the same time, because these respondents are not heterosexual, their unions do not evoke the same depth of cultural anxiety as do Black men with White women or Black women with White men.

Conclusion

Romantic partners in this study use racework to construct identities in the presence of negative images of interracial intimacy. In this chapter, I have examined how couples engage in boundary work to construct identities for themselves and for their relationships outside and apart from these images. To affirm their relationships as positive and legitimate, interracial partners erect boundaries to separate them from negative stereotypes and to blur boundaries that distinguish them from normative modes of intimacy.

Some of this boundary work addresses stereotypes about the type of person who enters an interracial relationship. Black partners are especially concerned with stereotypes about the cultural politics of interraciality. They erect exclusionary boundaries to differentiate themselves from the stereotype of the confused or "inauthentic" Black person who is trying to be White. By affirming their racial pride and critical politics, these partners construct a Black self that is not diminished by interracial intimacy. White partners, in contrast, are more concerned with longstanding racial-gender stereotypes that mark White interracial partners as trashy and immoral. Heterosexual White women are the most visible targets of this imagery, but other White partners also construct symbolic boundaries against the bundle of stereotypes associated with interracial intimacy.

Other forms of boundary work enable partners to more broadly disassociate themselves from negative notions of interracial intimacy. In other words, couples do boundary work on their joint, couple identity. Some partners employ colorblind language to separate themselves from presumed deviancy and to blur the distinctions between themselves and same-race couples. These partners explain that they don't "see race." Race is merely happenstance. Others disarm the specter of deviance by squarely acknowledging how race shapes everyday interactions, including intimate ones.

Sexuality too shapes partners' construction of intimacy. It mediates access to symbolic resources that diffuse racial judgments. Heterosexual partners are in a unique position to make appeals to heteronormative colorblindness, claims that they are "just a couple" or "just a man and a woman in love." These assertions help close the gap between them and same-race couples, emphasizing a shared normalcy. This brings up a tension that runs through these narratives—heterosexual Black/White couples receive more negative attention because of their racial difference, but they also have access to symbolic resources to shield them from this negativity. Put differently, heterosexual Black/White couples are particularly disadvantaged by their heterosexuality, but they are also uniquely rewarded by it.

In contrast, lesbian and gay partners generally do not claim that they are "just a couple." Even gays and lesbians who frame their relationship in colorblind terms do not have access to this additional resource with which to claim that their intimacy is normative. Instead, for lesbians and gays, sexuality compounds, eclipses, or diffuses racial difference in intimate relationships.

In this chapter and those that have preceded it, I have used interracial narratives to show four separate but related forms of racework in which Black/White partners engage. These stories point to when and in what ways racial difference is important. In the next chapter, I step away from the concept of racework and use insights from social-psychological research to explore how interracial intimacy shapes individual racial identities. This change in perspective allows us to examine the durability of racial orientations themselves.

CHAPTER 6 | White Racial Identities through the Lens of Interracial Intimacy

I'm very much empowered [as a White person] more so than [Mabel] is as an African American, as a Black woman in society. ... When we go to New Hampshire, we go through the whole summer and maybe see ten other Blacks, twenty at most. ... I'm surrounded by Whites. I think that's a problem for her. I don't *think*, I'm *sure* it is. ... They'll actually come up and want to get close to her and see her hair. But even that is hard, to be different. For me to be different is an exciting adventure. I'm the man, I'm strong. [In majority Black settings,] people look at me and think I'm a lawyer when I'm the only one in the room and I wear a tie; they thought I was a lawyer or elected official. I'm empowered greatly by my Whiteness, unfortunately; it's unhealthy and it doesn't feel good. It puts me on a level that I'm trying to get out of because I want to be on the same—I want to level with people. I want to communicate with folks.

WITH THESE WORDS, we can see that Hank Renault's racial orientation differs from the White racial habitus of most Whites in this study. A forty-five-year-old community activist and politician, Hank is also the White husband of Mabel Renault, an African American woman. The Renaults have been married for thirteen years and have three mixed-race children under ten years old.[1] The family lives in the same neighborhood where Hank grew up—a racially diverse community in a historically integrated area of Philadelphia.

Hank knows that he lives in a racially stratified society, but unlike many other Whites in my study, he understands that as a White man, he benefits from this stratified system. He explains: "When you are White you have a tremendous amount of power. ... That power ... play[s] such a role in how we trust one another and work together." He has no illusions that Whiteness is an invisible category. Intimate relationships with people of color have been crucial in helping Hank understand his own Whiteness. He has developed his critical perspective over time, through close friendships with African American men and his relationship with Mabel.

Hank's experience suggests that interracial intimacy has the potential to recast racial identity—not because he thinks of himself as something other than White, but because he has learned to think of his Whiteness differently than most Whites do. This raises important questions: Does interracial intimacy shape the racial identities of other White interracial partners in a similar manner? Does it have a similar effect on Black partners? The narratives of participants in this study show some of the ways in which individual racial identities are experienced in the context of interracial intimacy. Among Whites, intimacy has a varying influence on racial identity. For partners like Hank, intimacy strongly affects how they think of their own Whiteness; for other partners, it seems to have no influence; and for a third group, the effects fall somewhere in between.

Among African American partners, interracial intimacy has much less of an impact on racial identity. The heavy weight of social structure ensures that they think about their racial identity, whether they are in an interracial relationship or not. Most are reminded daily that being Black matters. It matters in how others see them and in the resources and spaces to which they have access. Yet Black partners have heterogeneous identifications with Blackness. There is considerable variability within the double-consciousness that characterizes Black racial habitus. The ability to see oneself as both a racial subject and a racial object is a defining feature of the racial orientation of African Americans in the United States, but the importance that individual Black respondents in this study attach to Black cultures and communities differs. Some Black partners have friendship networks made up almost exclusively of other African Americans or people of color, while others have social circles that are almost exclusively White. For both groups, however, interracial intimacy appears to have little impact on how they interpret their own Blackness. Among those with what identity researchers call "high-salience" identities, racial identity is too central to be shifted or swayed by their intimate relationship with a White person. Black respondents with "low-salience" identities may have been significantly influenced by interracial contact, but this effect often began during their youth rather than in an adult romantic partnership.[2] These respondents' close relationships with Whites over the course of a lifetime probably do influence how they think of their Blackness, but the effect each new relationship has on their racial identity is small.

I begin the analysis in this chapter by contextualizing White narratives within social-psychological research on Whiteness and then turn to an examination of the mixed impact that interracial intimacy has on White partners' racial identities. I focus the analysis on the racial identity of White partners in part because only Whites showed significant variation with respect to the influence of interracial intimacy on racial identity, and in part because that variability has significant potential consequences for theories that propose interracial contact as a means of gradually dissolving White racial prejudice. The narratives in this chapter offer an opportunity to examine more carefully that idea.

To explore how interracial intimacy shapes individual racial identities, I temporarily set aside the sociological concept of racework and use a social-psychological perspective. In this chapter, I analyze partners' experiences in terms of the concept of "identity," because this is the approach psychologists and social psychologists have used to understand how individuals think of their own Whiteness and Blackness. Although I connect this psychological perspective to the concept of racial habitus discussed in chapter 4, racial identity and racial habitus are not the same. When Pierre Bourdieu developed the concept of habitus, he envisioned a socially situated disposition, an orientation shaped by one's position in the social structure. Psychologists, in contrast, are more concerned with the steps and pathways individuals follow as they form their identities. Unlike Bourdieu, these researchers generally do not attempt to connect identity formation to larger questions of inequality. But making these connections between individual racial identities and broader racial structures is critical. As we see in this chapter, Whites' tendency to think of themselves as having no racial identity is typically coupled with an inability to see how Whiteness itself gives them resources and advantages that are unavailable to non-Whites. This pattern suggests that for most Whites in the United States, the formation of racial identity is deeply entwined with the persistence of systemic inequality.

Examining Whiteness

Sociologists of race and ethnicity have demonstrated that Whiteness is a clumsy category for classifying individuals from various European, Asian, and Middle-Eastern origins.[3] Like other racial categories, it includes persons of diverse ethnic origins, native tongues, and immigrant statuses. What unites generations of "Whites" are the everyday benefits and intergenerational advantages that come from being White in a White supremacist society. As I have shown, Whiteness embodies a position of both material and symbolic privilege mediated by social class status, gender, and sexuality, among other things. Most Whites, conditioned by a White racial habitus, do not feel that they inhabit a racial identity—they are "just human" (see chapter 4 for a discussion of racial habitus). Although Whites are afforded a common set of symbolic and structural privileges, this does not negate their heterogeneity.[4] There are multiple ways of interpreting, inhabiting, and performing Whiteness.

Sociological perspectives provide valuable insights into the social meanings of Whiteness by grounding it within a broader set of structural relationships. Social psychologists offer a different, but also useful, perspective that allows us to examine the specific processes by which racial identities develop and change. In the 1980s and 1990s, Janet Helms outlined what has become the most influential model in the area of White racial identity development. Her theories illustrate how Whites can move from a view of the world in which they are naturally superior toward a perspective that sees White dominance as the result of institutional and cultural racism. Helms's model shows how Whites can unlearn racism and develop a "positive" (i.e., nonracist) racial identity. [5]

For Helms, this movement from racism to nonracism is a linear process: Whites abandon individual racism, learn to recognize and oppose cultural and institutional racism, and develop a nonracist White identity. Her model has been critiqued and amended by others, but both it and the theories of subsequent researchers emphasize dissonance (the psychological discomfort that arises from trying to maintain two conflicting beliefs simultaneously) as an important factor in moving Whites from one type of racial thinking to another.[6] Helms argues that interracial contact undermines the assumption that Whites enjoy more resources (better homes, access to better education, more wealth) because they have worked harder than other racial groups and thus have earned those resources fairly. Because interracial contact is considered a primary cause of dissonance in racial understandings, it is seen as a necessary catalyst for the re-evaluation of old racial attitudes in light of new information and alternate racial perspectives.[7]

Helms's supposition that the juxtaposition of White and Black racial perspectives has the capacity to spur significant growth among White individuals resonates with later research on White antiracism. In her study of White antiracists, sociologist Eileen O'Brien shows that empathy can propel Whites toward a critical examination of race and racism.[8] Whites who develop close relationships with people of color may witness acts of discrimination firsthand or hear stories of racial suffering to which other Whites remain largely oblivious. These experiences can promote empathy, leading Whites to challenge White supremacy. Like identity theorists, O'Brien implicitly emphasizes the role of dissonance in moving Whites toward antiracist action. Subsequent research has shown that Whites can also be catalysts that move other Whites toward antiracism, and that not all people of color possess ideologies or experiences that create dissonance in the minds of Whites.[9]

White racial identity models make a powerful case for the potential of interracial contact to create the dissonance that motivates Whites to rethink racism. Yet many questions remain. The models do not specify what kind of contact is necessary to put this change into motion. Recent work on antiracism shows that not all interracial contact spurs Whites toward a critical consciousness. In the next section, I assess the attitudes of White partners in my study. Specifically, I examine whether interracial intimacy recasts these partners' sense of their own Whiteness and their racial attitudes in general. I describe three positions on a spectrum of White racial identities, spanning from one endpoint, in which Whiteness is rarely examined and its consequences are unexplored, to another, in which Whiteness is recognized and scrutinized. In the middle is a group of Whites who have progressed from not recognizing that they have a race, but who have not yet reached the critical awareness of race that Twine has termed "racial literacy."[10] I begin with partners whose Whiteness remains unexamined.

Whiteness as Usual: Interracial Intimacy and the Resilience of White Racial Identities

Among some White interracial partners, having a romantic relationship with an African American partner has little or no effect on the meanings or significance they attach to being White. This group's perspectives represent the "typical" or "default" mode of Whiteness discussed in sociological research on Whites in same-race relationships or families.[11] In their everyday lives, Whites in this group are rarely conscious of being White. For them, Whiteness is an invisible, empty category. African Americans and other people of color have a race; Whites are just people. Kirk Belton-Davis provides an example. Kirk and his Black partner, Walter Belton-Davis, live outside of Philadelphia. Walter's description of his relationship to Kirk provides the opening to this book. When we first met, Kirk and Walter were one year shy of their twenty-fifth anniversary. Kirk was raised in Philadelphia in a middle-class Irish-Catholic family. He is one of six children. Growing up he did well in school—he refers to his younger self as an "egghead"—and played sports. He hated high school, though, because he already knew he was gay and felt that he did not fit in. He came out the first semester of college and met Walter through friends two years later.

When I ask Kirk about his racial identity, he asserts that of all the ways in which he thinks of himself, his Whiteness is the least meaningful. "I'm a gay male who happens to be White. That would be how I identify myself. … I think it's cool that I have that Irish background, that my grandmother came from Ireland, but I identify as gay first, male second, and White third." Like others in this category, Kirk experiences his Whiteness as a low-salience identity, or what is sometimes termed a "thin" identity.[12] He knows he is White, but this identity is not something that he feels shapes his social activities, social networks, or daily interactions. In contrast, he experiences his sexual identity as directly influencing whom he spends time with and how he organizes his life.

Yet there is a tension in Kirk's description of the relevance (or irrelevance) of race in his relationship. On the one hand, he describes race as a "nonissue" in his life with Walter. He sometimes thinks of his relationship as a raceless space.

> [I have] no cognizance of my racial makeup being with him at all. … Only if [I was] out at the bar and there were other non-Whites there I would be aware of the fact that I'm a White guy. If we were hanging around his family a bit, it would come to my mind, you know something that floats to the front and back. But in my day-to-day existence with him, not at all.

Like other Whites in my study, Kirk feels his Whiteness mostly when he is in the presence of people of color. Recognizing their racial status, he is reminded of his own, especially when his race places him in the minority. In most other settings, however, his Whiteness is invisible to him. At the same time, and in seeming contradiction to his insistence that race is not relevant in his relationship with Walter, Kirk admits that his sexual preferences are racialized. During their decades-long relationship, he and Walter have gone through periods of non-monogamy, and both speak openly about the kind of people to whom they are attracted. Kirk tells me candidly that he prefers young African American men who are "smooth" and "lean"; he says Walter is almost exclusively attracted to White, blond-haired men.

When I ask Kirk about these racialized desires, he explains that "I don't have a problem with it. I mean you can't help who you are attracted to."

Kirk seems to be aware of this duality in how he interprets racial difference. In one sense it is irrelevant, but in another, it is part of his desire for Walter and for the other Black partners he has had:

> I guess part of me thinks like maybe interracial couples are more advanced socially than other couples. We were able to get beyond something so meaningless. I had no choice being Irish and White or male, I had no choice. It's such a nonissue—even though in everyday [life] I know it's not a nonissue. I just kind of live my life like it is. Yet I'm mostly attracted to people of color. So it isn't a complete nonissue.

The inconsistencies in Kirk's perspective are less stark if we consider not *whether* or *when* he sees race, but *how* he interprets it. For him, it is one kind of commodity in a sexual marketplace—something to be appraised, exchanged, and consumed. It is an aesthetic quality, just like being tall or muscular are aesthetic qualities. All are types of social currency with a particular exchange value. Kirk sees Whiteness as a form of capital not because of the material and symbolic privileges Whites are afforded through White supremacy, but because Whiteness has particular value in a sexual market where individuals seek and offer specific characteristics. As aesthetic commodities, the value of both Whiteness and Blackness depend upon who is seeking what in a given sexual market. Viewing race in transactional terms leads him to focus on the exchange of pleasure between two equal actors. Kirk cannot see his desire for Walter and other Black men as part of a long history in which Whites have eroticized and exotified men and women of African, Asian, and Native American descent. Though he clearly understands race as a commodity, he does not perceive the commodification of racialized "Otherness" as a form of racism.[13] In my study, gay men were not the only partners whose sexual preferences were distinctly racialized, but as a group, they were the most likely to express these desires explicitly.

It is notable that Kirk and other White partners who eroticize racial difference do so without fear that this desire for Blackness might reflect self-loathing or a rejection of their racial group. White partners do not appear to wrestle with how interracial intimacy affects their claim to an "authentic" White identity; nor do they struggle with whether their love for an African American might symbolize a latent conflict within their own self-concept.

Another characteristic of Whites in this group is a reluctance to talk about race. This often stems from the belief that being White means having no race. Laurie Lewis, for example, is ill at ease talking about race, especially when it comes to articulating what it means to be White. Laurie is a forty-four-year-old White lesbian; her Black partner is thirty-eight-year-old Kayla Carson (both were introduced in chapter 3). Laurie grew up in a middle-class family in a small town in Virginia that she refers to as a "professional hippy enclave." She had her first sexual experience with a woman in college; she has had a few relationships with men since then. She refers to herself as a lesbian and describes herself as "butch"—a term that describes not only her gender presentation but also her attraction to traditionally "feminine" women.

During our initial phone conversation, Laurie tells me that she has her "share of White guilt." When we meet, I ask her to expand on that.

> Being really sort of super-conscientious about what I say. ... Not wanting to say the wrong thing and offend somebody; not wanting to have my racial prejudice come into play. ... I think that being with Kayla has helped me be a little easier with that.

After being with Kayla for three years, Laurie has become somewhat more comfortable talking about race. But she confesses that even as recently as a year ago, she would have been too "uptight" to take part in the kind of interview in which we were then engaged.

Part of Laurie's unease comes from an awareness of her own prejudices and a fear that others will recognize them. But she also feels that her Whiteness does not imbue her experiences with any real authority when it comes to everyday racial conversations. Because she is White, she is not an "authentic" racial subject. "I don't have Black experience. I kind of follow Kayla's lead [in conversations about race] and sometimes I don't say anything because I haven't formed an opinion or haven't allowed myself to form an opinion." Even in intimate social settings with friends, when race comes up in conversation, Laurie is likely to just listen. The perception that she lacks the authority to speak about race may stem from her tendency to view Whiteness as an abstraction. Laurie says that she sees Whiteness "not as an individual but sort of [a] political" matter. As other scholars of Whiteness have suggested, White partners like Laurie often deny their own racial perspective because, as members of the dominant racial group, they do not think they "have" a race.[14] Within this logic, normative categories become invisible. Only people of color have a race, just as only women have a gender, and only lesbians and gays have a sexual orientation.

When I ask about her experiences as a White person, Laurie describes Whiteness as more of an absence than a presence, an empty category in want of a culture or history:

> I sometime feel I don't have a sense of like my heritage … like [I'm] identity-less or—not identity-less. … I basically know where our family came from, someone has done our genealogy. … Sometimes I think if I was like Latino or if my grandmother came over from El Salvador [or if] I could trace my roots back to some African country, I would have more of a sense of who I am. … Is that [being] White or just not knowing my genealogy?

The underlying assumption here is that Laurie's identity as a White person with European heritage is mundane or bland in comparison to ancestry that originates in South America or Africa. Here Whiteness is stigmatized for precisely the traits that mark its dominant position as the status quo—it is boringly normative.[15] This view may also be connected to Laurie's sense that White people do not "have" a race, or in this case—ethnicity. It also may derive from a common stereotype that people of color have more life experience or live life more intensely.[16]

Despite feeling that she has no formal opinions or authority to speak about race, Laurie is aware of the advantages afforded to Whites as a group. She tells me that the only time she feels White is "when I am a part of some group that is either privileged or … is associated with a group that has oppressed other people." But for Laurie it is easier to see Whiteness as a group identity than as an attribute she benefits from in her daily life. The failure to see their own position in the racial hierarchy is characteristic of Whites at this end of the spectrum of White racial consciousness.

Kirk and Laurie are part of a large group of White interracial partners. Nearly half of the White partners in my study did not view interracial intimacy as a spur to re-examine or reconsider their own experiences of Whiteness. Instead, their narratives reflect fundamental characteristics of a White racial identity. Kirk's account draws attention to the invisibility of Whiteness for many who possess it. Whites often become conscious of having a race only in the presence of people of color. Additionally, Kirk interprets Whiteness (and Blackness) as an aesthetic quality, devoid of material or symbolic value. Laurie's comments capture the uneasiness that many Whites experience articulating a White racial perspective and show Whites' tendency to deny that their race is imbued with cultural or historical substance. Both partners fail to see that they benefit from the same racial system that marginalizes people of color.

Discovering Whiteness through Blackness: Moving toward a Critical Lens

For a second group of White respondents, interracial intimacy has prompted the beginnings of a new racial perspective. These partners comprehend that African Americans and other people of color are disadvantaged by White supremacy, and they are starting to see how their own Whiteness confers benefits. This understanding falls short of that found among partners in the racial literacy category that I introduce shortly, but it does reflect forward movement. Nancy Taylor is an example of Whites in the intermediate group. Nancy and her Black partner, Nadine Allen, live in Washington, D.C. Both were introduced in previous chapters. Nancy grew up in Missouri, in a "very well-off" family. She attended a racially mixed public grade school, and her mother was part of the "desegregation force" in their school district. By ninth grade, however, her parents had moved her to a private high school. She describes her high school self as "boy crazy"; she began having relationships with women during her last year of college. When she came out, she "threw [herself] into it," attending radical protests and "those outrageous things." She remains conscious of certain privileges of heterosexuality, such as being able to kiss enthusiastically in public without being harassed, and she chafes when people "read" her as straight because of her traditionally feminine appearance.

Even before meeting Nadine, Nancy was sensitive to racial issues. She recalls being confused by personal ads that describe an ideal match in great detail but also state that "race is not important." This, she feels, does not indicate openness; it shows an unawareness of the significance of race. "It's an important aspect of the person. It's key. ... So when I placed an ad once, I said 'any race' because I thought that was more appropriate. ... "

Yet even with some understanding of race's significance, before her relationship with Nadine, Nancy had only an abstract notion of the everyday realities of anti-Black racism. Now racial inequality is real. She describes an incident that made her "upset" and "angry." Note that she includes herself among the "Black folks" as she tells me this story.

> We were with [Nadine's] nieces who are both Black and we went to this pizza place down the road which is in a White neighborhood. ... We were the only Black folks in there. ... Well we waited and we waited and we

waited and we waited and we waited and we waited and then Nadine went up to the bar and got us menus. And we waited and we waited and we waited and we waited. "Can we have some water?" "Just a minute we're in between shifts." ... But all these guys sitting at the bar are being served. ... It was like five o'clock on a Saturday afternoon in the summer. ... They gave us like plastic cups with no ice. No ice ... I was just like, "Oh, my God," and Nadine looked at me and said, "We're leaving. This is just unacceptable." So we walked out and wrote letters to the manager and filed with the Justice Department.

Subjecting people of color to indignity and disrespect in restaurants or other public settings is a common form of everyday discrimination. Indeed, for middle-class African Americans like Nadine, incidents of this kind are not-so-subtle reminders that their economic privilege does not shield them from racism. Yet Nancy was taken aback by Nadine's reaction. Usually "tough as nails," Nadine was "so upset about the girls having to experience that." Nancy describes her own incredulousness. "I couldn't believe it. I thought that kind of stuff was a myth. ... There are like all these sorts of things that I thought were myths but I'm finding out are not. ... I knew of some of it like with the [difficulty hailing] taxis. ... But this was the first time I had really experienced it firsthand. ... It had never happened to me before like that. I'm guessing this is not the first time Nadine has experienced this."

Nancy's earlier supposition that racial discrimination was largely a "myth" or an exaggerated perception of reality resonates with the way that many Whites think about racial issues. Recall Keith Fischer, for instance. Keith (introduced in chapter 4) is a White gay man in his mid-sixties who takes a historical interest in race but brushes off contemporary claims of racism as manifestations of a "victim complex." Witnessing everyday discrimination with her own eyes created dissonance with Nancy's then-current racial worldview. Her old racial framework could not account for these new, firsthand observations. This dissonance has propelled Nancy away from comfortable assumptions about discrimination as "myth" toward a more critical racial consciousness. But she is not fully there yet.

Like others in this middle group, Nancy is beginning to understand the privilege embodied in Whiteness, but she cannot quite see herself as a recipient of these benefits. She can recognize Whiteness most easily as it is embodied in the young, heterosexual women at the local bus stop. "I go to the bus stop and I'm surrounded by White girls in pink skirts and pink, pointed-toe like high heels." She is disdainful of their designer handbags (her own designer bag, she explains, is from a thrift store), "cute little clothes," and group shopping trips. Nancy connects these women's White-ness to an economic status she has disavowed. But she also associates their racial privilege with their heterosexual status. She says, "In my mind, they go together." She continues, "I don't really, I'm a White girl, but I don't really, I'm not a White girl. ... I'm a dyke. I don't think dykes could nec-essarily be White girls." Because she sees Whiteness connected to social identities with which she no longer identifies—economic affluence and heterosexuality—she has renounced it.

Unlike Laurie and Kirk, Nancy identifies Whiteness as a form of social power. However, she cannot yet perceive herself as wielding this power or as being implicated in its workings. Her relationship with Nadine has enabled her to develop a more critical perspective, but she is still learning to see herself as a part of the racial system that surrounds her.

Ulrich Drescher shares this middle position with Nancy. Ulrich (intro-duced in chapter 3) is a White gay man who was born and grew up in a small city in Germany. Now a forty-three-year-old college professor, he was twenty-five when he had his first serious relationship with another man. Ten years later, he moved to Michigan to pursue postgraduate work in chemistry. He met his Black partner, Marvin Nelson (introduced in chapter 5), seven years ago. They live in an old Victorian house in Phila-delphia.

Interracial intimacy has enabled Ulrich to see race differently. Ongoing conversations with Marvin have reshaped Ulrich's perspective on race and racism in the United States. For example, when the two men were house-hunting in Michigan, Marvin asked the real estate agent not to reveal his race to potential sellers, explaining to Ulrich that racial discrimination had to be anticipated. Ulrich has begun to internalize some of Marvin's insights. He explains, "I learned a lot of things through Marvin. ... I begin to look through his eyes and I see things even if he doesn't point it out to me. And it is very upsetting." Seeing the world through the racial lens of his Black partner reveals relations of privilege that Ulrich previously had not considered. "The more that you hear, the more you ... sort of lose your innocence about things."

When Whites in this category examine race critically, they begin to read the racial dynamics of social settings in a new way. Ulrich is learning to think of himself not only as a racial *subject*, but also as a racial *object*. This is akin to the double-consciousness that characterizes Blacks' racial habitus. Ulrich now anticipates how his Whiteness will be perceived by others in various social settings. He considers how the status embodied in his Whiteness shapes his social interactions. The racial dynamics at his workplace present opportunities to practice this critical analysis:

> You know, a lot of our security forces are African American, so now I can pick up on how it is different. ... To them I am a White guy, relatively high up in the pecking order, so that I can feel that they are treating me different. ... Each party can set up a relationship to become somehow influenced by race. It is not that both have to agree on, "Let's make this a racial issue." Either side can do that. So I can see how people can have issues. Everyone has issues here.

Ulrich now realizes that his Whiteness confers status, which is a form of social power. And yet, he does not *feel* powerful. It makes him uneasy to think that his Whiteness may be central to how others look at him. He tells me, "I think about myself as other things [besides White]." When I ask him about feeling conscious of himself as a White person, he says, "I don't like it if it happens because it feels so not me. ... Like someone else's expectation may influence how I feel about me. ... I realize in comparison or in someone else's eyes I am like the White person. It is not like we can ignore that." As we continue talking, he likens this reluctant acknowledgment of racial privilege to a realization he has had as an international traveler in developing nations. He tells me:

> You travel to a third-world country and you realize that people look at you as rich, because you are. In that sort of comparison and that relationship, you *are* rich because you could travel there and they can't travel to your country. So in that sense you are. And that is the same kind of thing. The moment that happens, that someone approaches you as that rich foreigner, it is not like you can pretend you aren't.

Ulrich's comparison between racial status and economic status is telling in that it positions both forms of power as obvious in one type of setting and invisible in another. International travelers from first-world nations may not feel wealthy in their everyday lives, but in a more global context, their relative affluence is undeniable. Similarly, his own Whiteness is always with him, but it is only in the context where others cannot claim that same status that he must reckon with its meaning. Likening White privilege to being "rich" also demonstrates his growing, if still reluctant, awareness that Whiteness is a form of racial capital.

It may be significant that Ulrich is learning about how race works in the United States from the vantage point of a White man from Germany. He views himself as "fortunate" to have grown up in Europe because it spared him from the "baggage" that Americans have around race. He acknowledges that this "doesn't mean that I don't have prejudice," but he positions himself as "different." In talking about his relationship to race and racism in Germany, he slips back into portraying Whiteness as invisible. He does not view the dominant Whiteness of his hometown or schooling as having any racial character. He explains, "When we go to high school in Germany, we learn English and they touch on these things but it is so theoretical. ... The whole race issue is what you read in a book or a teacher tells you about it. ... Then you come here and it is happening." For Ulrich, "the whole race issue" is symbolized by racial difference and interracial conflict. Like Whites in U.S. suburbs, he cannot see race "happening" in his small hometown. Looking back, he fails to perceive the Whiteness of his grade schools and everyday local environment. As Ulrich continues to develop a critical lens, he may begin to interpret his past through his new perspective. For now, his ability to identify Whiteness in some situations but not in others reflects his intermediate location in the range of White racial consciousness.

Interracial intimacy has enabled Nancy and Ulrich and other partners who occupy the middle zone on the continuum of White racial identities to witness everyday racism, to think more carefully about their partners' experience of Blackness, and to reflect upon their own White racial identities. These partners are in the beginning stages of a process of social learning and are starting to develop a form of double-consciousness that will enable them to see themselves through the racial gaze of others.

Transforming Racial Habitus, Cultivating Racial Literacy

Bourdieu's notion of habitus rightly emphasizes the commonalities in "schemes of perception, thought, and action" that create classes of people. His model has been justly criticized, however, for theorizing social reproduction as nearly impervious to change. We may make use of Bourdieu's insights but also note patterns of exception that his concept of habitus does not fully acknowledge. Sometimes people establish dispositions that are quite different from those typical of their class. For example, some White partners in my study have pushed beyond White racial habitus. They have developed the kind of critical racial stance that

France Winddance Twine calls "racial literacy."[17] Based on her research in the United Kingdom on White mothers and their children of African descent, Twine conceptualized racial literacy as an umbrella term that includes the cultural strategies and practices parents employ to equip their children with important racial sensibilities and a positive self-identity. This concept has been extended in later work to describe how some White partners in interracial relationships develop a racial vision akin to double-consciousness.[18]

Take, for instance, Norma Tanner, a heterosexual White woman in her mid-forties. She is married to Myron Tanner, a fifty-year-old Black man (the Tanners were introduced in chapter 3). They have been a couple for fourteen years and married for five. When I meet Norma, she and Myron are living in a small city not far from Manhattan. Norma tells me that she grew up in "a little bit rural" working-class town in upstate New York. She describes her family as "very simple country folk," noting that her brother is a "closeted bigot" and her father is "Archie Bunker personified." But Norma feels that she has always been a little different. She explains:

> I've always been more open-minded and always wanted to get out of that life that they all wanted to stay in. The small town life, just stay in that area, get jobs there, you know? I always wanted out. I always wanted bigger and better. I wanted to travel. I wanted to meet people. ... I've always been interested in other cultures and people who are different. ... I just wasn't close-minded. ... I never ever felt that White is better.

Her intimate relationship with Myron has furthered the process of opening Norma's mind by giving her access to an insider's perspective on how racial stratification operates in the United States. She observes the daily forms of discrimination enacted upon people of color, especially the way that racism limits Myron's options as the owner of a construction company.

> All of the prejudice that there still is in the world, and you know, if Myron's trying to get a certain job, get a certain contract, and they find out he's Black, I mean I don't know how many times he's lost contracts because they found out he was Black. They hear him over the phone, they look at his résumé, "Oh, you're great, you're the best." And then when they find out he's Black, like if he goes to towns, like lily-White towns, like Storch or somewhere, and tries to get a job, um, and it just doesn't matter how good his résumé is.[19] He's Black and that's that.

Developing a close relationship with a Black person has directly exposed Norma to the reality of racial injustice and everyday racism and has fundamentally changed how she relates to the reality of racial hostility and marginalization. She explains, "I never really was aware of the prejudice. I mean I was, in the sense that I heard my father making racial remarks, but it never really affected me until I fell in love with someone that experienced it. Then I saw it firsthand—that was very different. I just, it just started opening up my eyes, slowly but surely." Norma shares in Myron's anger and frustration, almost as if this discrimination were happening to her. She is also saddened. She tells me that her "heart breaks for him." Hearing stories of everyday racism or witnessing it firsthand are common ways for Whites to establish empathy with people of color.

Like others who develop racial literacy, Norma has also worked to recognize that she profits from the same racial system that disadvantages Myron. In describing social interactions she has as a teacher at a preschool program for low-income families, the majority of whom are Black, Norma notes the effects of her Whiteness. She flinches as she talks about how she is treated with noticeably more respect than the two West Indian women who assist her in the classroom. She believes that their expertise is disregarded and her status elevated, not only because they are her assistants, but also because she is White:

> The parents ... they all want to speak with me, you know, if [my assistant] answers the phone, "No, I want to speak to the teacher. I want to speak to Miss Norma," you know, um, it's weird. I'm uncomfortable with it. You know, I don't want them to treat me like that or look at me like I'm just so superior. I mean [my assistant] for God sakes was a third-grade teacher in her country for twenty-three years. And here she is, her credentials didn't transfer, and she's an assistant at [this program]. You know, she's way more educated and experienced than I am. ... And um, you know, I can't say for sure if that's their attitude, you know, White is right or superior. But that's what it appears to be.

These new insights and emotions have changed Norma's racial perspective. She tells me, "Sometimes I feel like I'm impersonating a White woman." Interpreting race and racism with a critical lens has made it more difficult to relate to people with whom she used to be close.

> I told Myron, I joked one time. I said, you know, "You've ruined my whole life. You've shattered my lily-white world." Now I have to go around, it's

affected all my friendships because, because I'm so aware now of racial tension and prejudice, I want everyone to feel it. I want everyone to know it. And my [White] girlfriends don't. They haven't experienced it. And it's really affected my relationship with my best friend to the extent that I no longer even consider her my best friend because she's just so close-minded about things.

Norma acknowledges some ambivalence about her newly acquired perspective. She sees pieces of her old self in the racial disposition of her friends and recognizes that being able to ignore the enormity of racial suffering is a privilege of Whiteness. "It's not that it's a negative thing; it's just that I'm aware of it. I'll never be the same again. I'll never—I kind of look at it as a good and a bad thing. I mean, sometimes ignorance is bliss." Racial "ignorance" is a critical element of a White habitus. It spares Whites the discomfort of acknowledging that they are granted unearned advantages in our racial system. Clinging to this ignorance spares Whites from dealing with feelings of guilt or anger, and from a responsibility for trying to dismantle the system that privileges them.

For some White partners, including Leslie Cobbs, parenthood necessitates racial empathy. Leslie (introduced with her partner in chapter 2) describes herself as "passionate, overly responsible, intellectual, and kind of insecure." She met Sylvia Chabot, her African American partner, at a queer student conference seven years ago. They live together in a predominantly Black neighborhood in New York City.

Five months after I first met Leslie and Sylvia, Sylvia became pregnant through alternative insemination. By definition, this approach to creating a family gives partners some influence over how their child will be racialized. For same-race couples, the process of choosing a donor from their racial group may be so automatic that it does not register as a "choice."[20] Yet for interracial couples like Sylvia and Leslie, selecting a White donor so their child would be "mixed" was a deliberate decision. They had long discussions about whether to choose a Black or a White sperm donor. Ultimately, they decided to use the sperm from a self-identified White man because they "felt like it was important that the baby be both races."

Leslie has shifted her racial lens as she anticipates becoming the transracial mother of what she calls "a child of color." Part of this process involves the emotional labor of educating herself through reading and extensive conversations with others. "I mean, I think it's going to be um, challenging you know, I feel like um, you know there are ways in which it calls for me to be able to like hold both perspectives as much as possible.

Like I mean obviously I am a White person and that's my life experience, but to also be thinking all the time about how is, how is whatever is happening affecting my child as a child of color." Leslie explains that she has always been attuned to other people's feelings and opinions, but since becoming involved with Sylvia, her racial awareness has grown "more sophisticated." She also notes that being gay adds "a layer of sensitivity," further necessitating a careful reading of the dynamics of social spaces.

Leslie is not alone in building on one type of critical perspective to create another. Indeed, this tendency to develop multiple modes of empathy, or multiple literacies, may account for why fully half of the White lesbians in my study developed racial literacy, more than any other group. This finding mirrors other research that finds individuals whose identities fall along several lines of oppression to be heavily represented among antiracist or progressive Whites.[21]

Conclusion

The narratives in this chapter have shown that interracial intimacy facilitates significant racial identity changes for some White partners. Among those who developed racial literacy, intimacy with a Black partner pushed them to think differently about race and their own Whiteness. It enabled them to see their own Whiteness through the eyes of others and engendered a more critical racial stance. It did not erase the benefits of being White or make their Whiteness less meaningful, but it allowed them to see their race more clearly. This kind of racial reorientation is what many social scientists would expect. Theories of White racial identity assume that interracial intimacy creates dissonance that presses Whites to develop a new racial lens. Contact theory predicts that close relationships across racial lines enable Whites to unlearn many of their prejudices and cultivate new perspectives. Yet White respondents who have this transformative experience are firmly in the minority in my study (constituting less than a quarter of all White respondents).

If we assume that interracial intimacy can create racial dissonance, then it is striking how little interracial intimacy changes some Whites' racial perspectives. Half of the White respondents treated their own race as meaningless, an empty category. This is not to suggest that these White partners had special prejudices or were in less loving relationships. It simply means that being very close to an African American partner did not change their perspectives on race or their awareness of their own Whiteness. There are several ways we might account for this pattern. First, like their Black counterparts, White partners enter interracial relationships with various interpretations about what it means to be White. Some have been active in political organizing or other activities in which their Whiteness has been made visible to them. Some also may have developed a critical way of thinking about race as part of contending with sexism, homophobia, or other forms of social inequality. Second, the stability of most Whites' feelings about Whiteness may reflect the inertia of dominant White identities. Most Whites develop their racial orientations, or racial habitus, early in life. Racial segregation prevents many Whites from establishing the interracial contact that might make them see Whiteness as a particular kind of racial identity, instead of as the absence of one. Further, the way Whites often talk about race—a White woman who writes for a newspaper is a "journalist," while a Black woman with that same job is a "Black journalist"—reproduces the invisibility of Whiteness, as do a multitude of media images.[22] It may take more than a single interpersonal relationship to change these deeply rooted attitudes. Third, as Black and White racial identities are variable, so too are the dynamics of racial difference within the relationship. Between White and Black partners who see race in a similar manner, interaction produces little dissonance. If perceptions of racial difference itself change from couple to couple, then not all experiences of racial difference will create the dissonance crucial to racial change.

In this chapter, I moved beyond the concept of racework to explore how interracial intimacy shapes individual racial orientations. In the final chapter, I return to some of the broad questions that sparked this study and explore what experiences of interracial intimacy can tell us about contemporary racial politics in the United States.

Conclusion: The Intimate Politics of Interraciality

PART OF THE CHALLENGE of examining interracial narratives is to nest all the ways in which racial difference matters within all the ways that it does not. The couples in this study share many qualities besides being Black/White. They experience the daily comforts of domestic life—of waking up next to the same person each day, of hanging up winter jackets in the same closet, and separating endless pairs of socks and underwear. I heard eighty-two accounts of how partners met. I was proudly shown dozens of photographs of weddings and commitment ceremonies—from formal events with black tuxedos and long, white wedding gowns to a vegan circus party with kazoos and candy. I heard stories that reflected bonds of trust, compassion, respect, admiration, and attraction, as well as occasional stories of jealousy and exasperation. The partners in this study have shared major life successes—the birth of children, the completion of educational degrees, the celebration of twenty-year anniversaries, the successful launch of a new business, and the celebration of religious conversions—as well as the more regular joys of everyday life—eating meals together, spending time with friends and family, laughing over stupid jokes, and simply enjoying each other's companionship. They have also faced some of the most difficult moments, as loved ones have died, divorced, or struggled with substance addiction.

The old but nevertheless enduring stereotype paints interracial partners as people who confuse racial exoticism for love. This hollow assumption does not characterize the interracial partners in this study. The women and men I met represent a wide variation within intimate relationships today. Some interracial partners, both heterosexual and same-sex, live lives as settled and traditional as any that could be found in heteronormative, middle-class America. They own houses in city or suburban neighborhoods and greet neighbors as they walk their dogs. Others embrace a queer sensibility in which racial difference is but one non-normative element of their relationship. These partners express their gender in nontraditional ways, are activists in their communities, or are experimenting with non-monogamy. Some partners deny that race plays any role in their sexual desires, whereas others openly describe their sexual attraction to people of different racial groups. Regardless of these relationship characteristics, the couples I interviewed have deep intimate connections, some lasting over twenty-five years.

Yet being interracial is significant. "I think that people in interracial relationships give up something, you know, give up an ease about living in some ways. ... Just, like, living without thinking about [race] in the same, in the same way." This is how Leslie Cobbs described her experience of eight years in a lesbian interracial relationship with her Black partner, Sylvia Chabot. Like many other interracial partners, Leslie's relationship has affected her life in broad ways—where she lives, how she thinks about motherhood, and her relationship with her family and her in-laws. It has also shaped her life in more specific, everyday sorts of ways—how she feels walking with her partner through their neighborhood and on other streets in New York City, how people interact with them as a couple, and what kinds of daily events they discuss after work and during dinner.

Interracial unions are still relatively unusual in the United States, especially those between Blacks and Whites. This rarity holds both for same-sex partnerships like Leslie and Sylvia's and for heterosexual unions. Yet some of the challenges these couples face reflect racial realities that are quite common for many Americans. Racial segregation in many city and suburban neighborhoods forces interracial couples to either pursue a (sometimes elusive) racially mixed environment or choose between living in a majority-White or majority-Black area. As one respondent succinctly stated, "[N]o matter where we live, one of us is going to be not in the right neighborhood." This segregation on city blocks and neighborhood streets bleeds into a homogeneity of other social spaces—schools, churches, families, lesbian/gay bars, and friendship circles. As interracial couples go about their everyday lives, they must often navigate racial boundaries along which partners alternate between insider-ness and outsider-ness.

For Leslie and Sylvia, the simple fact of their racial difference is significant in a context where interracial intimacy is both infrequent and disparaged, and where Whiteness is often symbolically and materially privileged over Blackness. As lesbian partners, their experiences of interraciality often differ from those of individuals who are in heterosexual Black/White relationships and sometimes differ from those of Black/White gay partners as well. The way they feel their intimacy to be profoundly unrecognized in public spaces is one such example. Leslie recounted how "gross" she feels when men approach her and Sylvia on the street and begin flirting with Sylvia, unable to see the women's intimate connection. Gay men also sometimes feel invisible, although they are more likely to expect that others will recognize them as romantic partners. Heterosexuals, on the other hand, are considerably more likely to assume that their intimacy is obvious to all onlookers. Other commonplace challenges that Leslie and Sylvia face are very similar to those faced by heterosexual and gay interracial partners. Together they must navigate the ups and downs of domestic life, though they possess racial worldviews that sometimes conflict. The contours of these convergences and divergences between heterosexual and same-sex interracial couples are meaningful because they show how sexual status shapes people's experiences in a racially stratified social system.

Understanding how interracial partners maintain intimate relationships across systems of stratification and how sexuality and gender affect these experiences provides an important glimpse into the contemporary relevance of racial boundaries in the United States at the beginning of the twenty-first century. In this final chapter, I reflect on the sociological meaning of these interracial stories by briefly focusing our attention backward, so that we might view our times in light of what has come just before. I then revisit the book's central argument and offer some concluding observations about intimacy and social structure.[1]

Interracial Biographies in Context

The interracial partners in this study live in a historical moment in which significant racial progress has been made in legal, political, and social realms. Until the 1960s, racial divisions in American life were sharply defined and protected by law. The same racial segregation and discrimination that characterized public places such as churches, hospitals, restaurants, and hotels also created barriers in employment. Although World War II had allowed African American civilians to enter semiskilled and skilled blue-collar professions from which they had previously been excluded, when White veterans and other White workers poured into urban areas after the war, African Americans were displaced and returned to lower-paying, less-skilled positions. By 1962, Black workers had an unemployment rate three times that of Whites.[2] Residential neighborhoods were also starkly segregated. Postwar government programs created opportunities for veterans to buy homes, but discriminatory lending practices and restrictive neighborhood covenants effectively excluded African Americans from taking advantage of these opportunities.[3] Americans' intimate lives were also shaped by racial divisions. As late as the mid-1960s, heterosexual interracial marriage remained illegal in sixteen states.[4]

By the mid-1960s, decades of legal efforts and political organizing forced important changes in America's social landscape. The 1964 Civil Rights Act extended desegregation policy to employment, federally funded programs, and public accommodations. A few years later, Congress enacted the Fair Housing Act, prohibiting the discriminatory housing and lending practices that had created Black inner cities and White suburbs.[5] Limitations on marriage were lifted in 1967 by the Supreme Court's *Loving v. Virginia* ruling. Landmark court cases and legislation represented the hard-won victories of African American leaders and laypeople alike. We live in a different world now. Yet even these successes represent only a partial attainment of the equality and racial justice that civil rights organizers envisioned.

In the early twenty-first century, the United States continues to be troubled by deeply entrenched racial inequalities. In this book I have provided a glimpse into how these racial structures shape interracial lives, but other researchers have documented these broad patterns in much greater detail. As a group, Blacks earn far less money per year than Whites. The typical income for Blacks, as measured by the median, is $32,500, compared with almost $54,500 for Whites.[6] But income figures capture only part of the story; they tell us how much someone earns. A much more stable measure of a person's financial standing is wealth. Wealth tells us about assets, how many resources a person has wrapped up in a home or other financial investments. The racial disparity in wealth is stark. The net worth of a typical Black family is only $5,700, compared with $113,000 for Whites. That means Black families hold only five cents for every dollar held by White families.[7] Part of this racial wealth gap comes from much higher rates of homeownership among Whites. Research shows that Black homebuyers continue to be discriminated against in the housing market. Regardless of their income, African Americans are more likely than Whites to receive riskier, subprime mortgages from nonregulated institutions.[8] As I have argued, Americans continue to live in racially segregated communities, and Blacks remain the most racially segregated group.[9] Because public schools educate children from surrounding neighborhoods, racially homogeneous communities create racially homogeneous schools. Over 35 percent of Black children go to schools in which between 90 and 100 percent of the students are children of color.[10] Racial disparities also shape Americans' likelihood of going to prison. African Americans are incarcerated at more than five times the rate of Whites. The lifetime risk of a prison term for Black young men is approaching 33 percent.[11] Once young Black men have criminal records, their job prospects plummet.[12]

Yet even in the presence of these profound disparities, over 40 percent of Americans do not consider racism an important social problem.[13] Some point to the election of a Black president as evidence that race and racism are ghosts of a racial past. Some suggest we have reached a turning point in race relations and that we are in the dawn of a postracial era.[14] In this social context, interracial intimacy is increasingly seen as a symbol of racial healing. Some people now believe that the tensions and conflicts that have long plagued interracial contact between groups can be smoothed by the bonds of empathy and trust that form within intimate romantic relationships. Further, the capacity of heterosexual interracial couples to produce children of mixed racial ancestry is thought to insure the blurring of racial divisions.[15] In this way, interracial intimacy and multiracial families are together framed as a positive sign of a less conflicted racial future. Many scholars of race and ethnicity are quite critical of this perspective, yet they make their own assumptions that support for or involvement in interracial relationships is a mark of "progressive" racial ideology.[16]

I have argued that increasing numbers of interracial couples should not be read as a promise of a more progressive racial era. But this notion of progress is a popular one, so it is worth addressing squarely. Why should we be cautious of interpreting interracial intimacy as an unambiguous sign of racial progress? First, although some interracial partners may be more racially progressive than people who oppose intermarriage, they are not necessarily enlightened subjects who have managed to "get beyond" race. They have racial prejudices and make false generalizations, just like Whites and Blacks in all types of relationships. Take, for example, Neil Chambers, who believes that his Black wife, Mary, is unusual because she is not aggressive and does not curse like other Black women. Or consider Jessica Merriam, a Black lesbian who is in a relationship with a White woman but believes that most Black people in relationships with Whites have issues with their own racial identities and suffer from internalized racism. For these partners and others, interracial intimacy is not a path to individual racial enlightenment, if such a thing exists. Instead, when their romantic choices contradict their racial beliefs, they position themselves or their partners as exceptions. Second, the women and men in this study do not live in race-neutral domestic zones. They sometimes wrestle with contrasting racial orientations. They may search for mixed-race communities but often find themselves in racially segregated neighborhoods where they must navigate grocery stores, laundromats, churches, playgrounds, and restaurants that are almost all White or almost all Black. They deal with interracial stereotypes and the racial judgments of others. These partners are not harbingers of a new racial future so much as they are lenses that refract a complicated vision of our racial present and past.

In sum, I want to be clear that the formation of an interracial relationship is not in itself a progressive act. Nor is it sufficient to contest a single social institution—the family—without also addressing others. Because racism is systemic, racial progress involves changing the multiple social institutions that reproduce racial inequality—schools, housing and lending, employment, the criminal justice system, and so on. Whether change of that order occurs depends in part on what people learn from interracial intimacy and what they do with these insights. When interracial intimacy leads to broader interracial coalitions that challenge existing social systems and demand racial justice, then intimacy can be a spark for progress. This happens when, for example, White partners who work to develop a critical racial consciousness, in part because of the direct and indirect experiences they have had as a partner to an African American, then take this insight and use it to work in coalitions with people of color toward racial equality. And it happens when Black partners take the skills they have practiced with their White partners and work to have a dialogue with other willing Whites and develop coalitions to enact sustained change. Racial progress involves institutional changes on a grand scale, and these changes can be best achieved by Blacks and Whites working together (with Latinos, Asian Americans, and other people of color).[17] Only when interracial intimacy impels people to work toward that change should we deem it to be truly "progressive."

The Practice of Intimate Racework

By emphasizing racework, this book contests the notion that intimacy is a site of racial transcendence. How can love relationships be "beyond race" when it is clear that interracial partners must negotiate racial differences, large and small, in everyday life? How could love see no color when feelings of trust, desire, admiration, and empathy are formed in a social context in which race matters so deeply? If our social positions shape how we perceive the world, how could domestic spheres ever be raceless (or classless or genderless) spaces? For many partners in this study, interracial intimacy represents not the end, but the beginning of a sustained process of negotiating racial differences. I have conceptualized those processes—the set of everyday actions and strategies through which individuals establish and maintain bonds of trust, love, and communication across systems of racial stratification—as racework. My central purpose has been to show that intimate relationships are not race-neutral spaces and that dealing with racial difference in everyday life requires racework.

Interracial partners engage in distinct forms of racework. Unlike Black/White friendships or parent-child relationships within multiracial families, interracial partners must negotiate not just the racialized status differences between them and the reality of racial segregation. They must also contend with racial prejudices and judgments about interracial intimacy. Put a little differently, interracial couples practice the same forms of racework as people with any other close interracial connection, plus they deal with the added burden of inhabiting a marginalized identity. The preceding chapters provided a detailed examination of four types of racework: navigating racial homogeneity, visibility management, emotional labor, and boundary work. To review briefly, I showed how status differentials inevitably arise from being Black/White in a society where Whiteness is privileged over Blackness. Because a White partner and a Black partner have more and less racial power, they are likely to perceive race and racism differently. I framed this as a conflict of racial orientations. Negotiating these contrasting racial perspectives inside the relationship requires *emotional labor*. This form of racework includes evaluating when to call attention to racial incidents and when to censor one's experiences or observations; considering how to explain one's own racial perspective to another; using humor to address race while simultaneously easing racial tensions; or strategically avoiding these conversations altogether. But status differentials also manifest in the spatial separation of Black and White environments. Racial segregation is an overtly visible result of deeply entrenched racism in the United States. Many interracial partners find these racial divisions within neighborhoods and social spaces particularly challenging. In these public spaces, racework therefore involves *navigating racial homogeneity*. This includes the energies that partners expend deciding which types of social environments are comfortable for each partner and managing the fatigue that comes from being one of the few persons of one's race in a given place.

Interracial stereotypes also necessitate racework for many interracial couples. Whether in public spaces or in the context of describing one's identity, interracial partners utilize racework to protect themselves from racial prejudice and judgments and from homophobia. In public spaces, lesbian and gay Black/White couples engage in practices of *visibility management* to prepare for or protect themselves from the harassment of others. By monitoring public displays of affection to conceal their intimacy from others or by actively asserting their intimacy through kissing or holding hands, partners attempt to control the dynamics of social situations in which they may be potentially vulnerable. But the same negative images that affect interracial partners when they are out in the world also shape the ways in which they think about their relationship and their own racial selves. At the level of identities, racework takes the form of *boundary work* through which partners create identities that distance themselves and their relationship from stereotypes of deviance. Using exclusionary boundary work, couples draw clear distinctions between "us" and "them," disassociating themselves from negative images of interracial couples. With inclusionary boundary work, interracial partners blur the boundaries between themselves and same-race couples, thereby emphasizing the "ordinary" nature of their relationship. As I discuss below, heterosexual couples have access to a special set of symbolic resources with which to make these claims.

The Intersections of Race, Sexuality, and Gender

In framing this study, I explained that research on interracial intimacy has become a field where assumptions of heterosexuality prevail. I asserted the importance of looking at gay and lesbian interracial partners for clues about the lived experiences of racial difference. Reflecting back upon these narratives, what do lesbian and gay experiences suggest about contemporary interracial life? First, and perhaps most importantly, they show us that in many social contexts, interraciality is recognizable only when it is embodied by heterosexual partners. A Black/White couple walking on the streets of Philadelphia or New York, or into a movie theater, restaurant, or shopping mall in Washington, D.C., is likely to attract the attention of others only if they are heterosexual. Whether the attention they receive is positive or negative, in most places Black/White couples are recognizable only when one person is a man and the other a woman. The exception, of course, is that in gay and lesbian spaces, racial difference can be profoundly visible. I have shown that lesbians and gay men face a unique set of interracial stigmas within their communities. Recall, for instance, Shawn Tarwick's disgust with the term "dinge queen," or Onika Marsh's reluctance to bring her White partner, Margaret, to a Black lesbian bar. Second, this research suggests that when same-sex interracial partners are made visible in public spaces that are not demarcated as lesbian or gay, homophobia may aggravate the effects of racial prejudice. Take, for example, Trina Stevens and Pamela Donato's antagonism in a New York subway. These complex intersections become apparent only when lesbians and gays are included in interracial research.

How does sexuality mediate the practice of racework? Sexuality influences racework mainly in contexts where negative images of interracial intimacy are especially prevalent. Heterosexual Black/White relationships, especially Black men with White women, are powerful historical symbols that have evoked unique anxieties within both White and Black communities. These negative characterizations have shaped how heterosexual interracial couples are viewed by the communities they live in and how they themselves think about what it means to be interracial. In public spaces, these couples generally feel that being interracial makes them conspicuous; they notice others noticing them. Yet they rarely modify their behavior in such spaces to avoid outright conflict or harassment. Some may have sufficient confidence in the visibility of their relationship to think it unlikely that modifying their behavior could conceal their intimacy. Others simply may not feel vulnerable enough to even consider such actions. Yet heterosexuals do attempt to manage others' impressions when it comes to the meaning of interracial intimacy, and for this they draw upon the symbolic resources attached to their heterosexual status. Assertions that they are "just a regular couple" or "just a man and a woman who love each other" draw on the normative status of heterosexuality to buffer the marginal status of interraciality. Both in face-to-face interactions with strangers and in defining their relationship apart from stereotypes, being heterosexual makes them more of a target, but it also provides them with the symbolic resources to diffuse negative assumptions.

Lesbian and gay interracial couples, on the other hand, exist in many ways outside and apart from the obsessive focus on interracial sexuality that has for so long haunted racial politics in the United States. As I have explained, in most public spaces, they are not visual triggers of painful racial realities. Instead, many same-sex couples, especially lesbians, seem to fade into the background. Their intimacy is rarely recognized in public interactions with strangers unless they are in physical contact or showing overt affection. This creates a peculiar contrast. In a social context where everyone is assumed to be heterosexual, lesbian and gay intimacy is difficult to see, because people assume it is not there. In this same context, as soon as same-sex partners hold hands or kiss each other, they are acutely visible. Their connection now stands out as different and unusual. There is evidence in these narratives that racial difference may accentuate the effects of homophobia for lesbian and gay Black/White couples. It may make their invisibility more pronounced or their harassment more intense.

In realms of social life where racialized status differences are especially salient, sexuality tends to play a minor role in how couples engage in racework. When interracial partners negotiate racial difference within the relationship, or when they navigate racially homogeneous environments, each partner's position as Black or White, woman or man, has great importance, but it generally matters less whether their relationship is lesbian, gay, or heterosexual. For example, Lucas and Thad reacted differently to the young Black man who was shot and killed by a New York City police officer, but their sexual identity as gay men did not figure prominently into their interaction. What mattered more was that as a Black man, Lucas was familiar with the danger of being assumed to be criminal, while Thad's life experience had not provided him with this perspective. In this and other examples of emotional labor, focusing on respondents' sexuality did not reveal markedly different behaviors or experiences. Thus, although race, sexuality, and gender always intersect, in certain moments or interactions some of these identities are more central than others.

Conceptualizing Racework in Other Contexts

The concept of racework is useful for understanding not only intimate relationships, but also other types of settings in which people may develop close interracial connections, such as schools, workplaces, community organizations, churches, and athletic teams. Examining racework in these contexts pushes us to consider how interpersonal relationships are shaped by and respond to racial stratification. It requires that we recognize that people who form a close connection across racial lines may experience conflicting racial perspectives as a result of their different racial positions, and that they may also be comfortable in different kinds of racialized spaces. For example, Black and White coworkers may have vastly different experiences in the workplace. Research shows that Black professional women often feel as if they are being unfairly judged in the workplace on their appearance, personal decorum, communication skills, and emotion management, and that they must repackage themselves in ways that are more palatable to White coworkers.[18] A focus on racework would lead us to consider how close interracial connections between coworkers are sustained amid these inequalities. Do Black women share with White coworkers their experiences with race fatigue and the impression-management strategies they use to try to achieve equitable treatment and promotion? When and under what circumstances do they initiate these conversations? Or do they practice what I have called "strategic avoidance"? How do their White coworkers respond? For another example we might consider the experience of Black and White members of multiracial congregations. As I have discussed, religious institutions in the United States have historically been racially divided—researchers have found that less than 10 percent of religious congregations are multiracial.[19] Still, an examination of how and when people engage in racework in these environments would be useful. It would shed light on how people in diverse voluntary associations where the express purpose is spiritual connection may still struggle with being racially different in a broader stratified society. Multiracial congregations sometimes draw from racially segregated neighborhoods, where people live and interact almost exclusively with others of their same race. Do tensions arise about which racial group holds leadership positions in the church? Or about how people should worship? Do Whites and Blacks talk to each other about the significance of racial diversity? Do they speak in colorblind language or do they address race squarely? These kinds of questions move us past thinking of interracial groups or settings as accomplishments in themselves and toward a critical examination of how race works in these spaces.

Scholars of race and ethnicity must continue to develop conceptual tools to better understand how racial stratification shapes interpersonal relationships. Researchers have provided sophisticated insights about the challenges that White parents face in raising children of color, given that their own racial upbringing does not equip them with the kinds of self-preservation skills their children will need. France Winddance Twine conceptualizes racial literacy to describe the critical racial perspective that some White mothers develop. In a moving autoethnography, Barbara Katz Rothman highlights the inevitable power imbalances involved in the practice of transracial adoption. These scholars show with great clarity that racial differences have significant consequences in family life. Research in the area of mixed-race families and friendships should explore these questions further, for they establish important links between social structures and intimate relationships. This kind of analysis displaces the multicultural view of difference mainly as a cultural aesthetic—for instance, in food, music, or holidays—and moves beyond the notion that racial conflict stems mainly from prejudice and misunderstanding. Instead, it sees differences in skin color as differences in racialized power.[20] It reminds us that race is a social structure and that people must contend with the consequences of that structure in interpersonal relationships.

This book is about interracial intimacy, but the stories I have recounted here speak more broadly to the significance of race in the United States at the turn of the twenty-first century. Racial inequalities have undoubtedly decreased in the past fifty years, and the taboo against intermarriage has been markedly eroded. Yet especially at a time when social pundits and commentators hail the dawn of a new racial era, interracial narratives point to the continued significance of race and racism in the United States. But interracial narratives are important beyond the simple evidence they provide that race still matters; many social scientific studies come to a similar conclusion. These narratives show that our position within an unequal racial system shapes more than where we live and the resources to which we have access. It also shapes our most intimate relationships. Love is not a raceless space in a deeply racialized world. Whom we love and desire and the intimacies we create are not merely personal, psychological, or spiritual—although they may be all of those things. They are also profoundly social. Understanding that our most intimate connections are shaped by social forces much larger than ourselves is crucial. There is much more to love than loving.

APPENDIX A | Research Methods

Researching Race

I began this study as a graduate student, but I have always had a strong investment in understanding social inequality. If pressed, I would trace this to having been raised by a strong feminist. I spent many hours of my childhood attending protests and eating cookies in other people's living rooms, waiting for my mom to finish her monthly meetings of the Syracuse, New York chapter of the National Organization for Women. By the time I got to Temple University as a graduate student, I was focused on how race and gender together shape women's experiences. I began to think critically about my own Whiteness and about how the largely White feminist movement my mother had been a part of had excluded particular experiences and ways of seeing the world. That there had been racial conflicts in the women's movement within which I had been enveloped struck a profound chord. I saw how power differences shaped "sisterhood." As I continued my studies, I became interested in how inequality shapes how we think, talk, and interact. When I met my Black partner, I began thinking about the everyday racial issues of interracial couples and families. Yet there was little written about what race means for unions like ours. Were lesbian experiences of racial difference similar to those of straight couples? In what ways where they different? These questions led to more questions and eventually to a dissertation and this book.

Being a White woman in a relationship with a Black woman inevitably shaped my role as a researcher. Every researcher brings her social position to each interview. In a study about race, gender, sexuality, and family, I embodied various forms of insiderness and outsiderness in relation to my respondents. Being in an interracial relationship may have allowed me to win the trust of some of the partners I interviewed. This was especially true when I interviewed lesbian and gay partners, as sexuality created an additional level of commonality. But I also interviewed respondents with whom I did not have a common gender or race or sexual identity. These similarities and differences were not inconsequential. Talking about race across racial lines can be difficult, especially with strangers. But as I became comfortable with the interview process, I was able to establish a rapport with my respondents.[1] Because I am aware that status differences shape social interactions, I tried to be always mindful of how racial, gender, and sexual differences could affect the interviews. Like any careful researcher, but especially because of my own interracial partnership, I looked for emergent themes in respondent narratives, cautious not to read my own expectations into what I observed. I looked for disconfirming evidence and patterns that surprised me or alerted me to perspectives I had not considered.

Research Design

This study is based on in-depth interviews with both members of forty Black/White couples, and two additional partners whose spouses were not interviewed, for a total of eighty-two individual interviews. I also conducted ethnographic observations with a subset of four couples from the original sample; the analysis in this book makes only limited use of the fieldnotes from these observations, however. Study participants were living in the metropolitan areas of New York City, Philadelphia, and Washington, D.C., at the time I interviewed them (2004–2005). Table A.1 shows the sample design.

In planning this study, I chose to treat individual partners, not couples, as the units of analysis. Asking for a couple's opinion of an interaction or event assumes that both partners see things in an identical manner. This is unlikely; regardless of their relationship, two people rarely experience

TABLE A.1 Design of Interview Sample

	SAME-SEX PARTNERS		HETEROSEXUAL PARTNERS		TOTAL
	LESBIAN	GAY	BLACK WOMAN/ WHITE MAN	BLACK MAN/ WHITE WOMAN	
Black	10	10	12*	10	42
White	10	10	10	10	40
Total	**20**	**20**	**22**	**20**	**82**

*The White husbands of two heterosexual Black women declined to be interviewed.

or interpret social interactions in the exact the same way. This may be especially true for heterosexual married couples, because as an institution, marriage has clearly structured expectations for wives and husbands. Family scholar Jessie Bernard called this the "his and hers" marriage.[2]

To capture each person's unique perspective, I interviewed partners separately. This strategy allowed me to observe different views—sometimes of a specific situation, but also of social life more broadly. I am convinced that this is the most productive way to study intimate relationships. Still, this approach has limitations. Joint interviews, though they may elicit a compromise between two points of view, allow the researcher to observe the couple interacting to construct a joint narrative. This process of negotiation is absent in a one-on-one interview. Further, interviewing intimate partners separately produces two narrative accounts of a single relationship, which introduces additional analytic complexity.[3]

Recruiting Couples

Interracial couples make up a very small percentage of all romantic couples. This is especially true for same-sex Black/White couples because lesbians and gays already account for such a small percent of the general population. To find couples for my study, I posted descriptions of the project on physical bulletin boards, including those at bookstores, grocery stores, coffee shops, gay and lesbian community centers, and a YMCA. I also posted on an Internet listserv for gay and lesbian alumni of a liberal arts college in the Philadelphia area and one for middle-class Black moms with small children; and I placed notices in a queer Internet newsletter aimed at women in New York City and in an online social events weekly bulletin for twenty- and thirty-somethings in Philadelphia. These strategies put me in touch with interracial couples from neighborhoods across New York and Philadelphia. After I had met and interviewed each partner, I asked whether she or he had any friends or acquaintances who might like to participate in the study. This snowball sampling method—recruiting participants from respondents' social networks—helped enlarge my sample and brought couples from Washington, D.C., into the study.

The Interview

In the in-depth interviews, my goal was to explore three main aspects of interracial intimacy: how interracial partners felt in various public spaces, how race worked inside their relationship, and how they thought about their own racial identities vis-à-vis their interracial relationship. Although experiences with their families of origin and their own children (if they had any) inevitably became part of these dialogues, these were not issues I prioritized during interviews.

It can be difficult for White people to talk about race with each other because the topic is so often avoided. It can also be difficult to talk about race across categories of racial difference because of a fear of saying too much, or of offending the other person. Thus, I consciously worked to build trust and rapport by beginning the interview with the less sensitive questions. I usually asked respondents about their backgrounds—where they grew up, what their family was like, where they went to school, and what they currently do for a living. I then asked them to tell me how they had met their partner and to describe their partner to me as if I had never met her or him. I asked if this was their first interracial relationship and, if not, to tell me about the others. We then moved to other topics: I asked about the neighborhood they lived in, about other parts of the city they frequented, whether they traveled, and how they felt others reacted to them in these places. I also inquired about how race shaped their own relationship, whether and when they talked about race, and whether they had learned anything about race from their partner. Finally, I asked about their own racial identities, posing questions like, "Has being in an interracial relationship changed the way you think of yourself? Has it changed the way you think of your racial identity? How?" These were the most sensitive questions of the interview process, but by the end of each interview, I felt comfortable asking them. Envisioning the interview process in three stages allowed me to explore how race shaped multiple levels of interracial life.

The Ethnography

In-depth interviews make up the largest part of this study, but the project also has an ethnographic component. In designing the study, I was influenced by the research and mentorship of Annette Lareau, who accomplished an ambitious investigation of how social class shapes the childrearing strategies of poor, working-class, and middle-class families. With a small team of research assistants, she observed each of twelve families during twenty visits carried out over the course of a month.[4] I was persuaded that my study too would benefit from the insights that come from "sitting in" on people's daily lives.

As I conducted the interviews, I began ethnographic visits with one couple from each of the sample groups—one gay couple, one lesbian couple, one Black woman/White man couple, and one White woman/Black man couple.[5] Over a period of four to five weeks, I observed couples during at least eighteen visits.[6] Each observation generally lasted two to three hours, although when a day included a special event, an observation could last up to five hours. These visits included activities such as walking to the grocery store, driving to garden supply outlets, attending an elementary school Halloween parade, sitting in doctors' offices, riding the subway to a baby shower, listening to children's stories at the neighborhood library, and sitting for countless hours in kitchens and living rooms as interracial couples carried out the mundane routines of family life. During these observations, I envisioned myself as a long-term houseguest—someone whose presence you notice at first but get used to over time. No social observer is ever completely invisible, but by the fourth or fifth visit, couples became visibly more at ease.

The ethnographic case studies complemented the in-depth interviews by allowing me to sit in on the lives of interracial couples, learning about how and when racial difference matters—or does not matter—in daily life. I learned a great deal from these visits. They were especially useful for observing connections between intimate life and the social and neighborhood environments in which it takes place. The visits helped me understand how social spaces like churches, dance classes, restaurants, subway stops, and libraries are shaped by the broader racial composition of neighborhoods, and to see how partners negotiated these spaces. I also witnessed race emerge in the most ordinary circumstances, in regard to children, for instance, or as couples discussed the daily news. But much of what I observed centered on planning dinner, debriefings about each partner's workday, getting children ready to leave the house or go to sleep, and so on. These observations were useful reminders that race is but one part of daily life.

The insights I gained from the ethnographic fieldwork unquestionably shaped my understanding of interracial intimacy. In this book, however, I draw almost exclusively on the interview data. As individual case studies, the field observations reveal different ways of thinking about race and racial difference, and they provide evidence of different types of racework practices. But four ethnographic cases capture only part of the variability of the larger sample. I therefore consider the interviews my primary data source and treat the observations as a complementary source.

Data Analysis

The interviews in this study were transcribed in their entirety and coded using qualitative coding software. Initially, I attached simple descriptive codes, like "talking about race" or "anticipating racism." I used these descriptive codes to categorize language, interactions, relationships, events, and interpretations I noticed in the interracial narratives. As I began analyzing the early interviews and started to identify emerging concepts, I developed more detailed analytic codes, such as "boundary work" and "managing stigma." Writing analytic memos as I went along helped me connect codes and concepts across interviews.

When I had completed the data collection, I reviewed all of the codes and organized them according to social realm—public spaces, intimate interaction, or identity. For example, all text attached to codes that had to do with visibility, invisibility, and managing stigma were combined into a category called "Navigating Public Spaces." I therefore had three families of codes, plus some miscellaneous codes representing themes not directly relevant to my main research questions. I then assigned each of the interviews to numerous families—heterosexual, same-sex, Black, White, women, and men. With both the interviews and the codes organized into families, I could review the text attached to specific research questions and consider the commonalities and divergences of experiences according to race, gender, and sexuality. This process of organizing, categorizing, and analyzing interracial narratives distilled an enormous amount of text into manageable chunks. In these later stages, I utilized data matrices to visually represent data from the entirety of the sample in relation to a specific research question. Creating a visual representation persuaded me of the validity of my conclusions and confirmed that I was not allowing a few particularly compelling narratives to influence my vision of the broader picture.

APPENDIX B | Respondent Characteristics

TABLE B.1 Social and Demographic Characteristics of Study Participants

NAME	RACE	AGE	LENGTH OF RELATIONSHIP (IN YEARS)	CHILDREN (AGE)	EDUCATION	OCCUPATION	COMBINED FAMILY INCOME
Lesbians							
Dionna Yates	Black	23	4	—	Bachelor's Degree	Drug Counselor	$60,000–$74,999
Lindsey Michaels	White	26	4	—	Bachelor's Degree	Director of Youth Services, Local Community Center	$60,000–$74,999
Jessica Merriam	Black	23	3	—	Bachelor's Degree	Grant Writer, Nonprofit Organization	$60,000–$74,999
Bryce Cook	White	22	3	—	Bachelor's Degree	High School Physics Teacher	$60,000–$74,999
Sylvia Chabot	Black	29	7	Patrice (1 month)	Master's Degree	High School English Teacher	$75,000–$89,999
Leslie Cobbs	White	37	7	Patrice (1 month)	Doctoral Degree	Family Therapist	$75,000–$89,999
Tara Hilliard	Black	27	1.5	—	Some College	Waitress	$60,000–$74,999
Kate Taurisano	White	27	1.5	—	Master's Degree	High School Guidance Counselor	$60,000–$74,999
Monique Gilliam	Black	35	2	—	Doctoral Degree	Child Psychologist	not cohabitating
Barbara DiBacco	White	41	2	—	Some College	Retail Saleswoman	not cohabitating
Katrina Stevens	Black	42	5.5	—	Bachelor's Degree	Case Manager, Social Service Agency	$75,000–$89,999
Pamela Donato	White	31	5.5	—	Master's Degree	Labor Doula	$75,000–$89,999

(Continued)

TABLE B.I (Continued)

NAME	RACE	AGE	LENGTH OF RELATIONSHIP (IN YEARS)	CHILDREN (AGE)	EDUCATION	OCCUPATION	COMBINED FAMILY INCOME
Terrina Nissar	Black	31	3	—	Bachelor's Degree	Retail Saleswoman	$30,000–$44,999
Maureen Wiley	White	30	3	—	Master's Degree	Fundraiser, Women's Health Care Organization	$30,000–$44,999
Kayla Carson	Black	38	3	—	Bachelor's Degree	Unemployed (formerly ran landscaping business)	$90,000–$104,999
Laurie Lewis	White	44	3	—	Some College	Specialty Foods Distributor	$90,000–$104,999
Nadine Allen	Black	47	2	—	Some College	Financial Aid Counselor	$45,000–$59,999
Nancy Taylor	White	37	2	—	Master's Degree	Consultant, International Health Organization	$45,000–$59,999
Onika Marsh	Black	26	1.5	—	Bachelor's Degree	Graduate Student	not cohabitating
Margaret Otterlei	White	30	1.5	—	Bachelor's Degree	Administrative Coordinator	not cohabitating
Gay Men							
Evan Cody	Black	29	1.5	—	Master's Degree	School Psychologist	$75,000–$89,999
Vance Dalton	White	24	1.5	—	Bachelor's Degree	Architect	$75,000–$89,999
Leonard Umbers	Black	40	12	—	Doctoral Degree	Clinical Psychologist	above $105,000
Victor Renford	White	50	12	—	Bachelor's Degree	Executive Director, Non-profit Organization	above $105,000
Lucas Tatum	Black	28	7	—	Master's Degree	Odd Jobs/Musician	$30,000–$44,999
Thad Thompson	White	46	7	—	Bachelor's Degree	Music Instructor, Local College	$30,000–$44,999

Name	Race				Education	Occupation	Income
Walter Belton-Davis	Black	46	24	—	Master's Degree	Social Worker/Supervisor	$75,000–$89,999
Kirk Belton-Davis	White	44	24	—	Bachelor's Degree	Insurance Salesman	$75,000–$89,999
Daniel Embry	Black	49	18	Chester(2), Kendall (9 months)	Some College	Playwright/Actor	above $105,000
Shawn Tarwick	White	49	18	Chester(2), Kendall (9 months)	Some College	Journalist, African American Newspaper	above $105,000
Tommy Smith-Donnell	Black	54	12	—	High School Degree	Unemployed (formerly janitor)	$45,000–$59,999
Brian Smith-Donnell	White	60	12	—	Some College	Mechanical Engineer	$45,000–$59,999
Zachary King	Black	49	28	—	Master's Degree	Financial Analyst	above $105,000
Keith Fischer	White	65	28	—	Master's Degree	Retired Vice President, Family Business	above $105,000
Marvin Nelson	Black	41	7	—	Master's Degree	Dean of Students, Small Liberal Arts College	above $105,000
Ulrich Drescher	White	43	7	—	Doctoral Degree	Chemistry Professor, Local College	above $105,000
Nelson Ingles	Black	56	11	—	Bachelor's Degree	Director, Social Service Agency	above $105,000
Edmond Springer	White	53	11	—	Bachelor's Degree	Retired	above $105,000
Ken Irving	Black	37	1	—	Bachelor's Degree	Graduate Student/Freelance Journalist	$60,000–$74,999
Chad O'Neil	White	26	1	—	Bachelor's Degree	Waiter	$60,000–$74,999

(Continued)

TABLE B.I (Continued)

Black Women, White Men

NAME	RACE	AGE	LENGTH OF RELATIONSHIP (IN YEARS)	CHILDREN (AGE)	EDUCATION	OCCUPATION	COMBINED FAMILY INCOME
Nakia Geiger	Black	30	8	—	Bachelor's Degree	Actress/Waitress	$45,000–$59,999
Warren Geiger	White	29	8	—	Bachelor's Degree	Filmmaker	$45,000–$59,999
Mary Chambers	Black	38	9.5	Nevin (8), Kim (6), Iona (1)	Bachelor's Degree	Homemaker (formerly teacher)	$75,000–$89,999
Neil Chambers	White	38	9.5	Nevin (8), Kim (6), Iona (1)	Master's Degree	English Teacher, Middle School	$75,000–$89,999
Mabel Renault	Black	43	13	Cartier (9), Lecia (6), Ervan (2)	Some College	Homemaker (formerly documentary filmmaker)	$45,000–$59,999
Hank Renault	White	45	13	Cartier (9), Lecia (6), Ervan (2)	Some College	Landlord/Independent Contractor	$45,000–$59,999
Kristie Kelley	Black	46	24	Ivy (14)	Master's Degree	Attorney	above $105,000
Burton Connell	White	49	24	Ivy (14)	Doctoral Degree	Research Scientist	above $105,000
Velena Julien	Black	30	10	Octavia (16 months)	Master's Degree	Choreographer/Dancer	$30,000–$44,999
Brent Isley	White	36	10	Octavia (16 months)	Master's Degree	Massage Therapist	$30,000–$44,999

Name	Race	Age		Children	Education	Occupation	Income
Wanda Maxwell	Black	30	6	—	Master's Degree	Private Therapist	$60,000–$74,999
Ethan Smolen	White	29	6	—	Master's Degree	Science Teacher, High School	$60,000–$74,999
Devon Keller	Black	35	13	Davina (12 months)	Some College	Homemaker	$60,000–$74,999
Oliver Ryan	White	44	13	Davina (12 months)	Bachelor's Degree	Website Developer	$60,000–$74,999
Morgan Townsend	Black	35	15	Henry (12), Marcus (8), Tonya(2)	Master's Degree	Homemaker	$75,000–$89,999
Charles Townsend	White	38	15	Henry (12), Marcus (8), Tonya(2)	Bachelor's Degree	Corporate Salesman	$75,000–$89,999
Aisha Tannous	Black	30	15	Orion (3), Max (5), Terrence (10)	Bachelor's Degree	Homemaker	$15,000–$29,999
Laurent Vivier	White	31	15	Orion (3), Max (5), Terrence (10)	Some College	Electrician	$15,000–$29,999
Nina Young	Black	40	3	Odessa (13 months)	Some College	Homemaker	$60,000–$74,999
Earnest Young	White	35	3	Odessa (13 months)	Bachelor's Degree	Civil Engineer, Utility Company	$60,000–$74,999
Kim Russell (partner not interviewed)	Black	38	6	—	Master's Degree	Adjunct Professor/Graduate Student	above $105,000
Brianna Simmons (partner not interviewed)	Black	25	4	Olivia (6), Serena (2)	Some College	Alumni Development Officer, Local University	$90,000–$104,999

(Continued)

TABLE B.1 (Continued)

NAME	RACE	AGE	LENGTH OF RELATIONSHIP (IN YEARS)	CHILDREN (AGE)	EDUCATION	OCCUPATION	COMBINED FAMILY INCOME
White Women, Black Men							
Frank Thomas	Black	29	2	—	Associate's Degree	Graphic Designer	$60,000–$74,999
Marie Thomas	White	32	2	—	Some College	Manager, Clothing Boutique	$60,000–$74,999
Kalvin Oster	Black	30	5.5	Becky (12) from previous marriage, Kaya (6 months)	Some College	Daycare Business Owner/Financial Analyst	above $105,000
Vera Oster	White	33	5.5	Becky (12) from previous marriage, Kaya (6 months)	Some College	Daycare Business Owner/Manager	above $105,000
Norman Crenshaw	Black	49	26	—	High School Degree	Structural Iron Worker	$90,000–$104,999
Trudy Crenshaw	White	56	26	—	High School Degree	Customer Service Trainer	$90,000–$104,999
Benjamin Walters	Black	57	3.5	Adult daughter from previous marriage	High School Degree	Community Advocate, Non-profit Organization	$60,000–$74,999
Helen Rutkowski	White	50	3.5	Jeff (17) and older son from previous marriage	Some College	Fiscal Director, Community Health Organization	$60,000–$74,999
Christopher Tomlinson	Black	25	2	—	Master's Degree	Vice-principal, Elementary School	not cohabitating
Lana Keyes	White	29	2	—	Master's Degree	Graduate Student/Special Education Teacher	not cohabitating

Name	Race	Age	Years	Children	Education	Occupation	Income
Scott Patterson	Black	32	3	—	Some College	Paralegal	$60,000–$74,999
Tamara Stills	White	30	3	—	Master's Degree	ESL Teacher	$60,000–$74,999
Bradley Tyson	Black	44	15	Valerie (9)	Some College	Vice President, Advertising Agency	$90,000–$104,999
Julianna Tyson	White	34	15	Valerie (9)	High School Degree	Homemaker	$90,000–$104,999
Myron Tanner	Black	50	14	Adult children from previous marriage	Bachelor's Degree	President, Construction Company	$90,000–$104,999
Norma Tanner	White	45	14	—	Master's Degree	Preschool Teacher	$90,000–$104,999
York Kearney	Black	33	13	Bethany (4) Taryn (6)	Bachelor's Degree	Commercial Pilot	$90,000–$104,999
Tricia Kearney	White	39	13	Bethany (4) Taryn (6)	Doctoral Degree	Professor	$90,000–$104,999
Lionel Ivers	Black	35	7	—	Associate Degree	Corporate Salesman	$90,000–$104,999
Meryl Agassi Ivers	White	35	7	—	Master's Degree	Guidance Counselor, High School	$90,000–$104,999

TABLE B.2 Social and Demographic Characteristics by Group

Black woman/White man (10 couples)*	Lesbian (10 couples)
Median age: 35.5 years	Median age: 30.5 years
% with (at least) college degree: 73%	% with (at least) college degree: 80%
Median income: $60,000 – $74,999	Median income: $60,000 – $74,999
Median length of relationship: 10 yrs	Median length of relationship: 3 yrs
% with children from this relationship: 77%	% with children from this relationship: 10%
White woman/Black man (10 couples)	**Gay (10 couples)**
Median age: 34.5 years	Median age: 46 years
% with (at least) college degree: 50%	% with (at least) college degree: 80%
Median income: $90,000 – $104,999	Median income: $90,000 – $104,999
Median length of relationship: 6.25 yrs	Median length of relationship: 11.5 yrs
% with children from this relationship: 30%	% with children from this relationship: 10%

* There are 22 individuals in this group—10 couples and two Black women whose husbands declined to be interviewed.

NOTES

Introduction

1. The names of all study participants are pseudonyms, and the names of some locations and occupations have been modified to protect respondents' privacy.

2. See Lofquist et al., *Households and Families*: 2010. The Census Bureau classifies a couple as "interracial" if one spouse or partner is not in the same single-race category (White; Black or African American; American Indian and Alaska Native; Asian; Native Hawaiian and Other Pacific Islander, or Some Other Race) as the other spouse or partner, or if at least one spouse or partner is in a multiple-race group. Within this classification, a marriage between one Hispanic and one non-Hispanic person is not defined as "interracial."

3. See U.S. Census Bureau, Appendix Table 1. Put slightly differently, only 14 percent of heterosexual *interracial* married couples were Black/White. Common interracial pairs included Asian/White, Some Other Race/White, and marriages between two people who identified as multiple-race.

4. Zhenchao Qian and Daniel Lichter explain that cohabitation rates are increasing generally and that, among interracial couples, cohabitation may have advantages over marriage in circumventing the tensions that come from joining racially or ethnically dissimilar friendship and family networks. See Qian and Lichter, "Social Boundaries and Marital Assimilation."

5. See O'Connell et al., "New Estimates of Same-Sex Households." Although the census does not directly ask citizens about their sexual orientation, enumerators do ask about the relationship of cohabiters. Therefore, in the 2000 U.S. Census and beyond, lesbian and gay couples can be quantified through the category of "same-sex unmarried partner households." See also Sears et al., "Same-Sex Couples."

6. See U.S. Census Bureau, "Hispanic Origin and Race of Female Unmarried-Partner Households" and "Hispanic Origin and Race of Male Unmarried-Partner Households." Because the American Community Survey does not report the racial composition of different forms of intermarriage, and as this book went to press, racial and ethnic breakdowns for same-sex marriage was not available from the 2010 U.S. Census, these data are from the 2000 U.S. Census.

7. For examples of popular media accounts of this postracial sentiment, see Padgett et al., "Color-blind Love"; Russo, "Families"; Zogby, "Barack Obama"; Rutten, "The Good Generation Gap"; *Wall Street Journal*, "President-elect Obama"; and MacKenzie, "Choice of Obama." Some broader scholarly treatments of this decline-of-race sentiment were written before the term postracial took hold. See, for example, Thernstrom and Thernstrom, *America in Black and White*.

8. For an intensive synthesis of the persistence of racial inequalities across various realms of social life, see Feagin, *Racist America*; Brown et al., *Whitewashing Race*; and Collins, *Black Feminist Thought*. For more specific studies and data, see Shapiro, *The Hidden Cost of Being African American*; Lipsitz, *The Possessive Investment in Whiteness*; Mauer and King, "Uneven Justice"; Oliver and Shapiro, *White Wealth/Black Wealth*; Pager, "The Mark of a Criminal Record"; DeNavas-Walt et al., "Income, Poverty, and Health Insurance"; and Iceland et al., "Racial and Ethnic Segregation."

9. For example, antimiscegenation laws in various U.S. states have at times included restrictions on White intermarriage with Native Americans, Chinese, Japanese, Hawaiians, and Filipinos, but *all* of these laws simultaneously restricted intermarriage with Blacks. See Sollors, "Introduction."

10. "Race work" is a term with a long history. My usage here differs from that of other scholars, however. At the turn of the twentieth century, this term was used by Black club women to refer to "productive activities that would ultimately be beneficial to 'the race.'" See Sharon, "Nannie Helen Burroughs." See also Higginbotham, *Righteous Discontent*, and Whitaker, *Race Work*. Rebecca Chiyoko King-O'Riain uses "race work" to describe how individuals attempt to align their biological notions of race with their thinking about culture. See King-O'Riain, *Pure Beauty*.

11. Scholars in the field of family and counseling psychology have given this subject more extensive attention. See Rostosky et al., "Interracial Same-Sex Couples"; Lockman Jr., "Ebony and Ivory"; Perlman, "Loving Across Race and Class Divides"; Greene and Boyd-Franklin, "African American Lesbian Couples"; and Long, "Incredibly True Adventures."

12. But see Dalmage, *Tripping on the Color Line*; Dalmage, "Finding a Home"; and Drake and Cayton, *Black Metropolis*.

13. See Bonilla-Silva, *Racism Without Racists*.

14. See Cancian, *Caring and Gender*.

15. See Swidler, *Talk of Love*, and Scott, "Jungle Fever?"

16. See Moran, *Interracial Intimacy*.

17. See Moran, *Interracial Intimacy*, and Scott, "Jungle Fever?"

18. See Gordon, *Assimilation in American Life*.

19. See Qian and Lichter, "Social Boundaries and Marital Assimilation."

20. Newer offshoots of classic assimilation theory have taken this into account and extended the theory in new directions. On the concept of segmented assimilation, see, for example, Portes and Zhou, "The New Second Generation," and Rumbaut, "The Crucible Within." For a neo-assimilationist perspective, see Alba and Nee, *Remaking the American Mainstream*, and Alba, *Blurring the Color Line*.

21. See Russo, "Families: When Love Is Mixing It Up."

22. See Coontz, "Marriage, a History."

23. In fact, some argue that many of the gender inequalities that exist in society originate in, or are justified by, gendered expectations of women's role within the family.

24. See Hochschild, *The Second Shift*; Bianchi et al., "Is Anyone Doing the Housework?"; Gupta, "The Effects of Transitions in Marital Status"; and Brines, "Economic Dependency, Gender, and the Division of Labor."

25. Gordon Allport first conceptualized the contact hypothesis in 1958 (see Allport, *The Nature of Prejudice*). Since then, numerous empirical studies have examined this theory, including Yancey, *Interracial Contact and Social Change*; O'Brien and Korgen, "It's the Message"; and Jackman and Crane, "Some of My Best Friends Are Black. ... "

26. See Childs, *Navigating Interracial Borders;* Dalmage, *Tripping on the Color Line;* Rosenblatt et al., *Multiracial Couples;* Judice, *Interracial Marriages Between Black Women and White Men;* Yancey, *Just Don't Marry One;* Smith and Hattery, *Interracial Relationships in the 21st Century;* Root, *Love's Revolution;* Porterfield, *Black and White Mixed Marriages;* McNamara et al., *Crossing the Line;* and Kouri and Lasswell, "Black-White Marriages."

27. But see Frankenberg, *White Women, Race Matters;* Rosenfield, *The Age of Independence;* and Bystydzienski, *Intercultural Couples.*

28. See Rubin, "Thinking Sex."

29. For an extended analysis of heterosexual privileges, see Carbado, "Straight Out of the Closet." Note, however, that Carbado misses the fact that, historically, heterosexual interracial couples have been denied many of these privileges. For a discussion of the racial prerequisites to heterosexual privilege, see Steinbugler, "Visibility as Privilege and Danger."

30. See Law, "Homosexuality and the Social Meaning of Gender," 195. For further discussion of these terms, see also Darren Lenard Hutchinson, "Dissecting Axes of Subordination," and Barry D. Adam, "Theorizing Homophobia."

31. For a historical analysis of institutional heterosexism, see Canaday, *The Straight State.*

32. Notable exceptions in the field of sociology include Frankenberg, *White Women, Race Matters*, and Judice, *Interracial Marriages.*

33. This makes my sample fairly typical of interracial couples more broadly. According to the 2000 U.S. Census, in 71.8 percent of heterosexual interracial couples and 81.6 percent of same-sex interracial couples, at least one of the partners had a college degree. See Rosenfield, *The Age of Independence.*

34. See Ancheta, *Race, Rights, and the Asian American Experience*; Rodriguez, *Changing Race*; Wu, *Yellow*; and Perea, "The Black/White Binary Paradigm of Race."

35. For an astute analysis of contemporary Asian/White relationships that supports this conclusion, see Nemoto, *Racing Romance.*

36. Many excellent empirical studies have put the study of family reactions or children's racial identities at the center of analysis. See Childs, *Navigating Interracial Borders*; Rosenblatt, *Multiracial Couples*; Naomi Zack, *American Mixed Race*; Rockquemore and Brunsma, *Beyond Black*; and Brunsma, *Mixed Messages.*

Chapter 1

1. The last legal barriers to heterosexual interracial intimacy fell in 1967 when the Supreme Court legalized interracial marriage by declaring antimiscegenation laws unconstitutional. See *Loving v. Virginia.*

2. There are, of course, historical examples of sexual relationships between White slaveholders and the African women they enslaved that may have been consensual and

even loving. The story of Sally Hemings and Thomas Jefferson is perhaps the most famous example. See Reed, *Thomas Jefferson and Sally Hemings.*

3. See Collins, *Black Sexual Politics.*

4. As early as 1664, the first laws against interracial sexuality were enacted in the state of Maryland. These antimiscegenation laws prohibited interracial sex and marriage, though this was in some ways redundant because enslaved Blacks were not permitted to marry other Blacks, let alone marry Whites. See Pascoe, *What Comes Naturally.*

5. See Feagin, *Racist America,* especially chapter 3, and Jordan, *White over Black: American Attitudes Toward the Negro, 1550–1812,* 96.

6. In *Black Reconstruction,* W. E. B. Du Bois pioneered the idea that Whiteness has a psychological wage, even for economically marginalized Whites. He wrote, "It must be remembered that the white group of laborers, while they received a lower wage, were compensated in part by a sort of public and psychological wage. They were given public deference and titles of courtesy because they were white. They were admitted freely with all classes of white people to public functions, public parks, and the best schools. The police were drawn from their ranks, and the courts, dependent on their votes, treated them with such leniency as to encourage lawlessness. Their vote selected public officials, and while this had small effect upon the economic situation, it had great effect upon their personal treatment and the deference shown them." See Du Bois, *Black Reconstruction,* 700. See also Roediger, *The Wages of Whiteness,* which extends Du Bois's argument.

7. See Davis, *Women, Race and Class.*

8. Ibid. See especially chapter 1 for a discussion of the sexual and economic exploitation of Black women by White men.

9. See Collins, *Black Sexual Politics.*

10. See Brown, *Good Wives.*

11. This was a marked departure from English legal tradition of paterfamilias, according to which a child's status followed that of the father. In 1662, Virginia instituted a new mandate—*partus sequitur ventrem*—that ensured that children born in the United States would inherit the status of the mother. See Higginbotham Jr., *In the Matter of Color,* 47–48.

12. Historian Martha Hodes argues that when slavery began to replace indentured servitude in Southern states during the last decades of the seventeenth century, White indentured servants and enslaved Africans worked in close proximity to one another. They sometimes became sexual intimates and even married. But tolerance of these intermarriages waned by the end of the seventeenth century, as they were increasingly seen as dangerous exceptions to the racial hierarchy. See Hodes, *White Women, Black Men.*

13. The word "miscegenation" originated during the presidential campaign of 1864, when Democrats made the issue of sex between White women and Black men a national political scandal by coining this term in order to disparage the Republicans as a party favoring racial mixing. See Pascoe, *What Comes Naturally,* 27–30.

14. See Davis, *Women, Race, and Class,* especially chapter 11.

15. In 1954, the Supreme Court's ruling in *Brown v. Board of Education* ended desegregation in public schools. In 1964, Congress passed the Civil Rights Act, which prohibited all remaining institutionalized forms of segregation, except marriage.

16. At one time or another, thirty-eight states had laws that regulated interracial sex and marriage between Blacks and Whites. See Moran, *Interracial Intimacy.*

17. For an account of this pattern, see Loewen, *Sundown Towns.*

18. The connection between lynching and interracial sex between White women and Black men during the post-Reconstruction period and continuing into the 1950s is complicated. Vigilante groups such as the Ku Klux Klan used interracial sex as justification for the murder and, often, castration of Black men. Sometimes these murders were clandestine attacks witnessed by few, but often they were public spectacles. Joy James argues that these "lynching bees" should be read as "prosecutorial performances" in which Whites expressed symbolic rage against fabrications of Black male sexual violence. See James, *Resisting State Violence*. During this same period, interracial sex and the myth of the Black rapist were sometimes used as an excuse for ritualized forms of racial violence enacted for other reasons. Martha Hodes shows that during the Reconstruction period, fears of the political and sexual agency of Black men were deeply intertwined. Black masculinity and sexuality were often equated with Black political rights. In this way, fears of Black participation in state and national politics engendered fear of the sexual autonomy of Black men and of the possibility of sexual relations with White women. In this context, by policing alleged sexual transgressions between White women and Black men, White men reasserted not only their own patriarchal control over White women, but also their racial and political privileges as Southern White men dismayed at the outcome of the Civil War. See Hodes, "The Sexualization of Reconstruction Politics." Stewart E. Tolnay and E. M. Beck also investigate ulterior motivations for lynching campaigns. They argue that racial terror was used to intimidate African Americans who were perceived as economic competitors, as well as political competitors. See Tolnay and Beck, *A Festival of Violence*.

19. See Garber, "A Spectacle of Color," 319.

20. The 18th Amendment to the Constitution prohibited manufacturing or selling alcoholic beverages in the United States. The amendment was passed by Congress in 1917 and ratified by three-quarters of the states by 1919.

21. Historian Kevin Mumford defines "slumming" as "traveling to 'foreign,' exotic, supposedly inferior cultures." Importantly, Mumford envisions slumming as an extensive practice that served many purposes. He therefore argues that "social reformers, intellectuals, sociologists, bohemians, white urban sophisticates—all can be understood as modern-day slummers." See Mumford, *Interzones*, 135. See also Heap, *Slumming*.

22. For an in-depth analysis of *Nigger Heaven*, including the ways in which Van Vechten simultaneously critiqued and perpetuated White participation in Harlem life, see Mumford, *Interzones*, chapter 8.

23. See Chauncey, *Gay New York*, 246–247.

24. Ibid., 247.

25. See Heap, *Slumming*.

26. See Drake and Cayton, *Black Metropolis*, chapter 6.

27. Ibid., 141.

28. See Yu, "Mixing Bodies and Cultures," 457.

29. For an excellent discussion of early sexology framed in relation to emerging discourses about race and eugenics, see Somerville, *Queering the Color Line*. For reproductions of primary documents from early sexologists such as Havelock Ellis and Richard von Kraft Ebing, see Katz, *Gay/Lesbian Almanac: A New Documentary*. See also D'Emilio and Freedman, *Intimate Matters*, and Rupp, *A Desired Past*.

30. This notion that expressions of sexual desire were not isolated actions but central to the organization of social life was a reflection of broader changes taking place in

America. By the turn of the century, the spread of a capitalist economy and growth of urban areas permitted many White men and some White women to detach themselves from a family-based economy and strike out on their own. The possibility of anonymity within large cities enabled individuals to pursue their sexual yearnings. As some women and men began to interpret their homosexual desires as a characteristic that distinguished them from others, a sexual subculture emerged. Notably, strict segregation and Jim Crow racism prevented African Americans with similar desires from exercising this same social mobility. For further discussion, see D'Emilio and Freedman, *Intimate Matters*, and D'Emilio, "Capitalism and Gay Identity." For a critique of the racial and gendered assumptions in D'Emilio's argument, see Bravmann, "Telling Histories."

31. See Ellis, "Sexual Inversion in Women" and *Studies in the Psychology of Sex*.

32. See Chauncey, "From Sexual Inversion to Homosexuality."

33. Charles H. Hughes, as quoted in Mumford, "Homosex Changes," 399.

34. Ibid., 399.

35. See Otis, "A Perversion Not Commonly Noted," 113.

36. Ibid., 113. For a later study that also notes the presence of interracial relationships between institutionalized women, see Ford, "Homosexual Practices of Institutionalized Females." For superb studies on interracial sexuality in women's prisons during this same time, see also Freedman, "The Prison Lesbian," and Kunzel, *Criminal Intimacy*.

37. See Otis, "A Perversion Not Commonly Noted," 113.

38. See Somerville, *Queering the Color Line*, 34–37.

39. See Mumford, *Interzones*, 80.

40. Ibid., 35.

41. Mumford, *Interzones*, 35. Scholars of contemporary lesbian and gay life have a similar analysis. See Rich, "When Difference Is (More Than) Skin Deep"; Martin, "Sexualities Without Genders"; Shokeid, "Erotics and Politics"; and Greene and Boyd-Franklin, "African American Lesbian Couples."

42. See Garber, "A Spectacle in Color"; Chauncey, *Gay New York*; Mumford, *Interzones*; D'Emilio and Freedman, *Intimate Matters*; and Heap, *Slumming*.

43. See Chauncey, *Gay New York*, 244.

44. See Mumford, *Interzones*, 79.

45. Ibid., 79.

46. See Romano, *Race Mixing*, 14.

47. Ibid., chapter 1.

48. For a thorough discussion of "social-equality scares," see Drake and Cayton, *Black Metropolis,* chapter 6.

49. African Americans' lists looked quite different. For them, discrimination that resulted in the inability to "secure land, credit, jobs, or other means of earning a living" and discrimination in the law and by police were the most important forms of inequality. See Myrdal, *An American Dilemma,* 60–61.

50. See Romano, *Race Mixing*.

51. As quoted in Romano, *Race Mixing*, 158.

52. This was, for example, the central question behind the 1967 film, *Guess Who's Coming to Dinner*, directed by Stanley Kramer. For a thoughtful discussion of the latent and overt racial issues in this film, see Romano, *Race Mixing*.

53. See Pascoe, *What Comes Naturally.*

54. Drake and Cayton characterize the restriction of intermarriage as an area of agreement between Blacks and Whites. See Drake and Cayton, *Black Metropolis*, 126. See also Romano, *Race Mixing*.

55. See Spickard, *Mixed Blood*, 283.

56. See Romano, *Race Mixing*, 178.

57. See Erskine, "The Polls," 292.

58. See Deburg, *New Day in Babylon,* 31.

59. See, for example, Carmichael and Hamilton, *Black Power*.

60. See Cleaver, *Soul on Ice*. Some leaders, though, were critical of the practice of judging others' racial authenticity with a Blacker-than-thou attitude. See Hamilton, "How Black Is Black," 47.

61. See Beemyn, "A Queer Capital"; Thorpe, "A House Where Queers Go"; Bérubé, *Coming Out Under Fire*; and Kennedy and Davis, *Boots of Leather*.

62. See Rupp, *A Desired Past*, 133.

63. Ibid., 149.

64. See Wolfe, "Invisible Women in Invisible Places."

65. Ibid., 147.

66. Ibid., 148.

67. See Thorpe, "A House Where Queers Go."

68. Beemyn also explains that many of the bars with substantial White male and bisexual patrons excluded White lesbian and bisexual women, as well as African Americans. See Beemyn, "A Queer Capital," 186.

69. Ibid.

70. Ibid. See also Thorpe, "A House Where Queers Go," and Kennedy and Davis, *Boots of Leather*.

71. Historians have documented the popularity of rent parties within the Black neighborhoods of New York City, Washington, D.C., Detroit, and Buffalo during in the 1920s to 1950s.

72. See Garber, "A Spectacle in Color"; Kennedy and Davis, *Boots of Leather*; and Beemyn, "A Queer Capital."

73. See Moore, "Black and Gay in L.A."

74. See Kennedy and Davis, *Boots of Leather*.

75. Ibid., 119.

76. Beemyn, "A Queer Capital," 203.

77. Gay folklore contains particular stereotypes for those who eroticize race. "Snow queen," for example, is a term for a Black man who is attracted primarily to Whites, while "dinge queen" is a term for a White man attracted primarily to Blacks. The racist connotations here are not subtle. While snow connotes something pure and fresh, dinge is dirty, unclean, shabby, or squalid. Explorations of these terms mix research with personal accounts. See, for instance, Shokeid, "Erotics and Politics"; Boykin, "One More River"; McBride, "Why I Hate Abercrombie and Fitch"; and Lockman, "Ebony and Ivory."

78. For a discussion of tensions surrounding interracial desire among Black gay men, see Scott, "Jungle Fever," and Pharr, "Dinge." For an analysis of how the notion of interraciality has figured into the Black gay and lesbian canon, see Dunning, *Queer in Black and White*. Dunning argues that rather than render its subject "less authentically Black," in key texts, the interracial is used to signify the idea of nation, of authenticity, and of Blackness (21).

79. Here I refer to a collection of texts that include Kennedy, *Interracial Intimacy*; Moran, *Interracial Intimacies*; Romano, *Race Mixing*; Sollors, *Interracialism*; Hodes, *Black Men and White Women*; and Spickard, *Mixed Blood*.

80. An exception involves evidence from colonial Virginia that racial difference may have intensified negative reactions to homosexuality. See Higginbotham Jr. and Kopytoff, "Racial Purity and Interracial Sex," 102.

81. Thorpe argues that historians' tendency to privilege Whiteness has led to the overemphasis of bar culture in the construction of homosexual communities in the 1940s, 1950s, and 1960s. Sustained attention, Thorpe suggests, to the lives of African Americans would lead historians toward the role of rent parties and other informal sites of sociability in the creation of same-sex communities. See Thorpe, "A House Where Queers Go." Similarly, Scott Bravmann argues that John D'Emilio's landmark piece on how capitalism facilitated the emergence of gay and lesbian communities in urban areas overstates the role of economic systems in creating these communities, because it fails to consider experiences of African Americans who, because of White racism and its exclusionary practices, had far less spatial mobility than their White counterparts. Instead of the migration patterns D'Emilio describes, many African Americans created gay and lesbian lives and institutions within their own Black communities. See Bravmann, "Telling Histories." For other important critiques on what scholars of sexuality miss when they focus only on the experiences of Whites, see Moore, "Lipstick or Timberlands?" and Beemyn, "A Queer Capital."

Chapter 2

1. See Logan and Stults, "The Persistence of Segregation in the Metropolis."

2. See Maly, *Beyond Segregation*; Helper, *Racial Policies and Practices*; and Bauman, *Public Housing, Race, and Renewal*.

3. See Maly, *Beyond Segregation*.

4. Ibid. Blockbusting is the practice of selling a house to a Black family, spreading fear among White residents that the neighborhood is about to change, buying the properties of these panicked Whites, and then selling those houses at a higher price to middle-class Blacks who are looking for a nice neighborhood.

5. For an in-depth discussion of how discriminatory housing and lending practices have created racially homogeneous neighborhoods and perpetuated the racial wealth gap, see Massey and Denton, *American Apartheid*; Oliver and Shapiro, *Black Wealth, White Wealth*; and Shapiro, *The Hidden Cost of Being African American*.

6. According to census data, less than 1 percent of married heterosexual interracial couples are Black/White, and less than 2 percent of all same-sex partner households are Black/White interracial couples. See the introduction to this book for more detailed data. Researchers who study friendships find that interracial friendships are significantly rarer than intraracial friendships, that they may be more difficult to maintain, that they tend to be less intimate, and that they are less likely to be reciprocated than intraracial friendships. See Hallinan and Williams, "Interracial Friendship Choices"; Billy and Udry, "Patterns of Adolescent Friendship"; and Vaquera and Kao, "Do You Like Me ... ?"

7. See Zubrinsky and Bobo, "Prismatic Metropolis," and Farley et al., "Stereotypes and Segregation."

8. See Zubrinsky Charles, "Processes of Racial Residential Segregation."

9. See Krysan, "Community Undesirability in Black and White."

10. See Dalmage, *Tripping on the Color Line.*

11. In this study, I use census tracts to approximate neighborhoods. The tracts, which typically contain between 2,500 and 8,000 residents, are probably closest in size to what most people think of as a neighborhood. Yet they are imperfect measures. Neighborhoods are social projections as much as they are spatial designations, and how residents define the boundaries of their neighborhood may be quite different. In addition, using census tracts as neighborhoods can obscure patterns of separation that occur within the smaller units of blocks. For a useful discussion of these challenges, see Ellen, *Sharing America's Neighborhoods*, 14.

12. Lee and Wood, "Is Neighborhood Racial Succession Place-Specific?" and Jargowsky, "Ghetto Poverty among Blacks," use this definition of integration in their studies.

13. Some scholars argue that a 50/50 definition of integration is not useful in a country where African Americans make up 13 percent of the general population. These researchers contend that a more reasonable definition of integration is one in which the racial composition of a given community reflects the racial composition of the general population, plus or minus a few percentage points. From this perspective, a neighborhood that is 13 percent Black and 72 percent White is perfectly integrated if the national population is also 13 percent Black and 72 percent White. Ingrid Gould Ellen uses a compromise between the 50/50 definition and one based on the general population. She defines a racially integrated neighborhood as one with between 10 percent and 50 percent Black residents. See Ellen, *Sharing America's Neighborhoods.* My aim is not to craft an alternative definition of integration, but rather to show that interracial partners are not the only ones who find variability in this term.

14. Woodsdale is a pseudonym.

15. Eduardo Bonilla-Silva finds a similar pattern among Whites who like the idea of having diverse social networks and therefore overstate the number or intensity of friendships they have with African Americans. See Bonilla-Silva, *Racism Without Racists*, chapter 5.

16. For a thoughtful discussion of why interracial families seek mixed-race neighborhoods and a critique of the racial politics in some stable, integrated communities, see Heather Dalmage, "Finding a Home."

17. Though 2010 data on neighborhood racial composition are available, these calculations come from the 2000 U.S. Census. Data from 2000 more accurately approximated the composition of couples' census tracts during the years in which I interviewed them. Three couples in my study were not living together at the time of the study; they are excluded from these calculations.

18. See Oliver and Shapiro, *Black Wealth, White Wealth*, and Shapiro, *The Hidden Cost of Being African American.*

19. Oakton is a pseudonym.

20. In its proximity to working-class and poor neighborhoods, the Chambers's Black middle-class neighborhood reflects a national pattern of inner-ring Black suburbs that Mary Patillo-McCoy described in her study of Black middle-class residents in the South Side neighborhoods of Chicago. See Patillo-McCoy, *Black Picket Fences.*

21. See Oliver and Shapiro, *Black Wealth, White Wealth*, and Shapiro, *The Hidden Cost of Being African American.*

22. Not all Whites live in majority-White neighborhoods or cities. See Hartigan, *Racial Situations,* for an analysis of how meanings of Whiteness are localized and how Whiteness gets marked in majority-Black contexts.

23. As I noted at the beginning of the chapter, most Whites describe their ideal neighborhood as one that is less than 20 percent African American, and studies of discriminatory housing practices reveal that real estate agents lead Whites toward majority-White neighborhoods. See Krysan, "Community Undesirability in Black and White;" Zubrinsky Charles, "Who Will Live Near Whom?"; and Bobo and Zubrinsky, "Attitudes on Residential Integration."

24. See Essed, "Everyday Racism," 203, and Essed, *Understanding Everyday Racism.*

25. See Fulani, *The Psychopathology of Everyday Racism and Sexism,* and Jackson et al., "Racism and the Psychical and Mental Health Status."

26. In her ethnographic study of Black middle-class suburbanites, Karyn Lacy describes similar efforts to establish class status and legitimacy. See Lacy, *Blue-Chip Black.*

27. See Conley, *Being Black, Living in the Red*; Cose, *Rage of a Privileged Class*; Feagin and Sikes, *Living with Racism: The Black Middle-Class Experience*; Graham, *Member of the Club*; and Lacy, *Blue-Chip Black.*

28. Lest it seem that Kristie's reading of the situation is "paranoid," consider whether in a casual conversation between strangers, a White person would be expected to be conversant about Appalachian folk songs.

29. Nadine also noted that her more masculine gender presentation likely shapes the racism she experiences. She tells me she thinks that White people appear "guarded" and "nervous" when they perceive her as a Black man.

30. Using data from the Multi-City Study on Urban Inequality, Krysan shows that over 70 percent of African Americans rated the communities of Troy (in Detroit), Newton (in Boston), and Glendale (in Los Angeles) as desirable. These three communities have relatively high median housing values according to 1990 census data, and each of these communities has less than 5 percent African American residents. See Krysan, "Community Undesirability in Black and White."

31. See Emerson and Smith, *Divided by Faith.*

32. Interview after his "Social Justice and the Emerging New Age" address at the Herman W. Read Fieldhouse, Western Michigan University (18 December 1963).

33. Drake and Cayton argue that a "separate Negro institutional structure," ordered by a system of social classes, has existed in America since the eighteenth century. See Drake and Cayton, *Black Metropolis,* 121.

34. See Dalmage, *Tripping on the Color Line.*

35. See Moore, *Invisible Families.*

36. Moore, "Black and Gay in L.A.," 194.

37. "Border patrolling" is how Dalmage conceptualizes the ways in which Black and White communities maintain and defend racial boundaries. She notes, however, that there are very different motivations for White border patrolling, which has historically enforced exclusionary practices of segregation, versus Black border patrolling, which has enabled Black communities to come together in racially separate spaces for the purposes of unity, pride, and safety. See Dalmage, *Tripping on the Color Line,* chapter 1.

38. See appendix B for details about the study participants and table B.2 for a demographic comparison between groups.

39. See Beam, *In the Life*; Riggs, *Black Is, Black Ain't*; Hemphill, *Brother to Brother*; McBride, *Why I Hate Abercrombie and Fitch*; and Pharr, *Black Gay Man.*

40. See King, "Multiple Jeopardy, Multiple Consciousness."

41. See Dalmage, *Tripping on the Color Line*, chapter 1.

42. See Beemyn, "A Queer Capital."

43. See, for example, Moore's work on Black lesbians and gays in Los Angeles ("Black and Gay in L.A.") and on Black lesbian families and their relationships to Black communities (*Invisible Families*).

Chapter 3

1. See Drake and Cayton, *Black Metropolis*. Groundbreaking in both its detail and scope, Drake and Cayton survey key elements of social life in Chicago's South Side in the late 1930s, including employment, religion, migration, community structure, and Black-White race relations.

2. See Bonilla-Silva, *Racism Without Racists,* for a discussion of colorblind racial ideology.

3. See Childs, *Navigating Interracial Borders,* for an analysis of the ways in which colorblind logic shapes how interracial couples are perceived on college campuses and by their friends, family, and church communities.

4. See Childs, *Navigating Interracial Borders*; Dalmage, *Tripping on the Color Line*; Judice, *Interracial Marriages*; Kreager, "Guarded Borders"; and Rosenblatt et al., *Multiracial Couples*.

5. See Datzman and Gardner, "In My Mind, We Are All Humans."

6. This trend dominates the sociological research on interracial intimacy, with the exception of Frankenberg, *White Women, Race Matters*, and Bystydzienski, *Intercultural Couples*.

7. See Goffman, *Stigma*, 3.

8. See Goffman, *Stigma*, 42.

9. Goffman calls these dyads "withs." He says that "a with is a party of more than one whose members are perceived to be 'together.'" See Goffman, *Relations in Public*, 19–27. His analysis of how withs interact in public is very useful for considering how intimate partners move through public spaces. However, when he references withs in relation to stigma, he locates stigma within one partner or the other: "To be 'with' someone is to arrive at a social occasion in his company, walk with him down a street, be a member of his party in a restaurant, and so forth. The issue is that in certain circumstances the social identity of those an individual is with can be used as a source of information concerning his own identity" (47).

10. For an extended critique on this point, see Link and Phelan, "Conceptualizing Stigma." See also Crocker et al., "Social Stigma."

11. I borrow the term visibility management from Lasser and Tharinger, who conceptualize it as the dynamic, ongoing process whereby gay, lesbian, and bisexual youths make careful decisions about when, how, and under what conditions to disclose their sexuality, as well as how they monitor the presentation of their sexual orientation in different social environments. See Lasser and Tharinger, "Visibility Management." These practices are akin to what Goffman calls "information control." See Goffman, *Stigma*.

12. Simmons and O'Connell, "Married Couples and Unmarried-Partner Households."

13. See Childs, "Looking Behind the Stereotypes," and Patricia Hill Collins, *Black Sexual Politics*.

14. A 2007 Gallup Poll reported that 85 percent of Blacks and 75 percent of Whites said that they approved of marriages between Blacks and Whites. While African Americans have long been more likely to support intermarriage (a 1958 poll showed approval at 56 percent), approval by Whites has grown steadily from a 4 percent approval rate in 1958.

15. See Childs, *Navigating Interracial Borders*; Dalmage, *Tripping on the Color Line*; Rosenblatt et al., *Multiracial Couples*; Kreager, "Guarded Borders"; and Judice, *Interracial Marriages*.

16. See Romano, *Race Mixing*.

17. Other researchers have also argued that interracial stigma may heighten presumptions of intimacy between men and women of different races. See, for instance, Datzman and Gardner, "In My Mind, We are All Human."

18. See Root, *Love's Revolution*.

19. See Childs, *Navigating Interracial Borders*, and Dalmage, *Tripping on the Color Line*.

20. See Carbado, "Straight Out of the Closet." For other analyses of the intersections between racial privilege and heterosexual privilege, see Cohen, "Punks, Bulldaggers, and Welfare Queens," and Ross, "The Sexualization of Difference."

21. Carbado does recognize that Whiteness amplifies heterosexual privileges; what he fails to acknowledge is that monoraciality may stand above interraciality in shaping access to certain fundamental heterosexual privileges.

22. The dynamic contrast between lesbians who present a traditionally feminine self and those who present a traditionally masculine self, often characterized as femmes and butches, bulldaggers, aggressives, or studs, respectively, has been an important part of the relationships and sexual politics of lesbian communities. See, for example, Loulan, *The Lesbian Erotic Dance*; Newman, *The Femme Mystique*; Joan Nestle, *The Persistent Desire*; and Moore, "Lipstick or Timberlands?"

23. On the paradoxical nature of visibility for interracial partners, see Steinbugler, "Visibility as Privilege and Danger."

24. Research indicates that at least among school-age children, the reverse is true. Boys' social networks are less likely than girls' to be composed of those from the same race, perhaps because boys are more likely to play in larger, less intimate groups. See Maccoby, *The Two Sexes*.

25. See Greene and Franklin, *African American Lesbian Couples*, and Shokeid, *Erotics and Politics*.

26. See Gramling and Forsyth, "Exploiting Stigma."

27. Other researchers also find that heterosexual interracial partners conceal their intimacy from others. Elizabeth Vaquera and Grace Kao report that interracial couples were just as likely as their same-race counterparts to have intimate physical contact, such as kissing or sexual intercourse, but they refrained from more public displays, such as hand-holding, telling others they are a couple, and meeting each other's parents. See Vaquera and Kao, "Private and Public Displays of Affection."

28. Sexuality scholars have argued that in public, same-sex couples are often expected to "pass" as heterosexual friends instead of same-sex lovers, and that this self-policing is particularly oppressive for gays and lesbians because it involves regulating even the most "innocent" forms of sexual affection. See, for example, Johnson, "Heteronormative Citizenship."

29. See Rothman, *Weaving a Family*.

30. Goffman calls this "voluntary disclosure." See Goffman, *Stigma*, 100–102.

31. Tommy and Brian wear their "Smash Racism" pins every day.

32. See Goffman, *Stigma*, 4.

Chapter 4

1. See the introduction for further discussion of the assimilation paradigm, contact theory (a related theoretical perspective), and love myths.

2. See Yu, *Mixing Bodies and Cultures*, 447.

3. See Oliver and Shapiro, *Black Wealth, White Wealth*; Roscigno, "Race and the Reproduction of Educational Disadvantage"; and Kim and Miech, "The Black-White Difference."

4. See Bourdieu, *In Other Words*, 122.

5. Ibid., 11.

6. Bonilla-Silva, *Racism Without Racists*.

7. Ibid., 104.

8. See Du Bois, *The Souls of Black Folk*.

9. Davis is a pseudonym.

10. Emmett Till was a fourteen-year-old Black youth who was lynched by a group of White men in Money, Mississippi, in 1955, for allegedly whistling at a White woman.

11. See Dewan and Healy, "On the Rooftop."

12. Later in this chapter, I analyze how partners use humor to deal with racial tensions in greater detail.

13. Bourdieu argues that we often "misperceive" qualities that are social in origin as individual. This insight leads him to assert that because habitus works to reproduce structured differences and inequalities, there is a symbolic violence involved when individuals are blamed for consequences that are actually social. See Bourdieu, *Practical Reason*.

14. My use of the term emotional labor (and/or emotion work) diverges from Arlie Hochschild's definition. She defines emotion work as the process of modeling our own emotions and bringing them in line with what we consider appropriate, either through surface acting (when we pretend to feel a particular way) or through deep acting (when we attempt to change our feelings). Hochschild distinguishes this type of emotion work from the "emotional labor" women do in the workplace as a part of their jobs. See Hochschild, *The Managed Heart*. I use these terms in a broader manner, to describe emotional efforts and strategies that partners use to deal with race and racism. For other examinations of the racialized dimensions of emotional labor, see DeVault, "Comfort and Struggle," and Mirchandani, "Challenging Racial Silences."

15. In his critique of colorblind racism, Bonilla-Silva argues that Whites' extreme residential segregation leads to the development of a corresponding social and psychological isolation that skews Whites' racial views. See Bonilla-Silva, *Racism Without Racists*.

16. When Evan's family arrived, they were the second African American family to move into the neighborhood. The first left when a cross was burned on their lawn. Evan assumes that it was because his father was "kind of known" as a professional athlete that something similar did not happen to them.

17. As chapter 3 shows, reading the dynamics of public spaces, managing the emotions evoked by those dynamics, and deciding on the appropriate response are strategies

that individuals use to manage White supremacy and homophobia in their everyday lives. These complex strategies have a significant emotional component, yet I distinguish them from the emotional labor described in this chapter because these individual efforts are not used to negotiate differences in racial habitus between partners.

18. For an analysis of how youths of African descent can develop a White cultural identity, see Twine, "Brown Skinned White Girls."

19. See Hartmann, "The Family as the Locus of Gender, Class, and Political Struggle."

20. Bourdieu uses this term in numerous writings. See, for example, *Practical Reason*, 25.

21. See Bonilla-Silva et al., "When Whites Flock Together."

Chapter 5

1. Romano, *Race Mixing*, and Nagel, *Race, Ethnicity and Sexuality*.

2. The assumption that only lower-class White women sleep with Black men may derive from class privilege that has allowed upper-class White women to hide such associations. See Romano, *Race Mixing*, and Hodes, *White Women, Black Men*.

3. Pascoe, *What Comes Naturally*.

4. See chapter 1. See also Davis, *Women, Race, and Class*; Elizabeth Fox-Genovese, *Within the Plantation Household*; and Brown, *Good Wives, Nasty Wenches, and Anxious Patriarchs*.

5. See Collins, *Black Feminist Thought*.

6. See hooks, "Representations of Whiteness in the Black Imagination."

7. See Collins, *Black Sexual Politics*.

8. See Lacy, *Blue-Chip Black*.

9. The classic Spike Lee film *Jungle Fever* is one of many media depictions of this image of illicit desire and short-lived attraction. For an analysis of contemporary media representations, see Childs, *Fade to Black*.

10. See Bonilla-Silva, *Racism Without Racists*.

11. These concepts were initially developed by Fredrik Barth in *Ethnic Groups and Boundaries*. Others who have used the concept of boundaries to study interracial intimacy include Dalmage, *Tripping on the Color Line*, and Childs, *Navigating Interracial Borders*. For broader applications of this concept to race and ethnicity, see Lamont, *The Dignity of Working Men*; Lacy, *Blue-Chip Black*; and Wray, *Not Quite White*. For a general discussion, see Lamont and Molnár, "The Study of Boundaries in the Social Sciences."

12. See Wray, *Not Quite White*, 83.

13. See Lacy, *Blue-Chip Black*, 100.

14. See Ponse, *Identities in the Lesbian World*.

15. For an astute analysis of how middle-class African Americans use exclusionary and inclusionary boundary work to maintain intraracial distinctions and emphasize their middle-class status, see Lacy, *Blue-Chip Black*.

16. The notion of promiscuity as a negative attribute is highly gendered. The accusation of having had many sexual partners is damaging for women, whose virtue is tied to either chastity or monogamy. Having had multiple sexual partners generally brings men increased social status and a reputation for virility and sexual mastery. Marie seems to have accepted this double standard. For her, being labeled a "slut" is a terrible insult.

17. Note that even though White males as a group are not the usual targets of inter-racial stereotypes, Neil protects his individual self-image by distancing himself from pejorative stereotypes of Black femininity.

18. This pattern also suggests a flaw in the logic of contact theory, which implies that intimacy with one person of a different racial or ethnic group will decrease Whites' prejudice toward other members of that group.

19. See Pettigrew, "The Ultimate Attribution Error."

20. Sociologist Philip Blumstein has argued that it is the "publicness of the display, the apparent felt necessity of locating oneself, one's partner, and the relatedness of the two in some kind of conceptual space that suggests that the relationship engenders or demands reality construction work that is separate and apart from the simple reporting on a preexisting reality." See Blumstein, "The Production of Selves in Personal Relationships," 308–309.

21. "Trash" is a term used by Scott Patterson, not by either Trudy or Neil. Scott, a Black heterosexual male mentioned in previous chapters and also discussed later in this chapter, chose this word when he was describing what he and Tamara supposed was the attitude of an older White man they met in a gas station in a poor White neighborhood near their house. Scott recalled, "We're both thinking this guy hates us because we're interracial. 'Black guy with a White girl—both of them are trash.'"

22. Ulrich is one of five partners (among eighty-two in the sample) who were not born in the United States. The other four include a Black heterosexual woman born in St. Lucia, a White lesbian born in Italy, a White heterosexual man born in Switzerland, and a White heterosexual woman born in Poland.

23. Some of my findings in this section resonate with the colorblind and race-conscious narratives that Childs examines in *Navigating Interracial Borders*.

24. Sociologist Mary Waters uses the experience of West Indian immigrants and their children to explore the intraracial distinctions within those racialized as Black in the United States. See Waters, *Black Identities*.

25. See Massey, "Residential Segregation"; McPherson et al., "Birds of a Feather"; and Oliver and Shapiro, *Black Wealth/White Wealth*.

26. Childs interviewed Black/White couples who make this same distinction between how race works in public versus private spaces. See *Navigating Interracial Borders*, 41.

27. Currently, same-sex couples are granted marriage licenses in six states (Connecticut, Iowa, Massachusetts, New Hampshire, New York, and Vermont), as well as the District of Columbia. In 2012, the legislatures in Maryland and Washington passed bills allowing same-sex marriages, but as of the time of this book's publication, those bills have not yet taken effect.

28. See Bonilla-Silva, *Racism Without Racists*, and Childs, *Navigating Interracial Borders*.

29. Historian Renee Romano documents that in mid-twentieth-century America, heterosexual Black/White couples engaged in similar forms of boundary work. When these couples spoke publicly about their relationships, they often stressed how "ordinary" and "normal" they were. Romano quotes one interracially married White woman as saying, "This is 1972 and people ought to have a right to do what they feel is constitutionally and morally right. We're just man and wife, that's all." This effort, Romano argues, likely helped couples downplay the very unordinary treatment they received in their everyday

lives. Further, presenting themselves as respectable and legitimate might reduce the social discrimination they experienced and diminish the negative stereotypes that both Black and White communities held about them. See Romano, *Race Mixing*, 176.

30. See Human Rights Campaign, "Hospital Visitation Laws"; "Parenting Laws: Joint Adoption"; and "Statewide Employment Laws & Policies."

Chapter 6

1. I use the term "mixed-race" because Hank emphasizes his children's mixed heritage. The term he and Mabel use when they talk to their young children about their race/ethnicity is "African-American-Italian-French."

2. This meshes with social science research on Black identities. See, for example, Smith and Moore, "Intraracial Diversity and Relations Among African-Americans."

3. See Haney-Lopez, *White by Law*.

4. See Lewis, "What Group?"

5. Arguably, to be White in the United States is to be already exposed to a multitude of positive images and histories that portray Whiteness in the most favorable light, but Helms uses terms like "positive" and "healthy" to connote nonracist White identities. For her, racial self-actualization is an ongoing process in which a person has abandoned their racist beliefs and is continually open to new ways of thinking about race and culture. See Helms, "Towards a Theoretical Explanation," and Helms, *Black and White Racial Identity*. This stage does not necessarily include an active resistance to others' racial beliefs or practices. Nonracism is not the same as antiracism, a distinction Eileen O'Brien makes clear when she defines antiracism as a commitment "in thought, action, and practice, to dismantling racism. ... Antiracists make it a point to notice and address racism regularly." See O'Brien, *Whites Confront Racism*, 4.

6. See, for example, Rowe et al., "White Racial Identity Models."

7. This perspective echoes some of the same tenets as contact theory (discussed in previous chapters), although contact theorists did not explore the psychological stages through which this re-evaluation takes place.

8. See O'Brien, *Whites Confront Racism*.

9. See O'Brien and Korgen, "It's the Message."

10. See Twine, "Bearing Blackness in Britain," and Twine, *A White Side of Black Britain*.

11. See Lewis, "What Group?"; Dyer, "White"; and Rothenberg, *White Privilege*.

12. On thick versus thin identities, see Cornell and Hartmann, *Ethnicity and Race*.

13. For a discussion of the sexualized consumption of racial otherness, see hooks, "Eating the Other."

14. See Frankenberg, *White Women, Race Matters*.

15. Some persons of mixed descent stigmatize Whiteness in a similar manner. See Storrs, "Whiteness as Stigma."

16. See hooks, "Eating the Other."

17. See Twine, "Bearing Blackness in Britain," and Twine, *A White Side of Black Britain*.

18. See Twine and Steinbugler, "The Gap Between 'Whites' and 'Whiteness.'" Note that developing racial literacy to move beyond a White habitus is a form of racework (emotional labor).

19. Storch is a pseudonym.

20. For analysis of the complicated decisions that lesbian parents make in creating a family, see Mamo, *Queering Reproduction*.

21. See, for example, Aptheker, *Antiracism in U.S. History*, and Bonilla-Silva, *Racism Without Racists*. Both studies show that working-class Whites and women tend to be overrepresented among antiracists and progressive Whites.

22. See Bonilla-Silva et al., "When Whites Flock Together"; Dyer, *White*; and Van Ausdale and Feagin, *The First R*.

Conclusions

1. My intent here is to address C. Wright Mills's central challenge: that social analysts examine individual biographies by placing them within the broader historical moment. See Mills, *The Sociological Imagination*.

2. See Feagin, *Racist America*, and Harris, *The Harder We Run*, 131.

3. See Oliver and Shapiro, *White Wealth/Black Wealth*.

4. See Fowler, *Northern Attitudes Towards Intermarriage*, 339–439.

5. It should be noted, however, that when the Fair Housing Act was enacted in 1968, the law was comprehensive but also barely enforceable. It allowed the Department of Housing and Urban Development (HUD) to investigate the complaints it received, but it did not endow HUD with the power to bring parties guilty of housing discrimination to court. See Lipsitz, *The Possessive Investment in Whiteness*, 28.

6. Here "Whites" refers to non-Hispanic Whites. See U.S. Census Bureau, "Income, Poverty, and Health Insurance," 6.

7. See Taylor et al., "Twenty-to-One."

8. See Feagin, *Racist America*; Shapiro, *The Hidden Cost*; and Beeman et al., *Whiteness as Property*.

9. See Logan and Stults, "The Persistence of Segregation in the Metropolis."

10. For an analysis of resegregation within public schools, see Orfield, *Schools More Separate*.

11. See Mauer and King, "Uneven Justice," 1.

12. Devah Pager explores the consequences of incarceration for the employment outcomes of Black and White job seekers and shows that Whites with criminal records received more favorable treatment than Blacks without criminal records. See Pager, "The Mark of a Criminal Record."

13. According to a 2008 USA/Gallup Poll, 42 percent of Americans believe that racism against Blacks is not widespread in America. The breakdown by race shows significant variation: 46 percent of Whites, 20 percent of Blacks, and 38 percent of Hispanics believe that anti-Black racism is not widespread. See Jones, "Majority of Americans Say Racism Against Blacks Widespread."

14. *New York Times* columnist Thomas Friedman, writing on the morning after the 2008 presidential election, declared Barack Obama's victory to be "the final chapter of America's Civil War" (as quoted in Alba, *Blurring the Color Line*, 1).

15. I argue that mixed-race children are increasingly seen as blurring racial boundaries between Blacks and Whites, even as the one-drop rule remains the dominant logic for classifying the children of Black and White parents.

16. Eduardo Bonilla-Silva, for example, has a structural analysis of race and rejects the notion that race or racism can be transcended. Yet he positions interracial partners as "racial progressives." See Bonilla-Silva, *Racism Without Racists*.

17. I do not mean to naively suggest that coalition-building is unchallenging or even always productive. Cross-racial coalitions themselves have historically been contested spaces, fraught with some of the same sorts of tensions that I have described in this book. To effect real change, coalitions must acknowledge the power relations at play within groups themselves.

18. See Durr and Wingfield, "Keep Your 'N' in Check: African American Women and the Interactive Effects of Etiquette and Emotional Labor."

19. See Emerson and Chai Kim, "Multi-Racial Congregations: An Analysis of Their Development and a Typology."

20. See, for example, Bratter and Zuberi, "As Racial Boundaries 'Fade': Racial Stratification and Interracial Marriage."

Appendix

1. I was aided at the beginning of this project by Damien Frierson, who provided outstanding research assistance. We paired up and simultaneously interviewed each partner separately. We each interviewed four partners in this manner. I conducted the remaining seventy-eight interviews myself.

2. See Bernard, *The Future of Marriage.*

3. See Hertz, "Separate but Simultaneous Interviewing of Husbands and Wives."

4. Lareau had already finished data collection and was in the writing process when I was a graduate student. For further details on her study, see Lareau, *Unequal Childhoods.*

5. The partners in my ethnographic sample include Sylvia Chabot and Leslie Cobbs; Walter and Kirk Belton-Davis; Mabel and Hank Renault; and Kalvin and Vera Oster.

6. In the case of three of the couples, I completed all observations within a period of five weeks. I observed the fourth couple over a fourteen-week period.

BIBLIOGRAPHY

Alba, Richard. 2009. *Blurring the color line: The new chance for a more integrated America.* Cambridge, MA: Harvard University Press.

Alba, Richard, and Victor Nee. 2003. *Remaking the American mainstream assimilation and contemporary immigration.* Cambridge, MA: Harvard University Press.

Adam, Barry D. 1998. Theorizing homophobia. *Sexualities* 1(4):387–404.

Allport, Gordon W. 1958. *The nature of prejudice.* Garden City, NY: Doubleday.

Ancheta, Angelo N. 1998. *Race, rights, and the Asian American experience.* New Brunswick, NJ: Rutgers University Press.

Aptheker, Herbert. 1992. *Anti-racism in U.S. history: The first two hundred years.* New York: Greenwood Press.

Baker, Nancy. 1984. *The beauty trap.* New York: Franklin Watts.

Bauman, John. 1987. *Public housing, race, and renewal.* Philadelphia: Temple University Press.

Beam, Joseph. 1986. *In the life: A Black gay anthology.* New York: Alyson Publications.

Beeman, Angie, Davita Silfen Glasberg, and Colleen Casey. 2011. Whiteness as property: Predatory lending and the reproduction of racialized inequality. *Critical Sociology* 37(1):27–45.

Beemyn, Brett. 1997. *A queer capital.* New York: Routledge.

Bérubé, Allan. 2000. *Coming out under fire: The history of gay men and women in World War Two.* New York: Free Press.

Bianchi, Suzanne M., Melissa A. Milkie, Liana C. Sayer, and John P. Robinson. 2000. Is anyone doing the housework? Trends in the gender division of household labor. *Social Forces* 79(1):191–228.

Billy, John O. G., and J. Richard Udry. 1985. Patterns of adolescent friendship and effects on sexual behavior. *Social Psychology Quarterly* 48(1):27–41.

Blumstein, Philip. 1991. The production of selves in personal relationships. In *The Self-society dynamic: Cognition, emotion, and action.* eds. Judith A. Howard and Peter L. Callero. Cambridge, UK: Cambridge University Press.

Bobo, Lawrence, and Camille Zubrinsky. 1996. Attitudes on residential integration: Perceived status differences, mere in-group preference, or racial prejudice? *Social Forces* 74(3):883–909.

Bonczar, Thomas P. 2003. *Prevalence of imprisonment in the U.S. population, 1974–2001*. Washington, DC: Bureau of Justice Statistics, U.S. Department of Justice, NCJ 197976.

Bonilla-Silva, Eduardo. 2003. *Racism without racists: Color-blind racism and the persistence of racial inequality in the United States*. New York: Rowman & Littlefield.

Bonilla-Silva, Eduardo, Carla Goar, and David G. Embrick. 2006. When Whites flock together: The social psychology of White habitus. *Critical Sociology* 32(2–3): 229–253.

Bourdieu, Pierre. 1998. *Practical reason: On the theory of action*. Stanford, CA: Stanford University Press.

Bourdieu, Pierre. 1990. *In other words: Essays towards a reflexive sociology*. Cambridge, UK: Polity Press.

Boykin, Keith. 1996. *One more river to cross: Black and gay in America*. New York: New York University Press.

Bratter, Jennifer L., and Tukufu Zuberi. 2008. As racial boundaries "fade": Racial stratification and intermarriage. In *White logic, White methods: Racism and methodology*. eds. Tukufu Zuberi and Eduardo Bonilla-Silva. Lanham, MD: Rowman & Littlefield.

Bravmann, Scott. 1990. Telling histories: Rethinking the lesbian and gay historical imagination. *Outlook* 8:68–74.

Brines, Julie. 1994. Economic dependency, gender, and the division of labor at home. *American Journal of Sociology* 100:652–688.

Brown, Kathleen M. 1996. *Good wives, nasty wenches, and anxious patriarchs: Gender, race and power in colonial Virginia*. Chapel Hill, NC: University of North Carolina Press.

Brown, Michael K. 2005. *Whitewashing race: The myth of a color-blind society*. Berkeley, CA; London: University of California Press.

Brunsma, David L. 2006. *Mixed messages: Multiracial identities in the "color-blind" era*. Boulder, CO: Lynne Rienner Publishers.

Bystydzienski, Jill M. 2011. *Intercultural couples: Crossing boundaries, negotiating difference*. New York: New York University Press.

Canaday, Margot. 2009. *The straight state: Sexuality and citizenship in twentieth-century America*. Princeton, NJ: Princeton University Press.

Cancian, Francesca. 2000. *Caring and gender*. Thousand Oaks, CA: Pine Forge Press.

Carbado, Devon W. 2000. Straight out of the closet. *Berkeley Women's Law Journal* 15: 76–124.

Carmichael, Stokely, and Charles V. Hamilton. 1992. *Black power: The politics of liberation in America*. New York: Random House.

Carroll, Joseph. August 16, 2007. Most Americans approve of interracial marriages: Blacks more likely than Whites to approve of Black White unions. *Gallop News Service*, http://www.gallup.com/poll/28417/most-americans-approve-interracial-marriages.aspx.

Carter, Prudence. 2005. *Keepin' it real: School success beyond Black and White*. New York: Oxford University Press.

Chauncey, George. 1994. *Gay New York: Gender, urban culture, and the making of the male world, 1890–1940*. New York: Basic Books.

Chauncey, George. 1982. From sexual inversion to homosexuality: Medicine and the changing conceptualization of female deviance. *Salmagundi* 58–59:114–146.

Childs, Erica Chito. 2009. *Fade to Black and White: Interracial images in popular culture. Perspectives on a multiracial America.* Lanham, MD: Rowman & Littlefield.

Childs, Erica Chito. 2005. Looking behind the stereotypes of the "angry Black woman": An exploration of Black women's responses to interracial relationships. *Gender & Society* 19(4):544–561.

Childs, Erica Chito. 2005. *Navigating interracial borders: Black-White couples and their social worlds.* New Brunswick, NJ: Rutgers University Press.

Cleaver, Eldridge. 1968. *Soul on ice.* New York: Delta Books.

Cohen, Cathy. 1997. Punks, bulldaggers, and welfare queens: The radical potential of queer politics. *Journal of Lesbian and Gay Studies* 3(4):437–465.

Collins, Patricia Hill. 2004. *Black sexual politics: African Americans, gender, and the new racism.* New York: Routledge.

Collins, Patricia Hill. 2000. *Black feminist thought: Knowledge, consciousness, and the politics of empowerment.* New York: Routledge.

Conley, Dalton. 1999. *Being Black, living in the red: Race, wealth, and social policy in America.* Berkeley, CA: University of California Press.

Coontz, Stephanie. 2005. *Marriage, a history: From obedience to intimacy, or how love conquered marriage.* New York: Viking Press.

Cornell, Stephen, and Douglas Hartmann. 1998. *Ethnicity and race: Making identities in a changing world.* Thousand Oaks, CA: Pine Forge Press.

Cose, Ellis. 1995. *The rage of a privileged class.* New York: HarperCollins.

Craig, Maxine Leeds. 2002. *Ain't I a beauty queen? Black women, beauty, and the politics of race.* Oxford, UK: Oxford University Press.

Crocker, J., B. Major, and C. Steele. 1998. Social stigma. In *The handbook of social psychology.* Vol. 2, 504–553. Boston: McGraw Hill.

Cross Jr., William E., Thomas A. Parham, and Janet E. Helms. 1991. The stages of Black identity development: Nigrescence models. In *Black psychology.* ed. Reginald L. Jones. 3rd ed. Berkeley, CA: Cobb & Henry.

Dalmage, Heather M. 2000. *Tripping on the color line: Black-White multiracial families in a racially divided world.* New Brunswick, NJ: Rutgers University Press.

Dalmage, Heather M. 2005. Finding a home: Housing the color line. In *Mixed messages: Multiracial identities in the "color-blind" era.* ed. David L. Brunsma. Boulder, CO: Lynne Rienner Publishers.

Datzman, Jeanine, and Carol Brooks Gardner. In my mind, we are all human: Notes on the public management of Black-White interracial romantic relationships. *Marriage and Family Review* 30(1/2):5–24.

Davis, Angela Y. 1981. *Women, race and class.* New York: Vintage Books.

Dawson, Michael C. 1994. *Behind the mule: Race and class in African American politics.* Princeton, NJ: Princeton University Press.

D'Emilio, John. 1983. Capitalism and gay identity. In *Powers of desire: The politics of sexuality.* eds. Ann Bar Snitow, Christine Stansell, and Sharon Thompson, 100–113. New York: Monthly Review Press.

D'Emilio, John, and Estelle Freeman. 1988. *Intimate matters: A history of sexuality in America.* Chicago: University of Chicago Press.

DeNavas-Walt, Carmen, Bernadette D. Proctor, and Jessica C. Smith. 2010. *Income, poverty, and health insurance coverage in the United States: 2009.* Washington, DC: U.S. Census Bureau, P60–P238.

DeVault, Marjorie. 1999. Comfort and struggle: Emotion work in family life. *The ANNALS of the American Academy of Political and Social Sciences* 561(1):52–63.

Dewan, Sheila, and Patrick Healy. 2004. On the rooftop, when reflex and customs clash. *The New York Times*, January 26.

Drake, St Clair, and Horace R. Cayton. 1945. *Black metropolis: A study of Negro life in a northern city.* Chicago: University of Chicago Press.

Du Bois, W. E. B. 1999 [1935]. *Black reconstruction in America, 1860–1880.* New York: Simon & Schuster.

Du Bois, W. E. B. 1990. *The souls of Black folk.* New York: Vintage Books.

Dunning, Stefanie K. 2009. *Queer in Black and White: Interraciality, same sex desire, and contemporary African American culture.* Bloomington, IN: Indiana University Press.

Durr, Marlese, and Adia Harvey Winfield. 2011. Keep your "N" in check: African American women and the interactive effects of etiquette and emotional labor. *Critical Sociology*, http://crs.sagepub.com/content/early/2011/03/26/0896920510380074.

Dyer, Richard. 1997. *White: Essays on race and culture.* New York: Routledge.

Ellen, Ingrid Gould. 2000. *Sharing America's neighborhoods: The prospects for stable racial integration.* Cambridge, MA: Harvard University Press.

Ellingson, S., and K. Shroeder. 2004. Race and construction of same-sex markets in four Chicago neighborhoods. In *The sexual organization of the city,* 93. Chicago: University of Chicago Press.

Ellis, Havelock. 1915. *Studies in the psychology of sex. Volume 2: Sexual inversion.* Philadelphia: F. A. Davis.

Ellis, Havelock. 1895. Sexual inversion in women. *Alienist and Neurologist* 16:141–158.

Emerson, Michael O., and Karen Chai Kim. 2003. Multi-racial congregations: An analysis of their development and a typology. *Journal for the Scientific Study of Religion* 42(2):217–227.

Emerson, Michael O., and Christian Smith. 2001. *Divided by faith: Evangelical religion and the problem of race in America.* New York: Oxford University Press.

Erskine, Hazel. 1973. The polls: Interracial socializing. *Public Opinion Quarterly* 37: 283–294.

Essed, Philomena. 2002. Everyday racism. In *A companion to racial and ethnic studies.* eds. David Theo Goldberg and John Solomos. Malden, MA: Wiley-Blackwell.

Essed, Philomena. 1991. *Understanding everyday racism: An interdisciplinary theory.* Newbury Park, CA: Sage.

Faderman, Lillian. 1992. *Odd girls and twilight lovers: A history of lesbian life in twentieth century America.* New York: Penguin Books.

Farley, Reynolds, Charlotte Steeh, Tara Jackson, Maria Krysan, and Keith Reeves. 1994. Stereotypes and segregation: Neighborhoods in the Detroit area. *American Journal of Sociology* 100(3):750–778.

Feagin, Joe R. 2000. *Racist America: Roots, current realities, and future reparations.* New York: Routledge.

Feagin, Joe R., Hernán Vera, and Pinar Batur. 2001. *White racism.* New York: Routledge.

Feagin, Joe, and Melvin P. Sikes. 1995. *Living with racism: The Black middle-class experience*. Boston: Beacon Press.

Ford, C. A. 1929. Homosexual practices of institutionalized females. *The Journal of Abnormal and Social Psychology* 23(4):442–448.

Fowler, Dan. 1987. *Northern attitudes towards interracial marriage: Legislation and public opinion in the Middle Atlantic and the states of the old Northwest, 1780–1930*. New York: Garland Publishing.

Fox-Genovese, Elizabeth. 1988. *Within the plantation household: Black and White women of the old South*. Chapel Hill, NC: University of North Carolina Press.

Frankenberg, Ruth. 1993. *White women, race matters: The social construction of Whiteness*. Minneapolis: University of Minnesota Press.

Freedman, Estelle. 1996. The prison lesbian: Race, class, and the construction of the aggressive female homosexual, 1915–1965. *Feminist Studies* 22(2):397–423.

Fulani, L. 1988. *The psychopathology of everyday racism and sexism*. New York: Harrington Park Press.

Garber, Eric. 1989. A spectacle of color: The lesbian and gay subculture of jazz age Harlem. In *Hidden from history: Reclaiming the gay and lesbian past*. eds. M. B. Duberman and M. Vicinus, 319. New York: NAL Books.

Goffman, Erving. 1971. *Relations in public: Microstudies of the public order*. New York: Basic Books.

Goffman, Erving. 1963. *Stigma: Notes on the management of spoiled identity*. New York: Penguin Books.

Gordon, Milton. 1964. *Assimilation in American life: The role of race, religion, and national origins*. New York: Routledge.

Graham, Lawrence. 1995. *Member of the club: Reflections on life in a racially polarized world*. 1st ed. New York: HarperCollins.

Gramling, Robert, and Craig J. Forsyth. 1987. Exploiting stigma. *Sociological Forum* 2 (2):401–415.

Greene, Beverly, and Nancy Boyd-Franklin. 1996. African American lesbian couples: Ethnocultural considerations in psychotherapy. *Women & Therapy* 19(3):49–60.

Griffith, D. W. 1915. *Birth of a nation*. Film.

Gupta, Sanjiv. 1999. The effects of transitions in marital status on men's performance of housework. *Journal of Marriage and the Family* 61:700–711.

Hallinan, Maureen T., and Richard A. Williams. 1989. Interracial friendship choices in secondary schools. *American Sociological Review* 54 (February):67–78.

Hamilton, Charles. 1969. How Black is Black. *Ebony* (August):47.

Haney-Lopez, Ian. 1996. *White by law: The legal construction of race*. New York: New York University Press.

Harley, Sharon. 1996. Nannie Helen Burroughs: The Black goddess of liberty. *Journal of Negro History* 81(1/4):62–71.

Harris, William H. 1982. *The harder we run: Black workers since the civil war*. New York: Oxford University Press.

Hartigan, John. 1999. *Racial situations: Class predicaments of Whiteness in Detroit*. Princeton, NJ: Princeton University Press.

Hartmann, Heidi. 1981. The family as the locus of gender, class, and political struggle: The example of housework. *Signs: Journal of Women in Culture and Society* 6 (3):366–395.

Heap, Chad C. 2009. *Slumming: Sexual and racial encounters in American nightlife, 1885–1940.* Historical studies of urban America. Chicago: University of Chicago Press.

Helms, Janet. 1993. *Black and White racial identity: Theory, research and practice.* Westport, CT: Praeger Publishers.

Helms, Janet. 1984. Toward a theoretical explanation of the effects of race on counseling: A Black and White model. *The Counseling Psychologist* 12(4):153–165.

Helper, Rose. 1969. *Policies and practices of real estate brokers.* Minneapolis: University of Minnesota Press.

Hemphill, Essex, and Chuck Tarver. 2007. *Brother to brother: New writings by Black gay men.* Washington, DC: Redbone Press.

Hertz, Rosanna. 1995. Separate but simultaneous interviewing of husbands and wives: Making sense of their stories. *Qualitative Inquiry* 1(4):429–451.

Higginbotham Jr., A. Leon, and Barbara K. Kopytoff. 2000. Racial purity and interracial sex in the law of colonial and antebellum Virginia. In *Interracialism: Black-White intermarriage in American history, literature, and law.* ed. Ed Werner Sollers, 102. New York: Oxford University Press.

Higginbotham Jr., A. Leon. 1978. *In the matter of color: Race and the American legal process.* New York: Oxford University Press.

Higginbotham, Evelyn Brooks. 1993. *Righteous discontent: The women's movement in the Black Baptist church, 1880–1920.* Cambridge, MA: Harvard University Press.

Hochschild, Arlie Russell. 1989. *The second shift: Working parents and the revolution at home.* New York: Viking.

Hochschild, Arlie Russell. 1983. *The managed heart: Commercialization of human feeling.* Berkeley, CA: University of California Press.

Hodes, Martha. 1997. *White women, Black men: Illicit sex in the nineteenth-century South.* New Haven, CT: Yale University Press.

Hodes, Martha. 1993. The sexualization of reconstruction politics: White women and Black men in the South after the Civil War. *Journal of the History of Sexuality* 3 (3):402–417.

hooks, bell. 1998. Representations of Whiteness in the Black imagination. In *Black on White: Black writers and what it means to be White.* ed. David R. Roediger, 38–54. New York: Shocken Books.

hooks, bell. 1992. *Black looks: Race and representation.* Boston: South End Press.

hooks, bell. 1992. Eating the other. In *Black looks: Race and representation.* Boston: South End Press.

Human Rights Campaign. 2011. *Hospital visitation laws.* Washington, DC.

Human Rights Campaign. 2011. *Parenting laws: Joint adoption.* Washington, DC.

Human Rights Campaign. 2011. *Statewide employment laws & policies.* Washington, DC.

Hutchinson, Darren Lenard. 2002. Dissecting axes of subordination: The need for structural analysis. *Journal of Gender, Social Policy & the Law* 11(1):13–24.

Iceland, John, Daniel H. Weinberg, and Erika Steinmetz. 2002. *Racial and ethnic residential segregation in the United States: 1980–2000.* Washington, DC: U.S. Census Bureau, U.S. Department of Commerce, CENSR-3.

Jackman, Mary R., and Marie Crane. 1986. "Some of my best friends are Black … ": Interracial friendship and Whites' racial attitudes. *Public Opinion Quarterly* 50: 459–486.

Jackson, J., T. N. Brown, D. R. Williams, M. Torres, L. Sellers, and K. Brown. 1996. Racism and the psychical and mental health status of African Americans: A thirteen-year national panel study. *Ethnicity and Disease* 6 (Winter/Spring):132–147.

James, Joy. 1996. *Resisting state violence: Radicalism, gender, and race in U.S. culture.* Minneapolis: University of Minnesota Press.

Jargowsky, Paul. 1994. Ghetto poverty among Blacks in the 1980s. *Journal of Policy Analysis and Management* 12:288–310.

Johnson, Carol. 2002. Heteronormative citizenship and the politics of passing. *Sexualities* 5(3):328.

Jones, Jeffrey M. 2008. *Majority of Americans say racism against Blacks widespread.* Gallup Poll, http://www.gallup.com/poll/109258/majority-americans-say-racism-against-blacks-widespread.aspx.

Jordan, Winthrop D. 1968. *White over Black: American attitudes towards the Negro, 1550–1812.* Chapel Hill, NC: University of North Carolina Press.

Judice, Cheryl Y. 2008. *Interracial marriages between Black women and White men.* Amherst, NY: Cambria Press.

Katz, Jonathan Ned. 1983. *Gay/Lesbian almanac: A new documentary.* New York: Carroll & Graft Publishing.

Kelley, Robin D. G. 1998. *Yo' mama's dysfunktional: Fighting the culture wars in urban America.* Boston: Beacon Press.

Kennedy, Elizabeth Lapovsky, and Madeline D. Davis. 1993. *Boots of leather, slippers of gold: The history of a lesbian community.* New York: Routledge.

Kennedy, Randall. 2003. *Interracial intimacy: Sex, marriage, identity and adoption.* Ann Arbor, MI: University of Michigan Press.

Kim, Jinyoung, and Richard Miech. 2009. The Black-White difference in age trajectories of functional health over the life course. *Social Science & Medicine* 68(4):717–725.

King, Deborah K. 1995. Multiple jeopardy, multiple consciousness: The context of a Black feminist ideology. In *Words of fire: An anthology of African-American feminist thought.* ed. Beverly Guy-Sheftall, 577. New York: New Press, distributed by W. W. Norton.

King-O'Riain, Rebecca. 2006. *Pure beauty: Judging race in Japanese American beauty pageants.* Minneapolis: University of Minnesota Press.

Kouri, K. M., and M. Lasswell. 1993. Black-White marriages: Social change and intergenerational mobility. *Marriage and Family Review* 19(3/4):241–255.

Kramer, Stanley. 1967. *Guess who's coming to dinner.* Film.

Kreager, Derek A. 2008. Guarded borders: Adolescent interracial romance and peer trouble at school. *Social Forces* 87(2):887.

Krysan, Maria. 2002. Community undesirability in Black and White: Examining racial residential preferences through community perceptions. *Social Problems* 49(4): 521–543.

Kunzel, Regina. 2010. *Criminal intimacy: Prison and the uneven history of modern American sexuality.* Chicago: University of Chicago Press.

Lacy, Karyn. 2007. *Blue-chip Black: Race, class, and status in the new Black middle class.* Berkeley, CA: University of California Press.

Lamont, Michéle. 2000. *The dignity of working men: Morality and the boundaries of race, class, and immigration.* Cambridge, MA: Harvard University Press.

Lamont, Michéle, and Virág Monlár. 2002. The study of boundaries in the social sciences. *Annual Review of Sociology* 28:167–195.

Lareau, Annette. 2011. *Unequal childhoods: Class, race, and family life*. 2nd ed. Berkeley, CA: University of California Press.

Lasser, Jon, and Deborah Tharinger. 2003. Visibility management in school and beyond: A qualitative study of gay, lesbian, bisexual youth. *Journal of Adolescence* 26(2) (April):233–244.

Laumann, Edward O., Stephen Ellingson, Anthony Paik, and Yoosik Youm, eds. 2004. *The sexual organization of the city*. Chicago: University of Chicago Press.

Law, Sylvia A. 1988. Homosexuality and the social meaning of gender. *Wisconsin Law Review* (March/April):187–235

Lee, Barrett, and Peter Wood. 1991. Is neighborhood racial succession place-specific? *Demography* 28:21–39.

Leiberson, Stanley, and Mary C. Waters. 1988. *From many strands: Ethnic and racial groups in contemporary America*. New York: Russell Sage Foundation.

Lewis, Amanda E. 2004. What group? Studying Whites and Whiteness in the era of "color-blindness." *Sociological Theory* 22:623–646.

Link, Bruce G., and Jo C. Phelan. 2001. Conceptualizing stigma. *Annual Review of Sociology* 27:363–385.

Lipsitz, George. 1998. *The possessive investment in Whiteness: How White people profit from identity politics*. Philadelphia: Temple University Press.

Lockman Jr., Paul T. 1984. Ebony and ivory: The interracial gay male couple. *Lifestyles: A Journal of Changing Patterns* 7(1):44–55.

Loewen, James W. 2005. *Sundown towns: A hidden dimension of American racism*. New York: Simon & Schuster.

Lofquist, Daphne, Terry Lugalia, Martin O'Connell, and Sarah Feliz. 2012. *Households and families: 2010*. Washington D.C: U.S. Census Bureau, U.S. Department of Commerce, C2010BR-14.

Logan, John R., and Brian J. Stults. 2011. The persistence of segregation in the metropolis: New findings from the 2010 census. Census brief prepared for U.S. 2010, http://www.s4.brown.edu/us2010.

Long, Janie. 2003. The incredibly true adventures of two women in love. *Journal of Couple and Relationship Therapy* 2(2):85–101.

Loulan, JoAnn. 1990. *The lesbian erotic dance: Butch, femme, androgyny and other rhythms*. New York: Spinsters Book Co.

Loving v. Virginia, 388 U.S. 1 (1967)

Maccoby, Eleanor E. 1999. *The two sexes: Growing up apart, coming together*. Cambridge, MA: Harvard University Press.

MacKenzie, Ross. 2009. Choice of Obama could make nation stronger. *Richmond Times-Dispatch*. November 9.

Maly, Michael T. 2005. *Beyond segregation: Multiracial neighborhoods in the United States*. Philadelphia: Temple University Press.

Mamo, Laura. 2007. *Queering reproduction: Achieving pregnancy in the age of technoscience*. Durham, NC: Duke University Press.

Martin, Biddy. 1994. Sexualitites without genders and other queer utopias. *Diacritics* 24 (2/3):104–121.

Massey, Douglas. 2001. Residential segregation and neighborhood conditions in U.S. metropolitan areas. In *America becoming: Racial trends and their consequences.* eds. Neil J. Smelser, William Julius Wilson, and Faith Mitchell, 391–434. Washington, DC: National Academy Press.

Massey, Douglas, and Nancy A. Denton. 1993. *American apartheid: Segregation and the making of the underclass.* Cambridge, MA: Harvard University Press.

Mauer, Marc, and Ryan S. King. 2007. *Uneven justice: State rates of incarceration by race and ethnicity.* Washington, DC: The Sentencing Project.

McBride, Dwight A. 2005. *Why I hate Abercrombie and Fitch: Essays on race and sexuality.* New York: New York University Press.

McBride, Dwight A. 1999. Can the queen speak? Racial essentialism, sexuality and the problem of authority. In *Black men on race, gender, and sexuality: A critical reader.* ed. Devon W. Carbado. New York: New York University Press.

McNamara, R. P., M. Tempenis, and B. Walton. 1999. *Crossing the line: Interracial couples in the South.* Westport, CT: Praeger.

McPherson, Miller, Lynn Smith-Lovin, and James Cook. 2001. Birds of a feather: Homophily in social networks. *Annual Review of Sociology* 27:415–444.

Mills, C. Wright. 1959. *The sociological imagination.* New York: Oxford University Press.

Mirchandani, Kiran. 2003. Challenging racial silences in studies of emotion work: Contributions from anti-racist feminist theory. *Organizational Studies* 24(5):721–742.

Moore, Mignon. 2011. *Invisible families: Gay identities, relationships, and motherhood among Black women.* Berkeley, CA: University of California Press.

Moore, Mignon. 2010. Black and gay in L.A.: The relationship that Black lesbians and gay men have to their racial religious communities. In *Black Los Angeles: American dreams and racial realities.* eds. D. Hunt and A. Ramon, 188–212. New York: New York University Press.

Moore, Mignon. 2006. Lipstick or timberlands? Meanings of gender presentation in Black lesbian communities. *Signs* 23(1):113–139.

Moran, Rachel F. 2001. *Interracial intimacy: The regulation of race & romance.* Chicago: University of Chicago Press.

Mumford, Kevin J. 1997. *Interzones: Black/White sex districts in Chicago and New York in the early twentieth century.* New York: Columbia University Press.

Mumford, Kevin J. 1996. Homosex changes: Race, cultural geography, and the emergence of the gay. *American Quarterly* 48(3):399.

Myrdal, Gunnar. 1944. *An American dilemma: The Negro problem and modern democracy.* New York: Harper and Brothers Publishers.

Nagel, Joane. 1994. Constructing ethnicity: Creating and recreating ethnic identity and culture. *Social Problems* 41:152–176.

Nagel, Joane. 2003. *Race, ethnicity, and sexuality: Intimate intersections, forbidden frontiers.* New York: Oxford University Press.

Nemoto, Kumiko. 2009. *Racing romance: Love, power, and desire among Asian American/White couples.* New Brunswick, NJ: Rutgers University Press.

Nestle, Joan. 1992. *The persistent desire: A femme-butch reader.* New York: Alyson Publications.

Newman, Leslea, ed. 1995. *The femme mystique.* New York: Alyson Publications.

O'Brien, Eileen. 2001. *Whites confront racism: Antiracists and their paths to action.* Boulder, CO: Rowman & Littlefield.

O'Brien, Eileen, and Kathleen O'Dell Korgen. 2007. It's the message, not the messenger: The declining significance of Black-White contact in a "colorblind" society. *Sociological Inquiry* 77(3):356–382.

O'Connell, Martin, Daphne Lofquist, Tavia Simmons, and Terry Lugaila. 2010. New estimates of same-sex couple households from the American community survey. Paper presented at the annual meeting of the Population Association of America. Dallas, TX. April 15–17, 2010.

Ogbu, John, and Signithia Fordham. 1986. Black students' school success: Coping with the "burden of acting White." *The Urban Review* 18(3):176–206.

Oliver, Melvin L., and Thomas M. Shapiro. 1995. *Black Wealth/White wealth: A new perspective on racial inequality.* New York: Routledge.

Omi, Michael, and Howard Winant. 1994. *Racial formations in the United States: From the 1960's to the 1990's.* New York: Routledge.

Orfield, Gary. 2001. *Schools more separate: Consequences of a decade of resegregation.* Cambridge, MA: The Civil Rights Project, Harvard University.

Otis, Margaret. 1929. A perversion not commonly noted. *Journal of Abnormal Psychology* 23:442–448.

Padgett, Tim, Frank Sikora, Anne Berryman, Jeanne Dequine, and Constance Richards. 2003. Color-blind love. *Time Magazine*, May 12.

Pager, Devah. 2003. The mark of a criminal record. *American Journal of Sociology* 108 (5) (March):937–975.

Park, Robert E., and Ernest W. Burgess. 1969. *Introduction to the science of sociology.* Chicago: University of Chicago Press.

Pascoe, Peggy. 2009. *What comes naturally: Miscegenation law and the making of race in America.* New York: Oxford University Press.

Pattillo-McCoy, Mary E. 2000. *Black picket fences: Privilege and peril among the Black middle class.* Chicago: University of Chicago Press.

Perea, Juan F. 1997. The Black/White binary paradigm of race: The "normal science" of American racial thought. *California Law Review* 85 (October):1219–1221.

Perlman, Sarah F. 1996. Loving across race and class divides: Relational challenges and the interracial couple. *Women & Therapy* 19(3):24–35.

Pettigrew, Thomas F. 1979. The ultimate attribution error: Extending Allport's cognitive analysis of prejudice. *Personality and Social Psychology Bulletin* 5:461–476.

Ponse, Barbara. 1978. *Identities in the lesbian world: The social construction of self.* Westport, CT: Greenwood Press.

Porterfield, Ernest. 1978. *Black and White mixed marriages.* Chicago: Nelson Hall.

Portes, Alejandro, and Min Zhou. 1993. The new second generation: Segmented assimilation and its variants. *Annals of the American Academy of Political and Social Science* 530:74–96.

Qian, Zhenchao, and Daniel T. Lichter. 2007. Social boundaries and marital assimilation: Interpreting trends in racial and ethnic intermarriage. *American Sociological Review* 22:68–94.

Reed, Annette Gordon. 1997. *Thomas Jefferson and Sally Hemings: An American controversy.* Charlottesville, VA: University of Virginia Press.

Reid-Pharr, Robert. 1996. Dinge. *Women & Performance* 8(2):75–85.

Reid-Pharr, Robert. 2001. *Black gay man: Essays*. Sexual cultures. New York: New York University Press.

Rich, Ruby. 1994. When difference is (more than) skin deep. In *Queer looks: Perspectives on lesbian and gay film and video*. eds. Martha Gever, John Greyson, and Pratibha Parmar. New York: Routledge.

Riggs, Marlon T., Nicole Atkinson, Christiane Badgley, Independent Television Service, California Newsreel, and Signifyin' Works. 2004; 1995. *Black is—Black ain't*. San Francisco: California Newsreel.

Rockquemore, Kerry Ann. 2002. Negotiating the color line: The gendered process of racial identity construction among Black/White biracial women. *Gender & Society* 16:485–503.

Rockquemore, Kerry Ann, and David L. Brunsma. 2007. *Beyond Black: Biracial identity in America*. 2nd ed. Boulder, CO: Rowman & Littlefield.

Rodriguez, Clara E. 2000. *Changing race: Latinos, the census, and the history of ethnicity in the United States*. New York: New York University Press.

Roediger, David. 1991. *The wages of Whiteness: Race and the mixing of the American working class*. London: Versa.

Romano, Renee. 2003. *Race mixing: Black-White marriage in postwar America*. Cambridge, MA: Harvard University Press.

Root, Maria P. P. 2001. *Love's revolution: Interracial marriage*. Philadelphia: Temple University Press.

Roscigno, Vincent J. 1998. Race and the reproduction of educational disadvantage. *Social Forces* 76(3):1033–1060.

Rosenberg, Morris. 1979. *Conceiving the self*. New York: Basic Books.

Rosenblatt, Paul C. 1995. *Multiracial couples: Black & White voices*. Thousand Oaks, CA: Sage.

Rosenfield, Michael J. 2007. *The age of independence: Interracial unions, same-sex unions, and the changing American family*. Cambridge, MA: Harvard University Press.

Ross, Josephine. 2004 The sexualization of difference: A comparison of mixed-race and same-gender marriage. *Harvard Civil Rights–Civil Liberties Law Review* 37:255–288. Available at SSRN: http://ssrn.com/abstract=508022.

Rostosky, Sharon S., Ellen D. B. Riggle, Todd A. Savage, Staci D. Roberts, and Gilbert Singletary. 2008. Interracial same-sex couples' perceptions of stress and coping: An exploratory study. *Journal of GLBT Family Studies* 4(3):277–299.

Rothenberg, Paula. 2004. *White privilege: Essential readings from the other side of racism*. New York: Worth Publishers.

Rothman, Barbara Katz. 2005. *Weaving a family: Untangling race and adoption*. Boston: Beacon Press.

Rowe, Wayne, Sandra K. Bennet, and Donald Atkinson. 1994. White racial identity models: A critique and alternate proposal. *The Counseling Psychologist* 22:129–146.

Rubin, Gayle. 1984. Thinking sex: Notes for a radical theory of the politics of sexuality. In *Pleasure and danger: Exploring female sexuality*. ed. Carole Vance. Boston: Routledge and Kegan Paul.

Rumbaut, Ruben G. 1994. The crucible within: Ethnic identity, self-esteem, and segmented assimilation among children of immigrants. *International Migration Review* 28(4):748–794.

Rupp, Leila J. 1999. *A desired past: A short history of same-sex love in America*. Chicago: University of Chicago Press.

Russo, Francine. 2001. Families: When love is mixing it up. *Time Magazine*, November 19.

Rutten, Tim. 2008. The good generation gap: The way that young people deal with race is a hopeful sign for our politics. *The Los Angeles Times*, February 6.

Scott, Darieck. 1994. Jungle fever? Black gay identity politics, White dick and the utopian bedroom. *GLQ* 1:299–321.

Sears, R. Bradley, Gary Gates, and William B. Rubenstein. 2005. Same-sex couples and same-sex couples raising children in the United States: Data from Census 2000. Los Angeles: The Williams Project on Sexual Orientation Law and Public Policy, UCLA School of Law.

Shapiro, Thomas. 2005. *The hidden cost of being African American: How wealth perpetuates inequality*. New York: Oxford University Press.

Shokeid, Moshe. 2010. Erotics and politics in the agenda of an interracial (Black and White) gay men's association in New York. In *The anthropology of values: Essays in honour of Georg Pfeffer*. eds. Peter Berger, Roland Hardenberg, Ellen Kattner, and Michael Prager. Delhi, India: Pearson Longman.

Simmons, Tavia, and Martin O'Connell. 2003a. Interracial unmarried-partner households: How do they compare with interracial married-couple households in census 2000? Presented at the Annual Meeting of the Population Association of America. Minneapolis, May 1–3.

Simmons, Tavia, and Martin O'Connell. 2003b. Married-couples and unmarried-partner households: 2000. Washington, DC: Bureau of the Census.

Smith, Earl, and Angela Hattery. 2009. *Interracial relationships in the 21st century*. Durham, NC: Carolina Academic Press.

Smith, Sandra S., and Mignon R. Moore. 2000. Intraracial diversity and relations among African-Americans: Closeness among Black students at a predominantly White university. *American Journal of Sociology* 106(1)(July):1–39.

Sollors, Werner. 2000. *Interracialism: Black-White intermarriage in American history, literature, and law*. Oxford, UK: Oxford University Press.

Somerville, Siobhan B. 2000. *Queering the color line: Race and the invention of homosexuality in American culture*. London: Duke University Press.

Spickard, Paul. 1991. *Mixed blood: Intermarriage and ethnic identity in twentieth-century America*. Madison, WI: University of Wisconsin Press.

Steinbugler, Amy C. 2005. Visibility as privilege and danger: Heterosexual and same-sex interracial intimacy in the 21st century. *Sexualities* 8:425–443.

Storrs, Debbie. 1999. Whiteness as stigma: Essentialist identity work by mixed-race women. *Symbolic Interaction* 22:205–224.

Swidler, Ann. 2001. *Talk of love: How culture matters*. Chicago: University of Chicago Press.

Tatum, Beverly Daniel. 1997. *Why are all the Black kids sitting together in the cafeteria? and other conversations about race*. New York: Basic Books.

Taylor, Paul, Rakesh Kochhar, Richard Fry, Gabriel Velasco, and Seth Motel. 2011. Twenty-to-one: Wealth gap rises to record highs between Whites, Blacks, and Hispanics. Washington, DC: Pew Research Center.

Thernstrom, Stephan, and Abigail M. Thernstrom. 1997. *America in Black and White: One nation, indivisible.* New York: Simon & Schuster.

Thorpe, Rochella. 1996. A house where queers go: African American lesbian nightlife in Detroit, 1940–1975. In *Inventing lesbian cultures in America.* ed. Ellen Lewin. Boston: Beacon Press.

Tolnay, Stewart E., and E. M. Beck. 1995. *A festival of violence: An analysis of southern lynchings, 1882–1930.* Champaign, IL: University of Illinois Press.

Twine, France Winddance. 1999. Bearing Blackness in Britain: The meaning of racial difference for White birth mothers of African-descent children. *Social Identities* 5:185.

Twine, France Winddance. 1996. Brown skinned White girls: Class, culture and the construction of White identity in suburban communities. *Gender, Place & Culture: A Journal of Feminist Geography* 3:205–224.

Twine, France Winddance. 1996. Heterosexual alliances: The romantic management of racial identity. In *The multiracial experience: Racial borders as new frontier.* ed. Maria P. P. Root. Thousand Oaks, CA: Sage.

Twine, France Winddance. 2011. *A White side of Black Britain: Interracial intimacy and racial literacy.* Durham, NC: Duke University Press.

Twine, France Winddance, and Amy C. Steinbugler. 2006. The gap between "Whites" and "Whiteness": Interracial intimacy and racial literacy. *Du Bois Review* 3(2): 341–363.

U.S. Census Bureau. 2003. Table 3, Hispanic origin and race of male unmarried-partner households for the United States: 2000. March 13.

U.S. Census Bureau. 2003. Table 4, Hispanic origin and race of female unmarried-partner households for the United States: 2000. March 13.

U.S. Census Bureau. 2012. Appendix Table 1. Interracial/Interethnic Married Couple Households: 2010. *Households and families. C2010BR-14.* Washington, D.C. http://www.census.gov/population/www/cen2010/briefs/tables/appendix.pdf

Van Ausdale, Debra, and Joe R. Feagin. 2001. *The first R: How children learn race and racism.* Lanham, MD: Rowman & Littlefield.

Van Deburg, William. 1992. *New days in Babylon: The Black power movement and American culture, 1965–1975.* Chicago: University of Chicago Press.

Vaquera, Elizabeth, and Grace Kao. 2008. Do you like me as much as I like you? Friendship reciprocity and its effects on school outcomes among adolescents. *Social Science Research* 37(1) (March):55–72.

Vaquera, Elizabeth, and Grace Kao. 2005. Private and public displays of affection among interracial and intra-racial adolescent couples. *Social Science Quarterly* 86(2): 484–508.

Wall Street Journal. 2009. President-elect Obama. November 9. A22.

Wang, Wendy. 2012. *The rise of intermarriage: Rates, characteristics vary by race and gender.* Washington, DC: Pew Research Center.

Waters, Mary C. 1999. *Black identities: West Indian immigrant dreams and American realities.* New York: Russell Sage Foundation.

Whitaker, Matthew C. 2005. *Race work: The rise of civil rights in the urban West.* Lincoln, NE: University of Nebraska Press.

Wolfe, Maxine. 1992. Invisible women in invisible places: Lesbians, lesbian bars and the social production of people/environment. *Architecture & Comport/Architecture & Behavior* 8(2):137–158.

Wray, Matt. 2006. *Not quite White: White trash and the boundaries of Whiteness*. Durham, NC: Duke University Press.

Wu, Frank H. 2002. *Yellow: Race in America beyond Black and White*. New York: Basic Books.

Yancey, George. 2007. *Interracial contact and social change*. Boulder, CO: Lynne Rienner.

Yu, Henry. 1999. Mixing bodies and cultures: The meaning of America's fascination with sex between "Orientals" and Whites. In *Sex, love, race: Crossing boundaries in North American history*. ed. Martha Hodes. New York: New York University Press.

Zack, Naomi. 1995. *American mixed race: The culture of microdiversity*. Lanham, MD: Rowman & Littlefield.

Zogby, John. 2009. Barack Obama: America's first global president. *Campaigns & Elections*, http://www.campaignsandelections.com/publications/campaign-election/2009/march-2009/barack-obama-americas-first-global-president/.

Zubrinsky Charles, Camille. 2008. Who will live near whom? *Poverty & Race* 17(5):1–7.

Zubrinsky Charles, Camille. 2001. Processes of racial residential segregation. In *Urban inequality: Evidence from four cities*. eds. Alice O'Connor, Chris Tilly, and Lawrence Bobo, 217–271. New York: Russell Sage Foundation.

Zubrinsky, Camille L., and Lawrence Bobo. 1996. Prismatic metropolis: Race and residential segregation in the city of the angels. *Social Science Research* 25(4): 335–374.

INDEX

Emboldened page ranges refer to chapters. Locators with an 'n' indicate a note.